LOCK LINKED
INTELLIGENCE-INSTINCT
-DREAMS-EDUCATION

LOCK LINKED INTELLIGENCE-INSTINCT -DREAMS-EDUCATION

Norris Ray Peery

Writer's Showcase
presented by *Writer's Digest*
New York San Jose Lincoln Shanghai

Lock Linked
Intelligence-Instinct-Dreams-Education

Writer's Showcase
presented by *Writer's Digest*
an imprint of iUniverse.com, Inc.

For information address:
iUniverse.com, Inc.
5220 S 16th, Ste. 200
Lincoln, NE 68512
www.iuniverse.com

The Front Cover, all Illustrations and Poetry are by the Author.
Most of the original Illustrations are in color, they have been
Reduced to gray scale for this print edition, V-7.52

ISBN: 0-595-15257-0

Printed in the United States of America

For my family and friends, with whose helping hands life has been mostly a joyous journey of Discovery

And

To

Hungry Minds

Contents

List of Illustrations

List of Poetry

Acknowledgments

Professor of Mathematics, James H. Case, for the many hours of pleasurable discussions concerning Intelligence and a lifelong friendship.

Electronic Engineer, Ahmad Attaie, for the wonderful discussions and speculations about every subject under the sun, and for his and his family's enduring friendship.

Teacher and friend Carol Anderson and her husband, Electronic Engineer, David W. Anderson for their insights, critics and discussions about Education and our friendship that has lasted a lifetime.

Teacher and friend, Judith N. Middleton, for her insights, criticism, and discussions about Intelligence and the Educational System.

Teacher and friend, Anne Middleton, for our discussions about Education.

Introduction

When at the University my mentor was a professor of Mathematics, James H. Case, who had for a great number of years pursued the ever-elusive search for the understanding of the mechanisms of Intelligence. His long sought after dream was to understand the mechanisms that might define an Artificial Intelligent System, and then be able to describe that system with an exact mathematical notation. He worked privately on this problem for over thirty years. Since we shared this common interest, we had many discussions and correspondences about Artificial Intelligence. I had many times encouraged him to take his ideas and write them in a version that would generate some popular enthusiasm for them, but he was a mathematician at heart and could not bring himself to publish something that was not absolutely concrete. He did publish in conjunction with another enthusiast a very long and tedious paper titled "Short Wire Theory" also known as "A Universal Three Dimensional Parallel Computer", which now lays sleeping somewhere in the Association for Computing Machinery Depository; he also obtained a patent covering much of the material described in that paper.

During the more recent years before his death, his ideas concerning Artificial Intelligence and my own ideas became divergent and for the last few years of his life our discussions were always about speculations on topics other than Artificial Intelligence.   I have long felt the need to write a book that would give the average reader some feeling of substance about the nature of Intelligence. For most people, Intelligence is such an elusive and abstract thing, they have no material visualizable structure of what it is, or even might be.

I believe it is important for a very general audience to find substance within the meaning of Intelligence. It is especially important that teachers have a real feeling of what physically might exist within the definition.

Although I have spent the majority of my working life in the field of electronics and was much involved with computers, electronic designs, and programming, I have always been contemplating what might make up the structures of an Intelligent System.

My speculations within this book are not to demonstrate the exact mechanisms of Intelligence and the exact details of their complicated interactions. Some important aspects of mental functioning I have left untouched, but in doing so, hopefully the readers will be inspired to their own speculations. I do not try to answer the question of the nature of Consciousness, but I do believe its nature is more elusive than it is complicated. Some clever reader might find a place to nestle it within the structures discussed here.

The exact intent of these speculations is to give the reader a feeling that they know something of this thing we call Intelligence, so that in the future they can approach it as a real material thing with which they are capable of wrestling by use of reason and speculation. Also, by considering the nature of Instincts and Dreaming along with Intelligence, we can see that they have a significant importance in understanding the needs of Education.

Foreword

It is the very nature of an economy that is in the midst of a technological revolution that society finds itself involuntarily caught up in the midst of another kind of revolution. It is the nature of powerful technological based economic revolutions that new demands are placed upon the existing Educational System; they are necessarily demands for talents that are not supplied by the existing System. They are demands whose basic requirements exceed the quality and quantity of knowledge that students have customarily been required to know.

It is during these times that pressures are put on the Educational System to deliver results that are applicable to the needs of the Real World. It is at these times that parents who have the monetary means are busy removing their children from the Public Educational System and are placing them in private schools as a means of fulfilling their desires for a better education. It is during these times that cries rise up from many in the population for any means to escape from the Public Educational System into any alternative that they believe can better deliver the educational results they desire.

Such times are dangerous times for a democratic society. They present situations whose unchecked direction can lead to exasperating the spread between those of sufficient economic means and those of minimal means, situations that lead to the further exaggeration of the distance between those with the knowledge to compete within the newly emerging economic world and those with little knowledge to aid in their economic survival.

Our greatest concern should be that this growing situation is self-reinforcing.

Unless timely steps are taken to correct its root cause, it will without doubt lead to an ever-increasing gulf between what will become just two identifiable classes within society, one class representing wealth in all its forms and one class representing poverty in all its forms.

There is an immediate need that steps must now be taken, so that we have some leverage of time towards making our Educational System one that delivers to society, students that are immediately prepared to take a meaningful place within the society and its ever-changing economy.

INTELLIGENCE

INTELLIGENCE

"In the Land of the Blind the One Eyed Man is King",
Until the Population in its Ignorance Destroys the Eye.

ORIENTATION

It is my intent here, to make an argument for a most basic platform and the mechanisms that would define the nature of Intelligence. It is to be understood that although I believe each mechanism to be common to the structures of Intelligence in all Creatures, it does not mean that all Creatures have the same capability for Intelligence, nor does it mean Creatures in the same species have the same capability for intelligence. There are many outside influences effecting the functioning of these mechanisms and how well they function for any individual. Some obvious things that affect the functioning of the mechanisms of Intelligence are: an individuals direct heredity, the world of chemicals, social and cultural pressures, injuries, nutrition, general physical and mental health, and the regular quality and quantity of sleep and dreaming.

Although the structures I will describe are the most basic ones for Intelligence to exist, these structures are greatly enhanced and augmented in the more complex Creatures of Nature. Shortly I will give a rather restricted definition of Intelligence. The current characterization of Intelligence seems to me to contain any and all higher mental functions that might be attributed to the Human Animal. It is my belief that it is of considerable importance to attempt to isolate the mental functions into their most basic components as a means of giving a clear insight into their individual complex functions. It is of particular importance to attempt a rational separation of functioning in any complex systems, especially when the overall system is both complex and poorly understood. Our best hope of understanding any complex system is to break it down to its smallest functional components and then work at understanding these individual components.

The current situation is much like Intelligence is thought of as: the whole Rose Garden, grass, walkways, fencing, irrigation systems, signs, rose beds, etc. What I would like to talk about is the Rosebush, as it is what is essential to the Rose Garden. All of the other features of the Rose Garden are secondary and separate. To understand the Rosebush, we must concentrate on the Rosebush. To understand Intelligence, we must separate it from other mental functioning and concentrate on it.

What I will describe here are the Major Overall Functions of the Mechanisms of Intelligence. You should realize, for each of the Major Mechanisms there are Multitudes of Minor Secondary Mechanisms. These Secondary Mechanisms perform the essential Housekeeping Jobs necessary for the orderly operation of all. Any attempt to weave into this story the details of all of those Housekeeping Mechanisms would so seriously complicate the story, as to make it unreadable for the general reader to whom this book is directed.

You might keep the following generalized picture in mind while reading this section "Intelligence", think of the Human Brain as being divided into two distinct volumes. These distinct volumes are not the Right and Left Hemispheres. Do not try to give these volumes names in terms that are associated with current anatomical knowledge.

Within one of those volumes reside the most Primitive Structures of the Brain, here, in Tightly Defined Structures are clumped together those mechanisms and their functions that are Solely Determined by

Heredity. These are the Mechanisms and Functions that have been very slowly evolving since the earliest times. All of a Creature's Sensory Organs have direct ties into this volume; within this volume are those Neural Structures that allow each Creature to control its most basic physical body functions and also the major elements that allow each Creature to exhibit Instinctive Reactions. Everything in this most Primitive Volume is hereditary and therefore is capable of being passed from one generation to the next.

In the second Volume there is quite an unusual situation, here a Major Part of the Volume is Not Dedicated to any particular function at all. Instead much of the volume is awaiting some stimulation to cause a tiny part of it to take up a dedicated purpose, also distributed within this volume are structures, mechanisms, that have ties to the most Primitive First Volume. These Mechanisms are the Mechanisms of Intelligence, they extract information from the First Volume, and they order and categorize that information and then direct it deep into the second volume. The Mechanisms of Intelligence use this captured information to cause changes in tiny parts that were previously without purpose, into memories, these memories represent timely happenings lying outside of the Brain, happenings from the Real World.

The Mechanisms of Intelligence for each individual, slowly over much of a lifetime, build the undedicated parts of the second volume into the memories that are the representations of what exists or existed for them within the Real World. These Memories consist of both learned events and learned responses to events. These memories are Nature's most powerful way of giving a more timely option, than the ancient process of forming fixed Inheritable Instinctive Memories and Responses.

The only draw back of this newly evolved Intelligent System of Nature is that the results of its lifetime's memories are not passable by heredity from one generation to the next. For an individual when that individual ceases to exist, all of the wonderful lifetime of learning also vanishes. Fortunately for humans, we have found ways to pass on much of a lifetime of learning by means other than heredity.

If you find this first section of the book "Intelligence" to be somewhat tedious reading, I assure you your final reward for persistence and patience's will far out weigh with delight any first sufferings.

PATTERNS

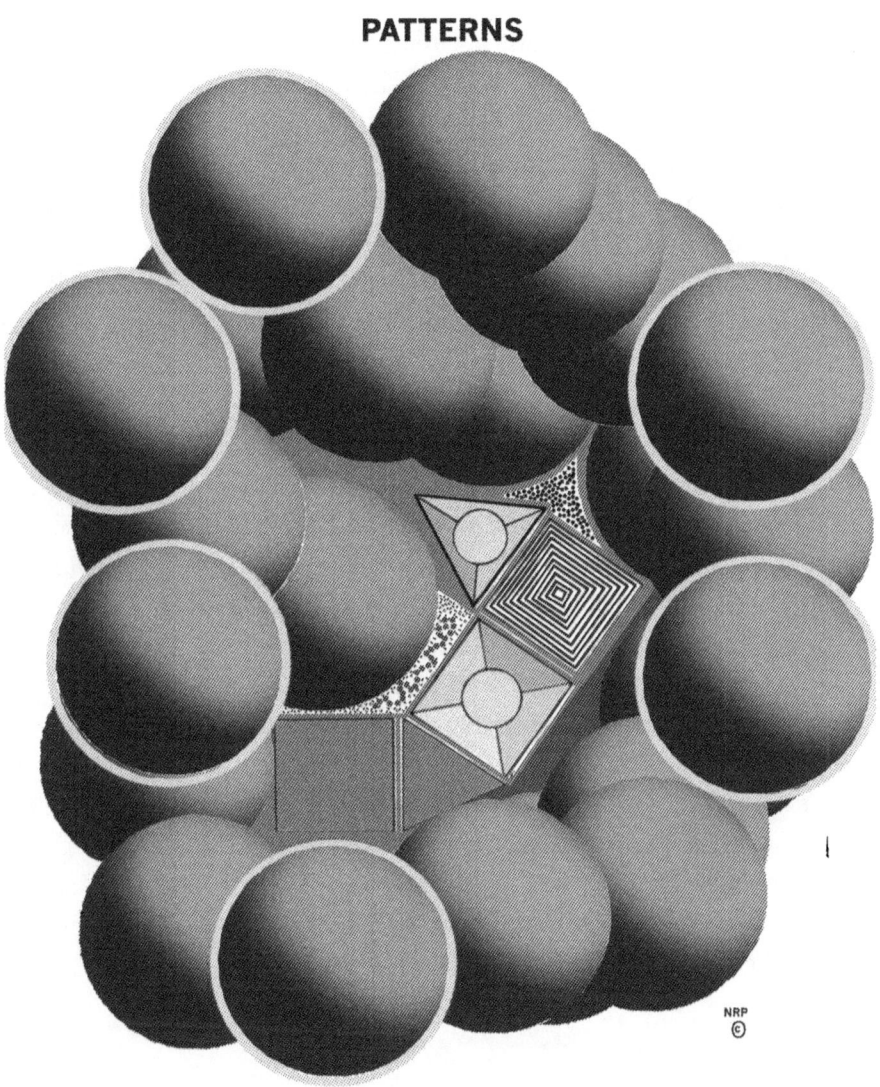

PATTERNS

Intelligence is primarily about a Creature's ability to function within the Natural Environment. It is about how Creatures detect the Real World Environment and what information they are able to separate and use from that Real Environment. To begin our understanding of Intelligence, we must first look at what exists within the Real World and to break it down into its smallest identifiable parts.

We must first realize that objects and phenomenon in the Real World are basically and essentially all made-up from just simple singular patterns that are repeated again and again in Nature. It is absolutely necessary to understand that repeatability is the primary element of this argument about defining what is a Simple Intelligible Pattern. It is the very fact that a Simple Pattern is a Repeating Pattern in Nature that makes it Intelligible, this can be understood in as much as any Simple Pattern that happens exclusively, only once in Nature, is of no value to any Creature that detects the pattern as it will never happen again and therefore can be of no further consequence to the Creature.

Within the Natural World of all Intelligible Patterns there are those whose structures are the simplest, we could think of these patterns consisting of the simplest structures as comprising a group that we might name "the Alphabet of Patterns." Such patterns might include those basic geometric forms as: a point, a line, two lines connected, a circle, a square and so on. It is the Set of most Simple Patterns, including Three Dimensional Simple Patterns that taken together would make up our Alphabet of Patterns.

VISUAL PATTERN ALPHABET SOUP

It is from this Alphabet of Patterns that the more complex patterns are formed. The next step up in the complexity of patterns, we might think of as analogous to the words of a language, from these words we can construct even more complex patterns and we might compare these to the sentences within a language. You can clearly see that the complexity of the patterns that we can construct is endless, and so in the Natural World all of the things that exist there can be related to Intelligible Patterns.

You have of course been understanding this argument in terms of visualizations, but an Alphabet of Patterns is also applicable to those things of the Real World that are detected by our other Senses.

Hearing, Feeling, Tasting and Smelling each have their own unique alphabet of basic simple patterns from which we are able to construct more complicated patterns that completely represent their way of knowing the Real World.

To know or recognize the more complex patterns of the Real World, creatures must first build up a repertoire within their memories of the simplest patterns from the Pattern Alphabet; they are then able through ever increasing the complexity of patterns contained in their memories to learn even more complex patterns.

We might consider here that the Nonvisual Senses and the patterns they are involved with are so very different from visual patterns, that they are not easily relatable in terms of words or images. Most different are those patterns associated with the senses of Feeling, Tasting and Smelling.

VISUAL PATTERN EVOLUTION

Their patterns are so different that early memories that are implanted by them might be difficult to describe with Human Language. Though a Human's memory is of a long duration it is interesting to realize how few exact memories we have from our earliest years of childhood. We may for a long time remember in terms of Feelings any traumatic experience from our earliest years, even those of our actual birth, but we can only remember them in terms of physical feelings and emotions and cannot relate them to any visual images and this is simply because the newly born child has no learned visual patterns that can relate to any Visual Sensory Input. It is also probably the reason we have very few visual memories from our early childhood. The pattern structures we are building in our minds at that age are of the simplest Alphabetical types and are not yet relatable to the complex pattern structures that make up experiences or events in the Real World.

Thinking about the proposition that patterns must be repeatable to be intelligible, the reader might say, what about one time patterns or things that happen only once to an individual and yet are of a significant importance to the individual, such as winning the lottery. These things are actually Complex Patterns or Events that are made up from simpler patterns, which are themselves, made up from the simplest patterns of the Alphabet of Patterns. These Complex Patterns or Events have no simple patterns within them, that are not repeatable patterns within Nature. The matter is actually this, the winning of the lottery involves a person using a very complex linking of simple patterns that when linked together makeup the total Event associated with the winning of the lottery.

SIMPLE VISUAL WORDS

Such basic patterns as: tickets, money, buying, sales, stores and on and on, that make up the whole complex of linked patterns involved in this Event are all well known by the individual. Also, all of the larger patterns, walking to the car, the drive to the store, to getting out of the car and walking to the store, to taking out the wallet and the money, to purchasing the ticket and all of the little in between details (little learned patterns) that fit between each of these actions, are all well known and common happenings. The one fact that is unique to all of the actions involved here is the winning of the lottery. But, even winning is a well-known pattern, if not a previously experienced pattern, a pattern that the individual has come into contact with again and again in life. The point of the argument here is that within the whole experience there are no one time exclusive patterns. The reader must be cautioned not to confuse basic or complex patterns (repeatable patterns) with patterns that happen only once in Nature. The winning of the Lottery is possibly a one time Event. There are many, many, one-time events that have great consequences for an individual. Many events are unique one-time happenings, but none of the basic patterns that compose them are unique one-time patterns in Nature. It just means that all of the patterns that make up this complex event were known before by learned experience or known vicariously. None of the patterns contained within the Event are patterns that occur only once in Nature.

The knowing of a pattern only in a vicarious way is considered as equivalent to knowing the pattern in reality. In our world being taught by a teacher is essentially a vicarious way of knowing patterns that may not have been experienced by an individual.

LARGER VISUAL WORDS

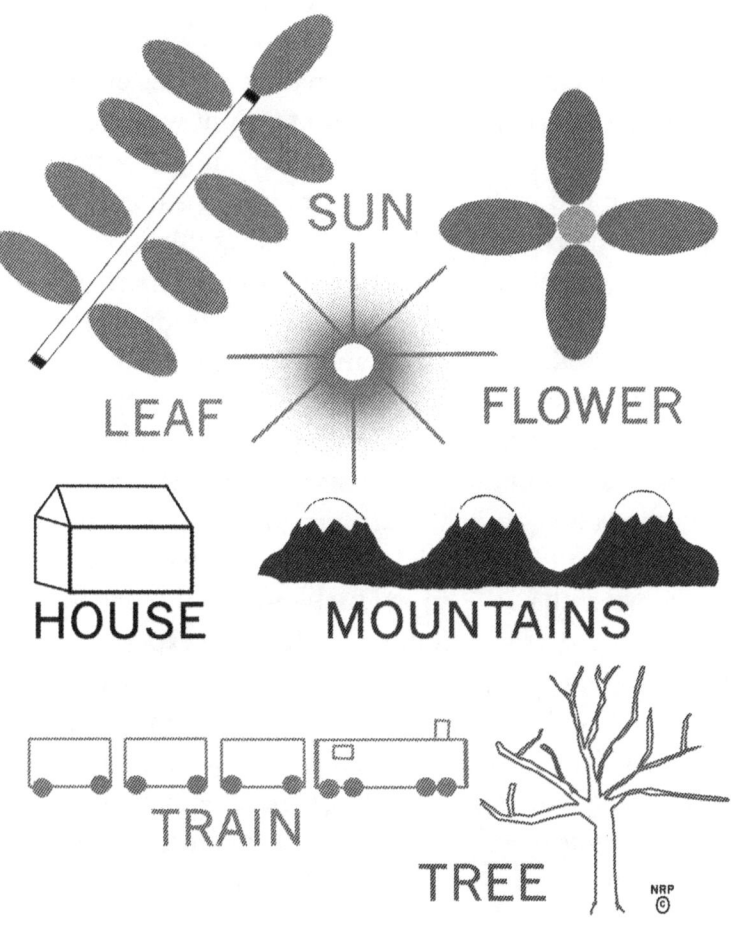

There is something of interest about all Complex Patterns or Events that lead to trauma for the individual. Almost all of these experiences involve simultaneous pattern inputs to all, or most all of the Sensory Detectors. What is important to note is, that the sequence of patterns that lead to trauma in an individual are remembered in great detail, usually for a lifetime. How is it that the set of patterns that lead to trauma are so well remembered for such long periods of time although the set may happen only once? As a counterpoint we have the situation of the classroom, wherein there are rather simple patterns that we repeatedly attempt to drill into the memories of students and we find they are so difficult to get in and so quickly forgotten.

So, as to the long remembrance of a traumatic experience, we might note that the simultaneous input of patterns from many senses has much to do with both the ease of remembering the patterns leading to trauma and the longevity of the memory. The intensity of the patterns surely has something to do with how long they are remembered; understanding what is involved could have important consequences for teaching methods and student learning. Although a pattern sequence that ends in trauma for an individual may only happen one time, it is generally reported that the individual re-lives the experience many times by the method of involuntary recall of the experience from their memory. My argument is this: that multi-sensory inputs, simultaneous multi-sensory inputs, the intensity of the patterns, involuntary recall of patterns, the voluntary recall of patterns, and dreaming are the prime factors in learning and the longevity of the memory of those learned patterns. These factors will be considered in more detail later in the section about Long Term Memory.

VISUAL PARAGRAPH

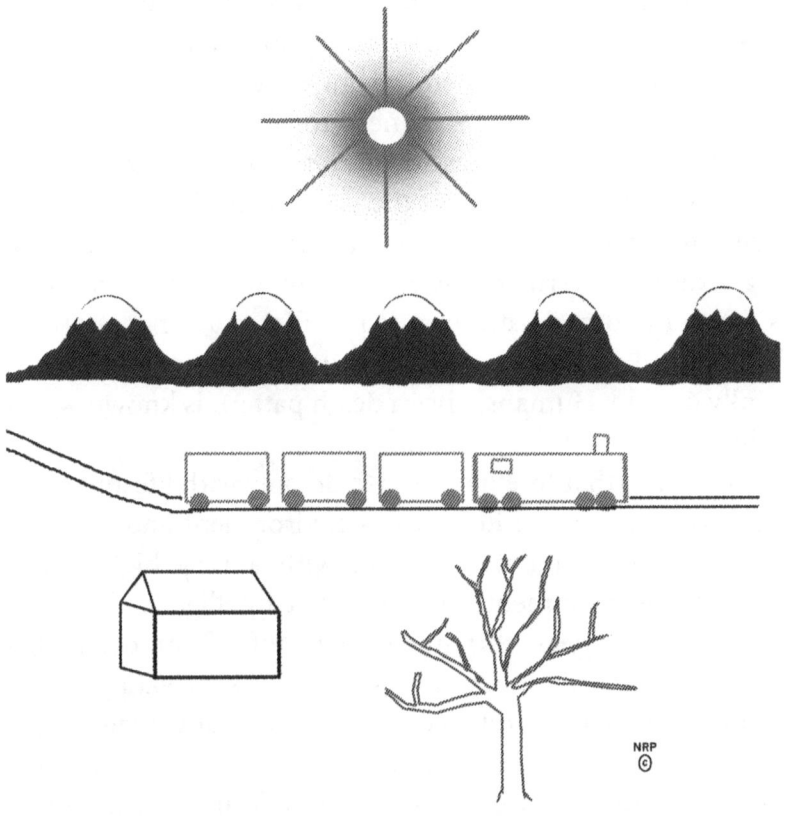

There is one more unusual traumatic event that we should consider, and that is the set of complex patterns whose end pattern is the death of the individual. Obviously the individual who directly experiences such a set of complex patterns can learn nothing from the patterns. Not knowing such patterns is a major cause of death for all young Creatures in the Animal Kingdom and knowing such a set of patterns, while still alive, is of extreme value to any Creature. It is clear that individuals do know some of these complex patterns. So, how is it that we can know such a set of death patterns? There are only three ways to know them. In the first way of knowing, we really need to rename the pattern as, "the almost death pattern" in this case the Creature by luck of action and/or Instinct escapes the final result of the pattern and in doing so successfully takes away the memory of the pattern. There is another way of knowing a death pattern that is a vicarious way, where the Creature detects (sees) the death pattern as it is inflicted against another individual. The third way of knowing this death pattern is the one most successfully used by Humans, once a death pattern is known we teach it to our children.

We must realize that Intelligence is to do only with life and life's drive to survive by knowing the Real World environment and being able to predict from one moment what will with a very high probability happen in the next moment. In saying that Intelligence is about life's drive to survive, I mean this in the sense of life or death. Because Intelligence is primarily a powerful system for survival against recognizable threats in Nature and a system for taking advantage of positive life enhancing patterns, this does not mean that there are no other consequences of Intelligence that are separate from immediate survival.

Just a quick word here about Creativity and Intelligence, Creativity has to do with manipulating learned patterns into new patterns that do or do not exist within Nature. Creativity surely has a great dependence on Intelligence, which is all about learning patterns from Nature. Certainly creativity without first having Intelligence is not possible.

Also, if some Creature is the most intelligent Creature in the Universe and the Creature does not have the basic structures that are necessary to be creative, that Creature will be superbly able to be successful in Nature's environment, but it will never significantly modify the environment of Nature. Whales may be the most intelligent Creatures in their environment, but they will never light fires, make arrowheads, or design airplanes. Intelligence by itself is not enough to purposefully change Nature. It is only enough to increase the odds of surviving within Nature and if a Creature can only do that, then Nature in the last resort always wins the final battle, always, Always.

Sadly in today's world Intelligence is believed to be responsible for all of Humankind's advances. This is mainly because in the past any and every advanced mental function was included under the cloak of Intelligence without questioning its possible exclusive nature, hopefully we can dispel that belief and lay the laurels for Humankind's advancements at the foot of a different Shrine.

THE DEFINITION OF INTELLIGENCE

Here I now give for the purposes of this paper a minimal definition of Intelligence. All other mental functions that do not lie within this definition are considered to be functions independent of Intelligence with their own special mechanisms that define their functioning.

Intelligence consists of mechanisms for:

1. Detecting
2. Filtering and Coding (Mapping)
3. Discovering
4. Memorizing
5. Characterizing
6. Predicting
7. Responding to

Patterns that are Repeatable in the Real World.

Once a repeatable complex pattern is identified and memorized and then later is again encountered, the intelligent Creature must be able once some unique structure of the pattern is detected to predict the next part of the pattern.

The World is filled with what appears to be order (Intelligible Patterns) and chaos (events with no apparent pattern or structure). There are two different types of Intelligible Patterns. One of these is fixed or static patterns, which are things like the Alphabet of Patterns and more complex patterns such as: rocks, cars, hats, wheels, mice and such, that can exist in time in a continuous static manner. The other patterns are complex patterns that exist only through time such as: a falling rock, a deer coming each morning to drink at a stream, the turning of a wheel, a hat blowing in the wind and all such events where a fixed pattern moves in time. These of course are very complex patterns that are made up from chaining together simpler patterns. We will call these chains of simpler moving patterns, "Events". You also need to realize, that in the strict sense the writing of an understandable sequence of symbols on a paper and or the reading of such a sequence of symbols is of this second kind, a pattern in time, since to understand the sequence it must be read through time in the same order as it was written. Spoken language since it is a sequential chaining of simple patterns through time is also a complex pattern or Event.

For an intelligent Creature it is important to be able to know the patterns of the first kind and it is of course essential that these be known before patterns of the second kind can be comprehended. It is clearly patterns generated through time that are of primary importance to living Creatures, for it is by knowing them that Creatures are able to recognize the unique beginning sequence of a pattern in time, and then by a kind of predicting into the future to know what the final realization of the pattern will be, this allows them to take an appropriate early action. It is of prime importance, once a pattern in time has been understood, that the Creature can predict the evolution of a pattern faster than the pattern actually develops in the Real World situation, this allows the Creature to prepare to take a timely action in response to the pattern and if Creatures could not do this, then the knowledge of the complete pattern would be of no value to them. Nature would always be rushing on past the helpless Creature, who would watch as it whizzed by with no understanding of what was going on. I think that in many cases, where the pattern is long and very complex and it is very fast at running its course from beginning to end, that Creatures do not in fact within their brains predict each step of the developing pattern to reach a conclusion before the pattern concludes its course. What they are able to do instead is, since the whole pattern is laid down in their memories, they simply see some unique part of the pattern and then jump to the final memory of the pattern's conclusion. (We will see how this is actually implemented in the section discussing Cross Address Linking) Of course, this method could be dangerous for a Creature. We call this method of knowing the future, jumping to conclusion. It is a method that is most frequently used and in almost all cases in Nature is safe. When we jump to conclusions concerning patterns that make up complex events that we have learned by observing the actions of other rational thinking Creatures, this can be very dangerous, for the obvious reasons.

JUDGING INTELLIGENCE

When we try to measure an individual's Intelligence or a Whale's or any other Creature's, it really has no meaning unless we do it in the context of the Creature's past experience environment. It is essential to keep this in mind that Intelligence is about life, about survival, not about anything else at least in its primary or primitive form. When I say "in the context of a Creature's environment" and when referring to Human Beings then I mean their complete real past experience environment. Any Creatures that come upon a situation where they have had no previous experience will not show some saving intuition that allows them to satisfactorily solve that new problem. This thing we call Intelligence will not spring forth with a magical solution to solve the new problem. The Creature may respond to a totally new situation with a reaction that is Instinctive. Later we will see how Instinct is a phenomenon that is essentially independent of Intelligence. Intelligence is the ability to experience a pattern, and to learn the pattern, and to deal with the pattern and its possible small variations in time. It is not the ability to predict the end result of an event that has never before been encountered. There is no name for this ability other than a lucky guess. By saying this, I do not mean that there is not any such thing as intuition.

Intuition might be considered to be a situation where a Creature comes upon a problem, where consciously the apparent pattern seems new and totally unknown, but subconsciously the new pattern contains clues that subconsciously relate it to known patterns and therefore bias the direction of the choice to a correct solution to the problem (new pattern). When any Creature comes face to face with an Entirely New Pattern, it is not realistic to judge the Creature's Intelligence on how well it handles the situation.

Consider a pod of Whales lounging on the ocean's surface while Whalers are slaughtering them. This has nothing to say about the Whales being stupid or Intelligent. It is simply an experience that the Whales have never before encountered, patterns they have never known. Their Intelligence can only deal with the patterns of the environment that they have learned since their birth.

By using your imagination and considering a fictitious situation, we can better understand the situation of the Whales. First imagine a fictitious Creature that we will name "Zimmy". We will give the Zimmy the following mix of characteristics:

1. A Zimmy can only see objects that are in motion. Any object within the Zimmy's visual field that is not moving becomes completely invisible to the Zimmy.

2. The Zimmy pursues with great speed and eats in one gulp anything that moves.

3. A Zimmy has an extremely short memory span. If the Zimmy is not continually visually stimulated into pursuit, then it completely forgets whatever it was doing and sits dormant until re-stimulated.

4. The Zimmy is extremely fierce looking, has a giant mouth that is big enough to swallow a whole person, fierce sharp extended claws and large legs that are built for the speedy pursuit of its prey.

5. Any similarity here to any person living or dead is not intentional.

Now to better understand the situation of the Whales. Imagine a California beach crowded with swimmers and sunbathers. Suddenly, a Zimmy comes out of the ocean and onto the beach. What happens next has nothing to do with how intelligent the people on the beach are supposed to be.

A somewhat similar and awkward situation exists for an individual who when taking an Intelligence Test comes upon a mathematical sequence of numbers and has never seen such a sequence before, in fact they have never seen anything even remotely similar to a such a sequence. The individual is at a loss as to what to do to complete the sequence as requested. The individual could actually fill in any numbers to complete the supposed sequence. There is a mathematical expression that could be written to show that their answer was a valid solution for the sequence. So does this actually demonstrate anything of significance? Most certainly it only demonstrates the outlook of an Educational System that assumes certain generalities should apply to everyone.

There are times after learning some simple or complex pattern that we might see the same pattern but with slight variations and we can understand what will be the final conclusion of the pattern. The reason for this is simply that all patterns in Nature have contained within them a degree of variation. As a simple example, a Cup viewed from slightly different angles gives us slightly different patterns to detect and remember. As we view the cup from increasingly different positions, the pattern that we see as the cup changes proportionately with our new viewing position. When we have seen the cup from every possible angle, then we know the cup as a set of continuously varying patterns. All patterns within Nature, as they exist within a Three Dimensional Universe, must be thought of as having variations within some fixed boundaries. And so any slight variations from any known pattern might be considered to be within the possible boundaries of the major pattern itself.

The learning of patterns beyond some basic minimum size can only be accomplished by slowly learning each of the smaller pieces that make up the total pattern. Most patterns in Nature are exceedingly large and we learn them only slowly a small piece at a time building our knowledge piece by piece until the whole pattern is known. We should understand that great new discoveries in Nature don't just happen out of the blue sky. They are in a sense snuck-up-on by understanding little bits and pieces that finally point and lead to a new discovery. In the truest sense newly learned bits of a complex pattern lead us by the nose on a path of slow learning until we are finally face to face with a new pattern that we can claim as a new discovery.

EXPERIMENTAL MINIMAL INTELLIGENT CREATURE

Within these discussions of the nature of Intelligence for clarity it will sometimes be necessary to speak in terms of a minimal system and the simplest patterns that can most clearly demonstrate the more complex natures of Intelligence.

Let's consider some thoughts about Intelligence in more detail. If we reduce the Real Universe and the Real World to an absolute minimal structure, this Simulated Real World will allow us the simplest environment in which to investigate the nature of some of the more complicated mechanisms of Intelligence. In our normal Universe of three dimensions, we understand that it is made up of those things we can know and understand and much that is not understandable which we will call chaos. In our Universe of chaos and recognizable patterns lets look at a Simplified Universe of one-dimensional objects happening one at a time (two dimensional if we consider time as a dimension). For the sake of giving these objects meaning in the context of the present World, our one-dimensional objects will consist of either a 1 (one) or 0 (zero). We will name either a one or a zero, a bit. In this system chaos would be represented by a completely random string of ones and zeros happening one at a time in time. Reading right to left with time represented as proceeding from right to left, chaos might look something like this:

101000100100101101110101000001110101011110010111110101 10111010

This string of bits was generated by the throwing of a pair of dice. If the dice came up with an even number it was recorded in the string as a zero and if the number on the dice was odd it was recorded in the string as a one. In a Universe of total chaos, one that contained no intelligible patterns, the string of chaos bits would continue without end. Let's now make a pattern that is intelligible or recognizable to an Intelligent Creature and then we will imbedded it in our Universe of chaos, such an intelligible pattern might look like this:

010011000111000011110000011111000000011111100

This pattern has some easily identifiable features. If this recognizable pattern is embedded intact within the string we called chaos it clearly remains easily identifiable. We must keep in mind that a pattern occurring in Nature to be of any value to any Creature must be a repeatable pattern. One of our primary arguments is that Intelligence is about identifying patterns that Nature repeats over and over again. If in fact, we have any exceedingly long sequence of random numbers making up our string of chaos, the intelligible pattern we synthetically generated will eventually appear in that sequence as a random occurrence, but that means nothing as concerns an Intelligent Creature. It is only if the intelligible pattern makes a frequent occurrence within the background of chaos, that it then can be intelligible to an Intelligent Creature. It must be understood that the intelligible pattern we synthetically generated here has a nice orderly structure, but an intelligible pattern in Nature does not necessarily have a nice looking orderly structure. It is not the nice, geometric, or symmetric nature of a pattern that makes it an intelligible pattern. The one, the only requirement for a pattern to be intelligible is that it is frequently repeated in Nature. This does not mean that nice, symmetric, or geometric patterns are excluded from being intelligible, they are plentiful in the Natural World and qualify as being intelligible with ease, but just because these patterns are so easily identifiable we must not assume that all intelligible patterns are in this category.

It is important to consider what are the most basic elements, which taken together could make up an intelligent system within a Little Creature existing within an absolute minimal Universe. Although to understand the nature of Intelligence, we will sometimes examine the problem from the viewpoint of a minimally complicated World, it is important that we relate our gained insights to Creatures in the Real World. Let's now begin examining in order, the individual pieces that might make up the intelligent mechanisms within our Little Creature and within us.

DETECTING

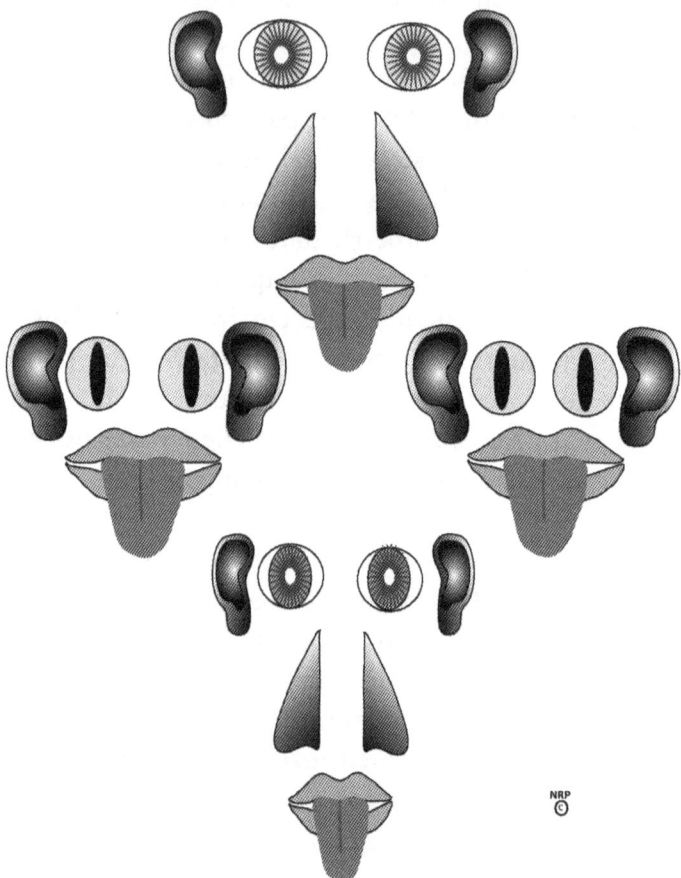

DETECTING

First, we need some sensory element that can detect the sequence of ones and zeros as they happen in our simplified Universe. Let's call this element the Detector. The Detector in our Little Creature is the simple equivalent of one of the sensory organs of a Real World Creature. (A Taste Bud, or Eye, or Ear, etc.). Let's let the Creature's Detector be the equivalent of a Real World Taste Sensor. I choose a sensor for taste because, I suspect that the evolutionary development and prioritizing of sensory mechanisms might have happened as a result of the need for detecting changes in a Creature's outside environment in relationship to their proximity and thereby immediate danger or value to the Creature. The ordering in time of the development of these senses might be as follows.

1. Taste, because the detected material is either adjacent to or actually entering the Creature.

2. Touch, because the detected material is directly adjacent to the Creature.

3. Smell, the detected material is within the immediate vicinity of the Creature.

4. Hearing, the detected material is actively moving, but can be at some distance from the Creature.

5. Sight, allows the detection of material that can be at a great distance from the Creature.

I think that it is not unreasonable to believe in this chronology of sensory development, if only from the viewpoint of survival against the dangers of the natural environment. It maybe that some of the senses developed simultaneously.

We need to keep in mind that although our Little Creature has but one Detector (a sensor for taste), for other Creatures that are one sensory step more complicated on the evolutionary scale they would have essentially the same mechanisms of Intelligence associated with each of their individual Sensory Organs. They would also have special mechanisms for relating the different patterns detected by each sensory organ. This is a topic we will cover more completely in the section on Long Term Memory, but here, consider that the types of data that each of our Senses detects within the Real World is very exclusive data. The kind of information that our Eyes must process is a world away from the kind of basic information that our Ears must process and this is true for each of our other Senses.

You might now be thinking that it is not economical for Nature to duplicate the basic mechanisms of Intelligence five times over and that this is against a kind of economy of Mother Nature's evolution. But evolution is about sorting out and selecting the best mechanisms that contribute to survival. In this case Mother Nature had no choice, if intelligible patterns of such diversity where to paint a picture of the Real World inside of a Creature's Mind.

Our Little Creature's Detector will simply detect the patterns of ones and zeros as they happen over time. If our Creature's Detector and the Universe it exists in were much more complicated than the one we propose, then the incoming data patterns might be very complex. When the Real World is very complex there is a need for some method of reducing the complexity of the data patterns to a more simplified form before the "Discovering" of repeatable patterns in the data stream can be performed. For our most simplified Creature there is no need to reduce the complexity of the stream of in coming patterns because they are as simple as can exist. However for the primary Detectors of Real World Creature's each sensor has as a part of its basic nature a strict limit on what and how much data it can detect. As example, the Human Eye is limited by its physical mechanisms to detecting patterns of electromagnetic radiation within a strict band of frequencies. The eye also has limited its area of high geometric and color resolution to a very small part of the actual visual field. Further the majority of the Eye's visual field is limited to detecting only the most rudimentary of changing light patterns and has little or no geometric or color resolution.

Each of the Detectors associated with the other senses also have strict bounds on the kinds and quantity of information that they can detect coming from the Real World.

The mechanisms of the Hearing put strong bounds on the range of audio frequencies that they can detect and also on the strength of the audio signal that is detectable. The Detectors associated with Tasting, Smelling and Feeling also have fixed limits on the range and intensity of patterns that they can detect.

These basic restrictions of the range of pattern data that can be detected by the individual sensory Detectors is a kind of First Filtering of the multitudes of patterns that are present within the World. These initial restrictions allow a Creature to only deal with the range of Real World patterns that evolutionary processes have found as necessary contributors to survival.

Within an advanced civilization of Creatures that require more detailed information from the Real World and specifically information of patterns that are beyond the ranges of their own limited sensory Detectors, they must resort to instruments that in essence can detect patterns that lie beyond their own sensory limits, Ultra Sensory Patterns. For persons to know these patterns, the patterns must be transformed into patterns that are within the bounds of their basic sensory limits. There is no other way for us to know all of those Ultra

Sensory Patterns within the Universe that lie outside of our basic Sensory Detector's limits. We should be conscious of the fact that the transformation of these Ultra Sensory Patterns is by necessity only indicative of the real Ultra Sensory Patterns that existed in the Universe. In fact, all of the patterns that we detect from Nature and think of as representing the Real World are only barely indicative of the patterns that actually exist there.

A final reduction of the complexity of incoming data (for higher animals) is performed by filtering and coding mechanisms that in my definition we will usually refer to as "Mapping" or "The Mapping Function". Once this further filtering and coding of the pattern information that has already been selectively filtered by the Detectors is completed, what we will have left is a minimal skeletal representation of the original pattern that existed in the Real World.

**FILTERING AND CODING
(THE MAPPING FUNCTION)**

FILTERING AND CODING
(THE MAPPING FUNCTION)

Imagine for a moment how complex is the visual data coming to the Eye of a highly advanced Creature like a mammal. Let's say that the image falling on the Eye's Retina represents a simple square of solid red color suspended on a background field of solid untextured blue. Between the Retina and before the first entry into the Brain's first memory areas would exist a neural network that is a Filter and Coding Mechanism, a Mapping Function. This mechanism changes the direct point-by-point relationships that visually and geometrically represented the square's image. The Mapping Function strips away all nonessential detail. The Mapping Function makes a code, a new pattern that no longer has a point-by-point relationship to the initial Visual Real World image, but is a code that contains only the essential elements that can unambiguously define a square and its related nuances. A code, that as an example and for simplification's sake, we will say is a code that means: four right angled corners connected by four straight line segments of equal length. This code is then a new pattern that is representative of the visual image from the Real World; it represents the visual image of the square. Even more to the point, the most significant part of the code that represents the square will be the same code for all and every square that is presented to the visual field of the Eye. The code will also contain in its least significant part, the information that in fact represents the nuances of the visual image of the square i.e., its color, its texture etc.

The code that is generated by the Mapping Function from the initial image of the square is in two parts, a most significant part that is a code representing those things that are the absolute minimal defining aspects of a square and a less significant part that represents the possibilities of color and texture and other nuances that only modify the appearance of the square, but always leave the square as a square. It should be quite clear that if the Mapping Mechanism cannot produce repeatable codes for repeatable patterns (images) that exist in the Real World, then if the other mechanisms of Intelligence are totally functional, there is little chance of a Creature successfully adapting to the happenings in their World. Remember now, back to what we have said about the Visual Alphabet of Patterns. The Mapping Function can generate a specific code for each of the members of the Alphabet of Patterns. These codes are not the patterns, but new unique patterns (codes} that represent those inflections that are the defining elements of those basic Visual Alphabetic Patterns.

Because the Real World is far richer in complex patterns than any intelligent mechanism can deal with and to reduce this complexity, the primary function of the Filtering and Coding Mechanism, the Mapping Function, is to resolve very complex patterns only to the point that they can be meaningfully distinguished from other complex patterns. Because of this kind of exclusionary filtering, all complex patterns received by the Senses are really cut down to a barest of skeletal representations as compared to what they actually represent in the Real World.

For very complex visual patterns only the parts of them that are most significant in allowing us, with certainty, to distinguish them from other similar complex visual patterns are what survive in the output of the Mapping Function. As an example we all know of the experience when we encounter a friend or associate and after a few moments of being together they say to us, "You didn't even notice my new hair cut". The point here is that the defining features by which we know any complex pattern are the minimum features that define it well. In this case, the friend's hair was not one of the primary defining patterns by which we would normally recognize them. We can understand that there were other features about them that were more primary to our recognition of them than their hairstyle.

THE MAPPING FUNCTION

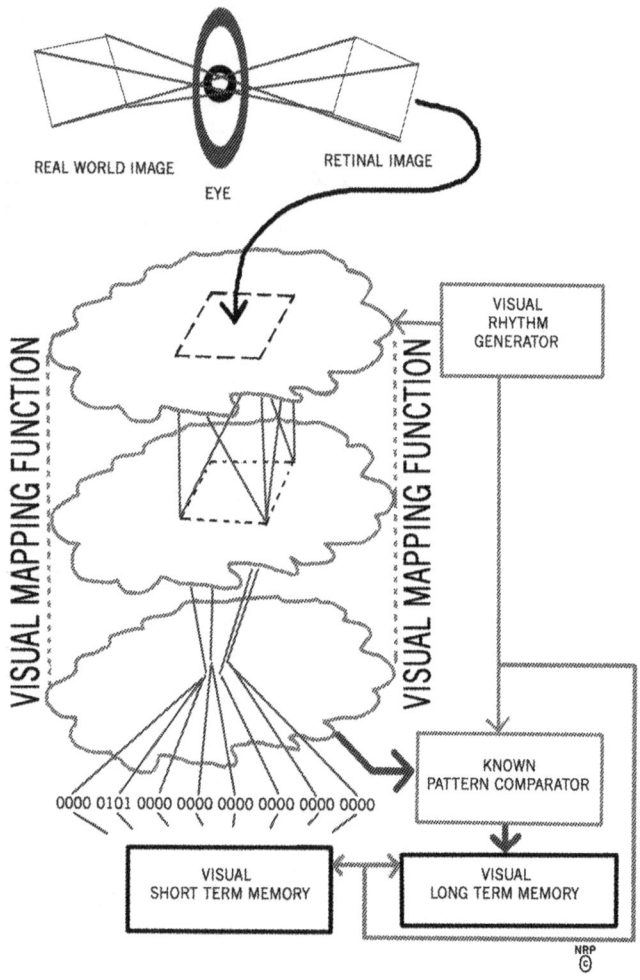

When small children are building their repertoire of patterns by which they can identify objects, we can clearly see how minimal are the features by which they decide recognition. As an example, if they have an older uncle who is bald, whenever they see any bald person in a crowd of people, they think they are their uncle.

You can prove this minimal skeletal structure proposition to your own satisfaction by considering the most familiar objects from the Real World and without having them in your view try to draw in exacting detail the visual details of those objects. You will find that even for relatively simple familiar objects that the details by which you can specifically identify them are extremely limited.   And even further, Seeing in and of itself or recognizing what we see is about comparing the output code of the Mapping Function with the previously learned codes that were outputted from the Mapping Function and were previously stored in memory and if there is something of minor difference between these two codes then we do not immediately recognize the difference.

So in the World of complex Creatures, if two similar but not identical complex visual patterns give the same output code from the Mapping Function, it is by directing the Eye to carefully gaze upon the visual object and by scanning more carefully the object, then the Mapping Function can resolve further defining features that can differentiate between the two complex patterns. It is by directing the sensory Detectors and prolonging their attention to complex patterns that we are able to know them in more and more defining detail. Artists, who are sometimes involved in trying to reproduce objects of the Real World in the realist terms, are persons who know complex patterns at their most defining levels. Further, when the Mapping Function resolves complex patterns and the coded output is stored into Long Term Memory, the Analytical resolution of the Mapping Function is only applied until the pattern can be distinguished from similar patterns. As an extreme example, the resolution of a complex pattern that represents a tree is only resolved to the most general structures: trunk, branches, leaves, and the general overall structural shape. To discern the patterns that distinguish one kind of tree from another kind, the further resolution is done to the next minimal point where the new encoding is sufficient to make the determination that they are different. A higher level of resolution might involve just a closer look at the leaves, or bark, or any other structure that is significant to differentiate between various types of trees. It is of a prime importance that an Intelligent System generalizes to the greatest possible extent, and therefore that the analysis and extent of resolution of a complex pattern be the absolute minimal that can define it as unique. The proposition that patterns are represented by the most minimal code that can determine their uniqueness, allows the Intelligent System two extremely important features:

1. The space required to designate the pattern's storage location in Long Term Memory is minimized.
2. Since the pattern's code is as minimal as possible, it is also in its most generalized form.

Pattern codes that are of a minimal size and therefore the most generalized can represent a whole set of objects, this makes them most useful to an Intelligent Creature. Highly generalized patterns are also the most useful for forming new complex patterns that might be used in solving a problem.

As an example: Consider a Chimpanzee, who sees another Chimpanzee using a long stick to swat at a tree's fruit to knock it to the ground. If the pattern that represents the stick is resolved and encoded and stored in memory as the most general code that can define it, then that code may represent any long thin stiff object, many different sticks can fit this minimal defining pattern. So, it is easy for the Chimpanzee to find another stick and to apply it to the solution of a similar problem. But, if the resolution and the encoding of the pattern for the stick were done to the maximum possible extent, then it would contain the details of every knot, every bend, every change of coloration, etc. In such a case, the Chimp would never be able to find another stick that was exactly in every detail like the original stick. So the Chimp could never find the same stick pattern that could be plugged into a new problem and thus allowing the fruit to be knocked down.

Most of us are extremely lazy at critically examining complex objects or events of the Real World and we therefore know only the most rudimentary features that can identify them. I am sure that persons, who are deaf and therefore must pay particular attention to the happenings within the Visual World, know it in much greater visual detail than those of us who see it and are able with our sense of hearing to help fill in the holes left there by our casual visual observance.

You should be remembering here that each of the Sensory Detectors has its own independent Mapping Function Mechanisms that produce codes that are essentially in two parts. Codes where the most significant part is dedicated to the most prominent and defining features of the incoming pattern and the least significant part is dedicated to the nuances that add secondary meaning to the primary pattern. Remember also that the codes themselves are unique for each of the senses. This is necessarily true because Ears do not smell Lemons, Eyes do not taste Triangles, Taste Buds do not know Squares and so on. This speculation that the mechanisms of detecting and mapping are discrete for each of the Senses is a necessary conclusion, because the information that they each receive from the environment is uniquely different for each of them. This fact alone dictates that each Sense's Detectors are unique and that the processing by filtering and coding of that data from each sensor is unique. But, the overall design of the Mechanisms of the different sensory Mapping Functions is essentially the same. Nature has just repeated the design for each of the unique Senses.

STICKS

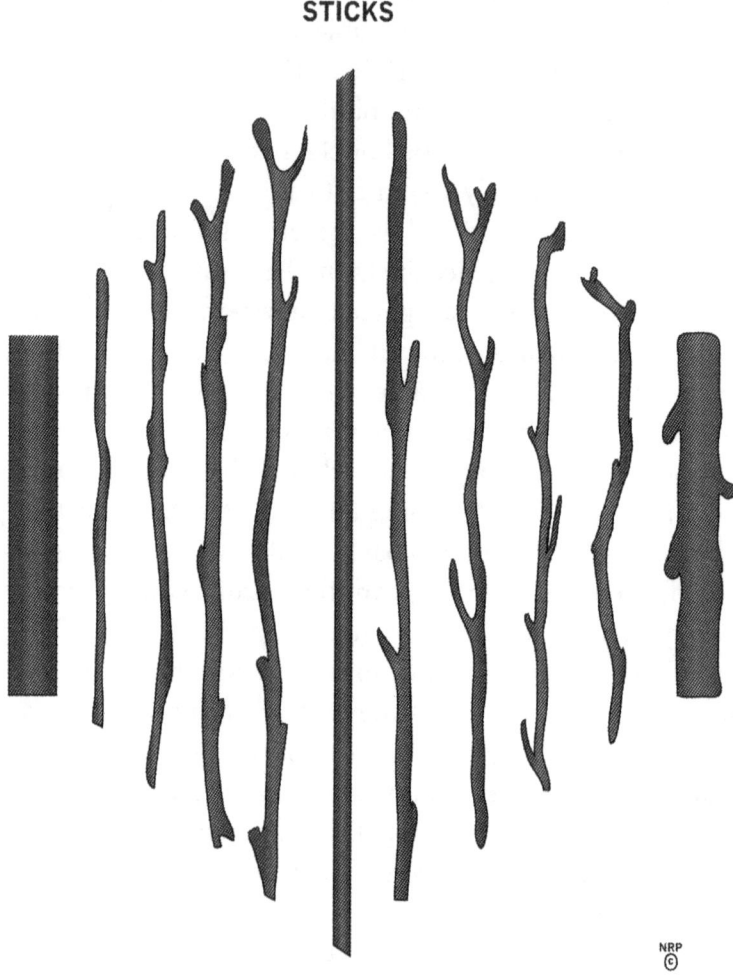

NRP
©

Looking a bit ahead of where we are in our observations, I will note here: That Short Term Memory for each of the Senses must also be Discrete, but not necessarily unique. Also the mechanisms that move Short Term Memory information to the Long Term Memory storage sites are discrete as their addresses are topographically unique. Long Term Memory although its mechanism is essentially common to all senses is topographically segregated for each Sense.

Yes, there is one more type of filtering that is applied to incoming sensory patterns. You might think of yourself and of your conscious examination of the Real World as a continuous process, but in fact it is not true. It cannot be a continuous process. Any continuous process for detecting dynamic moving patterns in the Real World would smear and blur the incoming patterns one into another and then all of the data would be chaotic and always unintelligible. The Mapping Function must take place as a rhythmic and cyclic process in time. We will name this process "Rhythmic Mapping". We will name the mechanism that produces the Cyclic Rhythm the "Rhythm Generator". As a result of this rhythmic sampling and filtering and encoding, what is finally produced is a code that represents a momentary snap shot of a Real World image. So in this final way the patterns detected by the sensory Detectors are time filtered. The nice thing about being time filtered is we don't realize that it is happening, so we believe we see the World in a continuous smooth and seamless existence.

This Rhythmic Mapping for some Creatures can be a deadly situation, for those Creatures who have the slowest Rhythmic Mapping; Creatures with a much faster rhythm snap them up and dine on them as a nice lunch, usually without wine.

Secondary Considerations

Those who teach should realize that by these arguments, if a student has a deficiency in learning through the mechanisms of one sensory input, then if the information can be directed to different or multiple sensory inputs, the learning might be facilitated. Sadly for very complex information all of the senses do not offer equal opportunities. The most primitive senses Smelling and Tasting have a limited ability for accepting complex patterns at a fast enough data rate to make them adaptable to uses for which they were not intended.

*   *   *   *   *

In the present day there are debates about the dangers of using mobile phones while driving a vehicle. The primary sense used in driving a vehicle is the visual sense. The primary sense to converse on a mobile phone is the sense of hearing. These two independent senses are totally capable of processing independent patterns without interfering with each other. We have been using the two of them simultaneously while driving vehicles and at other times long before there were mobile telephones. It should be obvious to this argument that the individual must stay alert to the visual field that is supplying the primary information necessary for driving and be able if required to use both of their hands. I would propose that if we had half of all frequent drivers wearing a small badge every time they were driving a vehicle, and every time there was a vehicular accident we checked to see if the driver was wearing a badge, there would be those who would claim the accident's fault belonged to the badge. We have a very serious problem within society of cause and effect being linked without the direct evidence of linkage. It is a condition that is rampant in today's World.

*   *   *   *   *

When any single sense is attempting to simultaneously capture two entirely different complex pattern strings, such as the attempt to listen to two different conversations about different subject matters, the sense will be severely defeated at trying to interlace between these different conversations.

If on the other hand you attempt to listen to only one conversation that is buried within the noise of many conversations, as long as that conversation of your interest is of a sufficient volume to be fully heard, the Mapping Function for the Ear can separate it out from the background without much trouble.

You might think of the situation this way. The Mapping Function for Hearing first maps the incoming sound spectrum at a rhythmic sampling rate on to an equivalent two-dimensional neural space. By this mapping, the Mapping Function is then able to differentiate between sources of sound in a similar manner to how the Eye is able to selectively examine the images within the visual field. The Mapping Function can isolate on a two dimensional canvas, what at first appeared as a one-dimensional stream in time. By this method the Mapping Function is able to concentrate on any part of the canvas and perform the mapping exclusively for that part as separate from other sound patterns that lay elsewhere on the canvas.

It would be reasonable to assume that this kind of first mapping to a two-dimensional canvas would also be appropriate for the other senses.

*   *   *   *   *

A Note of Caution:

When you are thinking about sensory patterns and how the mapping function might convert those sensory inputs into output codes, what you might be prone to believe is the most significant information (most significant parts) within the original sensory patterns will many times not be the most significant information. It is the Mapping Function that has evolved over great lengths of time that knows what are the significant and the less significant parts of any pattern. These are always necessarily related only to their importance for a creature's survival. Those features that are most important for survival are always the most significant part of the code.

SHORT TERM MEMORY

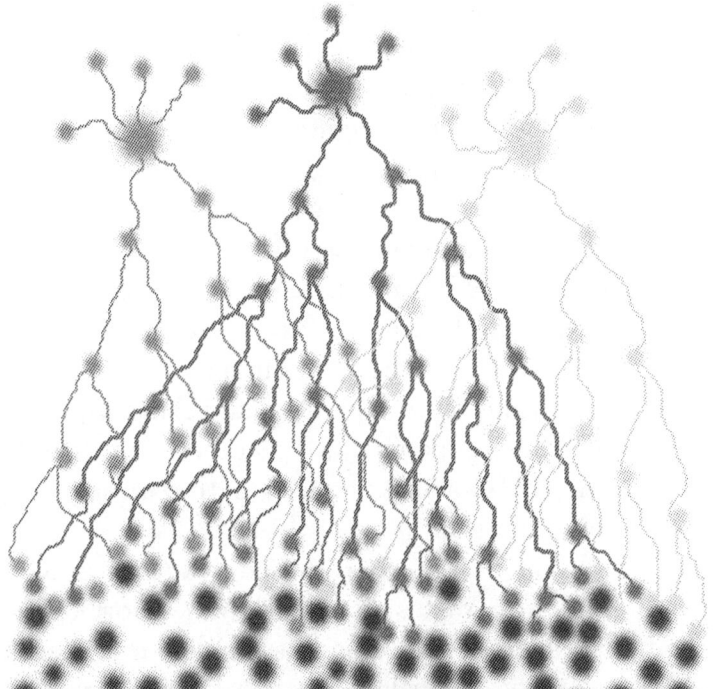

MAPPING FUNCTION

NRP
©

DISCOVERING AND SHORT TERM MEMORY LOOKING AT SOME THINGS IN TERMS OF THE LITTLE CREATURE

Clearly, the Intelligent Mechanisms of our Little Creature must contain some system of memory that can remember long sequences of ones and zeros that have happened over a period of time. Let's name this memory the Short Term Memory. Clearly, the Little Creature requires some mechanism that can compare the current happenings in its Minimal Universe to already learned patterns. This mechanism would allow the Little Creature to know when a known pattern that had just been realized (detected in real time) is an already known pattern. Let's call this mechanism the Known Pattern Comparator. In general a Comparator is a simple device that can contain any string of a predetermined length of ones and zeros (a pattern) and can compare each bit (a one or zero) in that string (pattern) to any other equal length string of ones and zeros, thereby allowing it to detect if the two strings (patterns) are identical or not identical.

Also the repertoire of Known (Learned) Patterns must be stored away in another memory that is distinct from the Short Term Memory. We will name this memory the Long Term Memory. The Long Term Memory is essentially equivalent to the Long Term Memory of Creatures in the Real Three Dimensional World. It should be noted here, that Known Patterns that happen in real time are easily determined as to being known patterns, because of a special scheme that involves the Known Pattern Comparator and their addressing within the Long Term Memory. This powerful scheme allows for the instant recognition, without the need for searching through Long Term Memory for any already learned pattern as it occurs in real time. We will look in detail at the Known Pattern Comparator and the Long Term Memory a little later.

The First Time Discovering of Patterns

The discovering of a new pattern in Nature for the first time is a difficult and time-consuming problem. This problem in our Real Three Dimensional World is called "Learning" and to accomplish this learning task even in our proposed One Dimensional World is still very complicated and very time consuming. It is important that we look at least briefly, at how this task of discovering for the first time an intelligible pattern might be accomplished. This process, even in its most rudimentary form in a One Dimensional World, will give us important insights into the mechanisms involved, mechanisms that we might not expect to be involved in learning. So here briefly is a description of the mechanisms involved in detecting a new intelligible pattern that is embedded within a background of chaos.

We of course need a simple Detector to detect each bit as it happens in our One Dimensional Universe. We also need a Short Term Memory. The Short Term Memory will record the data from the Detector, recording each one or zero exactly as it happens in our One Dimensional Universe. The Short Term Memory will contain, at the end of the day, an exact ordered record of the day's data (happenings). In keeping with current jargon, let's call the individual numbers, the ones or zeros at any time or any place within our Intelligent System, a "Bit" or "Bits". We need to note that we do not need to make use of the "Filtering and Coding" Mechanisms (the Mapping Function), this is simply because in the simplified One Dimensional Universe that we will be examining there are no patterns complicated enough to require Filtering and Coding. All possible patterns that can exist in this simplified One Dimensional Universe are as simple and condensed as they can be. At least this is true for the purposes of this discussion. Next we need a Comparator, but this is a special Comparator, different and separate from the Known Pattern Comparator. We will call this Comparator the New Pattern Comparator. We have not discussed how small or large a pattern we will use as our basic detectable pattern size; this of course would determine how many bits our New Pattern Comparator could contain at any one time. It is not important that we set an exact size for the Comparator at this time, but it is important to discuss generally what factors should be considered in determining its size. If we choose a size that is too small, we would not have any discretion at detecting patterns within a chaotic background. As an example, if the Comparator was just big enough to hold two bits every string of ones and zeros would look like a repeating pattern. In fact, the whole One Dimensional Universe would look as if it were made up of just four basic patterns, nothing else. In this case even the background of chaos would disappear and would seem like just four ever-repeating patterns.

In the case of choosing a Comparator that is too large, say larger than any detectable pattern in our One Dimensional Universe, then we would never find any patterns in existence. Everything would look like an endless string of chaos bits. So, there is a need to choose a large enough size for our Comparator, so that it is effective at filtering out the random bits of pure chaos. The Comparator must be small enough to detect the most basic patterns that would have a consequence to our specific Little Creature. Therefore the New Pattern Comparator must be large enough to contain enough bits that would be equal to the largest single pattern that our Little Creature can ever detect within its One Dimensional Universe. To make the New Pattern Comparator meet the requirements of also being small enough to detect the smallest basic patterns that are of consequence to our Little Creature, we simply place a lower limit on the number of bits that it is allowed to compare as a pattern. The reality for this New Pattern Comparator is that it could make comparisons of variable length strings of data. It could compare strings of some minimal length in a continuous manner and compare strings up to some maximal length. As an example it could compare a minimum of eight bits in a string, and then also nine bits, ten bits, eleven bits and so on up to the maximum size of the Comparator. It would seem believable, that depending upon their needs, different Creatures would have different sized New Pattern Comparators. By "size" here we mean the maximum number of sequential bits that the Comparator would be able to hold or contain at any one time. For Real World Creatures, their mechanisms for comparison are much, much more complicated, because they need to process multitudes of bits simultaneously. Without any doubt their only means of accomplishing such a great task is to process the data in a parallel processing mechanism.

Let's look at the complete process of detecting for the first time an intelligible pattern. As the day in our One Dimensional Universe begins, the little creature's Detector detects each bit of this Universe as it happens and stores them one at a time into the Short Term Memory. As each bit is stored in the Short Term Memory, the Short Term Memory Counter (This counter, we will consider as an integral part of the Short Term Memory) counts the number of bits as they come into the Short Term Memory. It counts each bit as one count.

Let's say that a day has just completed. The Short Term Memory will contain in sequence, bit by bit, an exact record of the detected happenings during the entire day in our One-Dimensional Universe. We also know by counting the bits as they entered the Short Term Memory, exactly how many in number there are within the Short Term Memory.

And so, we now will begin the process of searching for an intelligible pattern. (See Page 50 & 51) We take an ORDERED Copy of the first number of bits of the day's beginning, which entered the Short Term Memory, and transfer them into the New Pattern Comparator. We of course take the same number of ordered bits from the Short Term Memory as the New Pattern Comparator's number of bits, the number of bits that make up the maximum size of any pattern we would be trying to discover. We now move the whole compactor in an ORDERED Way to the left end of the Short Term Memory, where the last bits of the day's patterns are stored, and line up the first Ordered bit of the Comparator with the last ordered bit of the Short Term Memory.

New Pattern Comparator Searching Through Short Term Memory

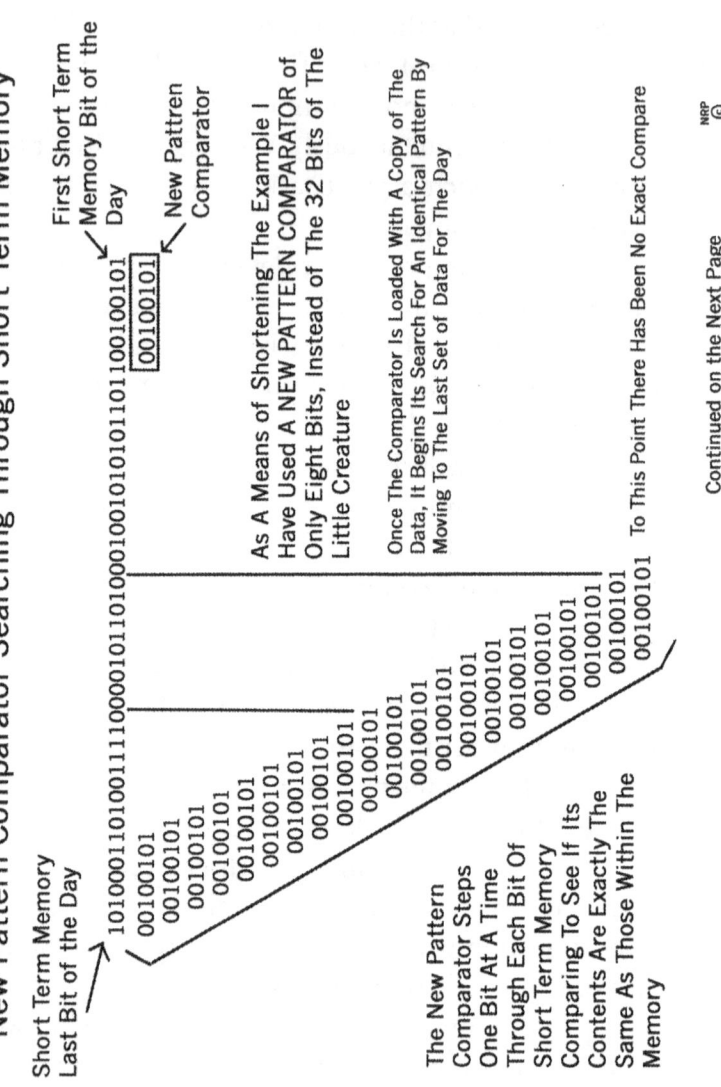

Short Term Memory
Last Bit of the Day

First Short Term
Memory Bit of the
Day

New Pattren
Comparator

As A Means of Shortening The Example I
Have Used A NEW PATTERN COMPARATOR of
Only Eight Bits, Instead of The 32 Bits of The
Little Creature

Once The Comparator Is Loaded With A Copy of The
Data, It Begins Its Search For An Identical Pattern By
Moving To The Last Set of Data For The Day

The New Pattern
Comparator Steps
One Bit At A Time
Through Each Bit Of
Short Term Memory
Comparing To See If Its
Contents Are Exactly The
Same As Those Within The
Memory

To This Point There Has Been No Exact Compare

Continued on the Next Page

NRP
©

=Continuation=

New Pattern Comparator Searching Through Short Term Memory

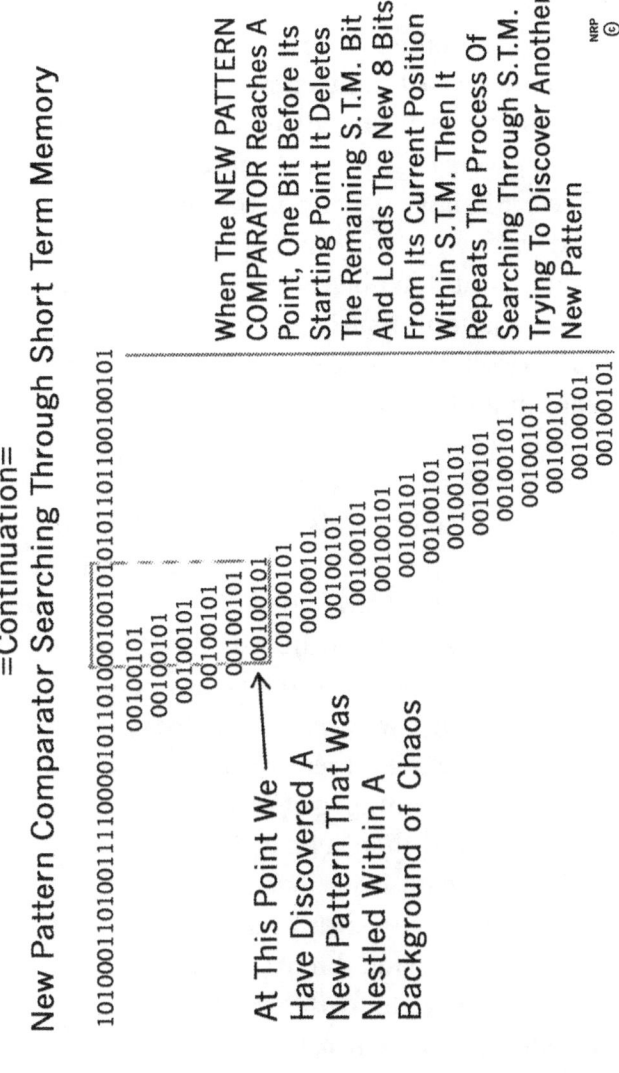

At This Point We ———→
Have Discovered A
New Pattern That Was
Nestled Within A
Background of Chaos

When The NEW PATTERN
COMPARATOR Reaches A
Point, One Bit Before Its
Starting Point It Deletes
The Remaining S.T.M. Bit
And Loads The New 8 Bits
From Its Current Position
Within S.T.M. Then It
Repeats The Process Of
Searching Through S.T.M.
Trying To Discover Another
New Pattern

NRP
©

We now compare bit for bit of the New Pattern Comparator with the ordered bits of our current position within the Short Term Memory. If there should be an exact comparison, each bit in order within the New Pattern Comparator is identical to each bit in order within the Short Term Memory, then we have found a repeatable pattern on our first try. It would mean that the very first string of bits that entered into the Short Term Memory were exactly identical to the last string of bits that entered Short Term Memory, a pattern that had repeated at least one time during the day. If we actually find a repeated pattern, then we do take a specific action, but don't be concerned here about what we do if in fact we do find a pattern, that is for little later in the discussion. If there is no comparison we move the Comparator in order one bit towards the beginning of the data (one bit to the right) in the Short Term Memory and again compare the ordered bits within the New Pattern Comparator to those ordered bits at our current position within the Short Term Memory. This routine would continue in exactly this manner until, either a pattern in the Short Term Memory compares exactly with the pattern in the New Pattern Comparator, meaning a new pattern has been found, or until we are exactly one bit from the beginning of the data (one bit away from the right end of the STM) in the Short Term Memory. When we are one bit from the beginning data within the Short Term Memory, then we stop at that point and decrement the count of the total number of bits in the Short Term Memory Counter by one count, and then reload the New Pattern Comparator with the ordered bits of data from its current position in Short Term Memory and delete the first currently existing bit within the Short Term Memory (the most right hand bit). We now test our Short Term Memory Counter, which contains the count of the number of bits in the Short Term Memory, to see if it is at zero. If it is not zero then we initiate the whole comparison process from the beginning. If the count is zero then we have completed our task of looking at every possibility of detecting a new pattern from the day's happenings. As can be clearly seen from this process, it is a slow drawn-out and laborious process to discover for the first time an intelligible pattern that is embedded within a background of chaos. We can easily understand that intelligible patterns of lengths longer than the primary detectable pattern length are simply just a summation of intelligible patterns and so are easily detected by just repeating the pattern detection scheme immediately after each part of the intelligible pattern is recognized.

With just these elements integrated in some way and contained in some Creature, we should be able to detect the occurrence of an intelligible pattern embedded within a string of chaos. But there are two important elements to still be considered for our Creature to be considered intelligent.

It is an absolute requirement that the Intelligent System or Creature must make an appropriate reaction into the Universe, whenever the System or Creature detects an intelligible pattern that is of a consequence to its survival. It is not sufficient to be considered Intelligent that a machine has contained within its structure the basic elements for detecting repeatable patterns in our Universe. This is not sufficient to be an Intelligent System. If these structures discover repeatable patterns and the Creature then waves some flag when an intelligible pattern is detected, this is not an Intelligent System. It is a prerequisite of a real Intelligence that the action it makes upon detecting a repeatable pattern is appropriate to the significance of the pattern to the Creature. This requirement is necessary because it is my claim that Intelligence is a condition of living Creatures and has only to due with benefiting the survival of living Creatures within the natural environment.

We must later discuss what exactly might be a meaningful reaction to the detection of an intelligible pattern and how that reaction is implemented. It would seem that the simplest forms of life have the basic elements of an Intelligent System and that these most simple most basic elements are certainly inherited.

LONG TERM MEMORY

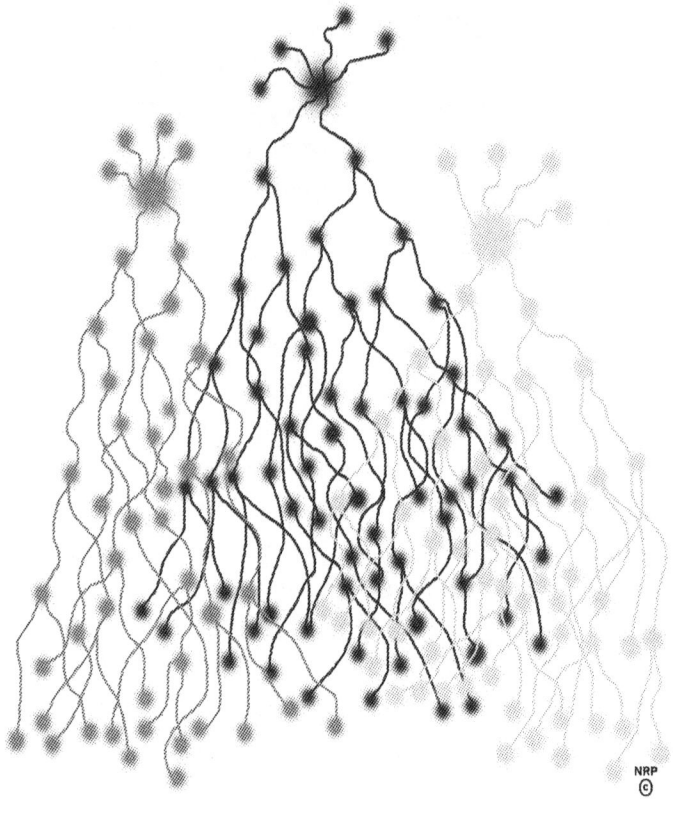

MEMORIZING
LONG TERM MEMORY

We now need to consider some things about another specific memory, one that is separate from the Short Term Memory, a memory that we have named the Long Term Memory. First let's examine the considerations that might determine its size. By size we will mean the number of individual memory locations that it contains and how many bits each memory location can hold. For now, we will not specify the size of the individual storage located at each Long Term Memory storage location. For the simplest of Creatures in Nature the size of the Long Term Memory would only need to be small. More complicated Creatures such as mammals with more refined sensory Detectors and therefore more known patterns and more complex patterns to be remembered and stored, they would require much larger Long Term Memories. Also the size of the Long Term Memory for mammals would be dependent on how complicated their interactions with Nature could be. For now and for our little One-Dimensional Universe let's choose an arbitrary size of our Long Term Memory, rather small at about four billion memory storage locations. This is a rather small memory, but it is of more than a sufficient size to clearly demonstrate what it is all about. It is a memory where any of the over four billion possible individual storage locations can be designated by using a thirty two bit binary number, we will refer to this number as the address of a specific storage location within the Long Term Memory. Consider if we sat down and began categorizing the things of the Real World, we could divide them into four billion different patterns and our proposed Long Term Memory would easily accommodate their storage, and as you will shortly see, it would also facilitate their instant identification for recall.

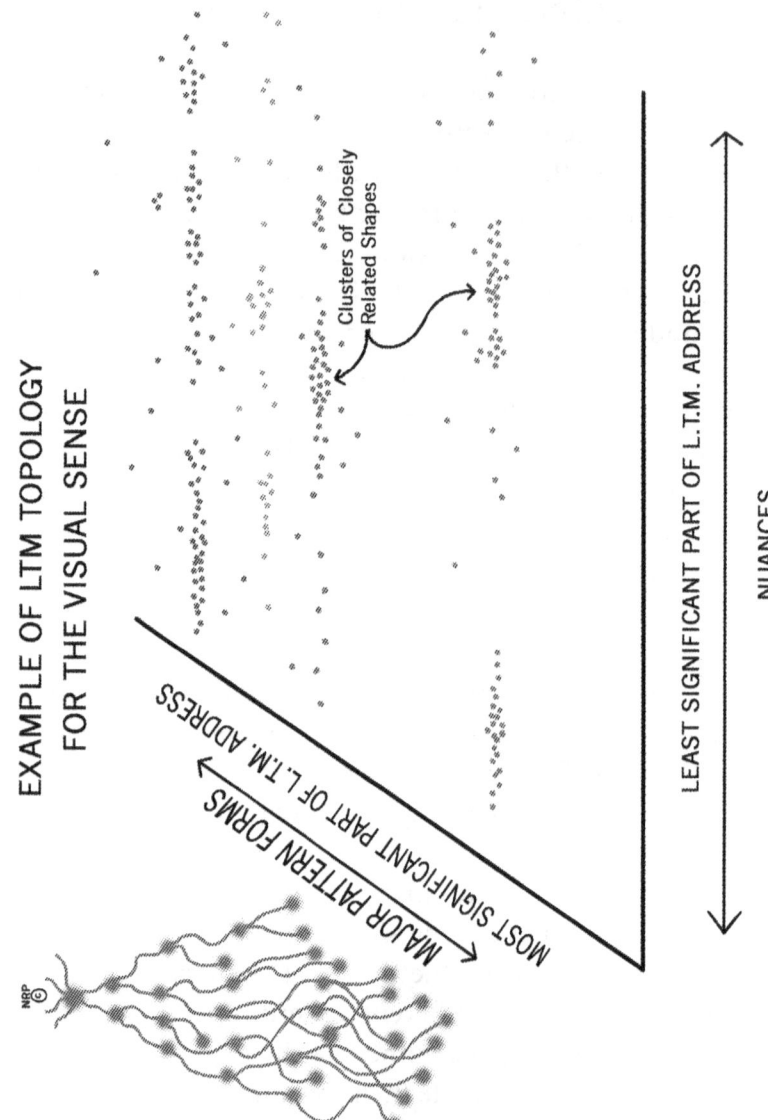

EXAMPLE OF LTM TOPOLOGY
FOR THE VISUAL SENSE

Clusters of Closely
Related Shapes

MAJOR PATTERN FORMS

MOST SIGNIFICANT PART OF L.T.M. ADDRESS

LEAST SIGNIFICANT PART OF L.T.M. ADDRESS

NUANCES

Addressing Storage Scheme

Now we come to a very interesting point to understand exactly how the repeatable patterns that our little Creature has discovered from the One- Dimensional Universe are stored within the Long Term Memory. We do not store the sequence of ones and zeros that make up the body of the detected pattern into the Long Term Memory as a means of remembering that we have detected that certain pattern. Instead we use that sequence of ones and zeros that actually make up the detected pattern as an address (a binary address) for a location within the Long Term Memory. It is at this address (the actual binary number that is the detected pattern or the encoded representation of a complex Real World pattern) where we will store a simple marker that means we have detected **the Pattern, which is This Address.** The pattern itself is just the address where a detection marker is stored. What I am saying is that the Address itself is the detected pattern sequence.

For a moment now think of addresses and mail in the Real World. Normally the address of a mailbox is where we place the mail as an envelope that contains information we want delivered to that particular mailbox. Later if we only know the information that was contained **Within** the **Envelope** and want to discover if it is in some mail box, then to find it we must search through every mail box until we finally discover which mail box it is in. In the system I am describing **the information in the letter is itself the mailbox address.**

The intelligible information contained within the pattern is simply just an address in Long Term Memory. This scheme allows the system (the Creature) a very, very powerful mechanism for immediately recognizing any known pattern that is again detected in Nature, as an already known pattern.

ADDRESSING STORAGE SCHEME

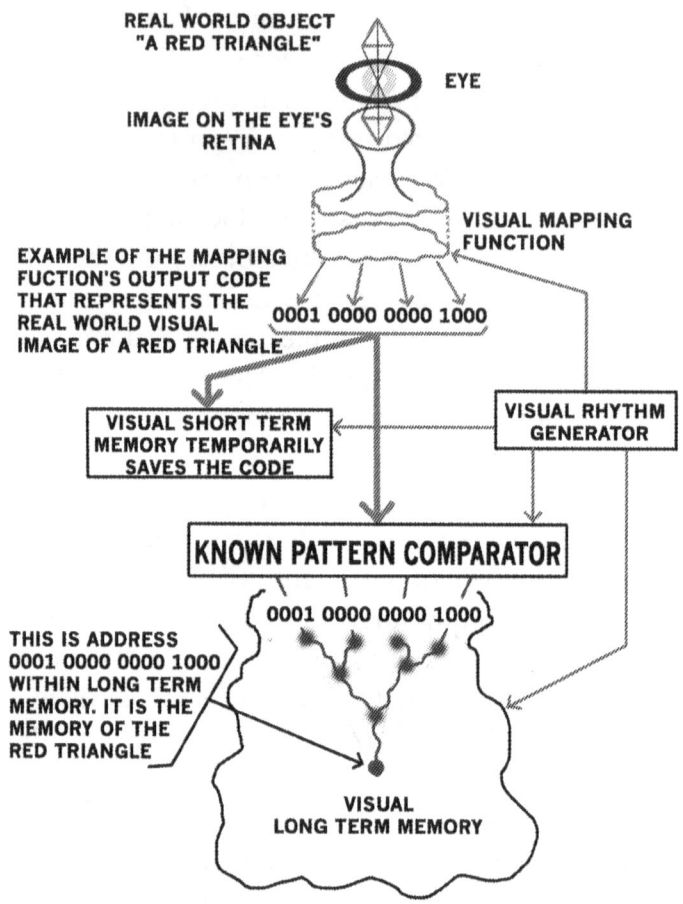

**REAL WORLD OBJECT
"A RED TRIANGLE"**

EYE

**IMAGE ON THE EYE'S
RETINA**

**VISUAL MAPPING
FUNCTION**

**EXAMPLE OF THE MAPPING
FUCTION'S OUTPUT CODE
THAT REPRESENTS THE
REAL WORLD VISUAL
IMAGE OF A RED TRIANGLE**

0001 0000 0000 1000

**VISUAL SHORT TERM
MEMORY TEMPORARILY
SAVES THE CODE**

**VISUAL RHYTHM
GENERATOR**

KNOWN PATTERN COMPARATOR

0001 0000 0000 1000

**THIS IS ADDRESS
0001 0000 0000 1000
WITHIN LONG TERM
MEMORY. IT IS THE
MEMORY OF THE
RED TRIANGLE**

**VISUAL
LONG TERM MEMORY**

Note: only sixteen bits of the mapping code are shown
as a means of simplifying the diagram

NRP

This system of the learned or known pattern actually being an address within Long Term Memory allows the Creature, the instant ability to always recognize it as a known pattern every time the pattern is again detected in Nature. There is no need for the mechanisms of Intelligence to begin searching through the more than four billion memory locations to discover if a pattern is identical to a known pattern. The immediate detection within Nature of an already learned pattern takes us directly to the memory address of that known pattern and we can know it is an already known pattern by a simple marker that is stored at that address.

You may think that I am over emphasizing this explanation, but I do so, because it is the most central kernel of all of the intelligent mechanisms that allows an Intelligent Creature to function as Intelligent within a very complex Real World.

Threshold of Memory

In truth there are other kinds of data, which we would like to store at these known pattern addresses within Long Term Memory. The Simple marker that we would store at the address of a known pattern would be a small number, a threshold number. The threshold number is like a counter value, which would give an indication of how many times the same pattern had been detected in the Real World. The Creature would use this threshold number, as an indication of how long the memory of a pattern would be retained in memory before it was forgotten. This threshold number for a particular memory would automatically be counted down to zero over some period of time. If the threshold number became zero, then the memory of that particular pattern would essentially disappear. Please keep in mind here, that the threshold number exists only in the Long Term Memory and realize that if the threshold number is very small, then the memory associated with it is weak and might soon be forgotten and in this sense, some memories within the Long Term Memory are truly short-term memories. The decay rate of the threshold number would probably be represented as a linear function of time. But, if the threshold number was large enough it would bypass the decay function and then the pattern would never be forgotten. That is, it would never be forgotten as long as the memory address remained physically healthy. In the Real World of Biological Long Term Memories the threshold number could be implemented as some strength of chemical binding between neurons or a physical proximity or other simple but potentially lasting physical or chemical features.

We should take note here that, as regards patterns from the Real World, we have considered them as things without intensity, but in fact all patterns from the Real World have an intensity associated with them. As an example, in the Real World of sound patterns, consider the sound from the clap of two hands as compared to the sound from a clap of thunder. It is quite certain that the intensity of a detected pattern effects the value of the threshold number at the memory location of the detected pattern. Another circumstance that can affect the value of the threshold number is when the Real World pattern from any sensory input is strongly and simultaneously associated with sensory inputs from other Senses. As I briefly mentioned about trauma, it is usual that it involves intense and simultaneous inputs to many Senses. These intense and simultaneous inputs have their direct effect on the longevity of their memory. They are probably intense enough to set the value of the threshold number above the bounds that allow the decay function to affect it. It is apparent that every kind of repeated exposure to any specific pattern or event including, voluntary or involuntary thinking about them, being re-exposed to the actual pattern in the real world or thinking of other patterns that are associated with them or might be associated with them, and even dreaming about them, all lead to an increase of the value of the threshold number and therefore the longevity of the memory of the pattern or event.

CROSS SENSORY ADDRESS LINKING

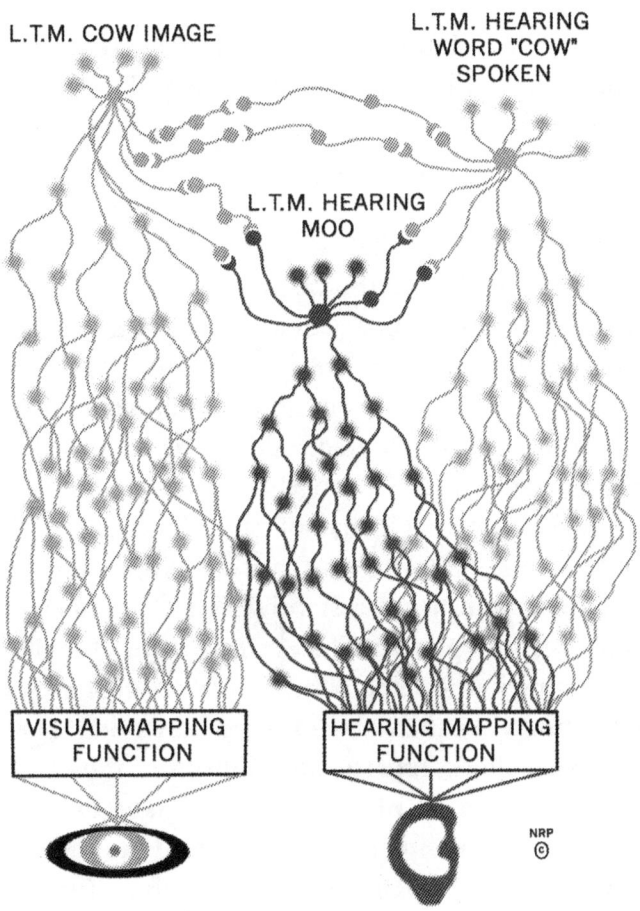

L.T.M. COW IMAGE

L.T.M. HEARING
WORD "COW"
SPOKEN

L.T.M. HEARING
MOO

VISUAL MAPPING
FUNCTION

HEARING MAPPING
FUNCTION

NRP
©

CROSS SENSORY ADDRESS LINKING

There are still other kinds of data that need to be stored at the address representing a known pattern. If, as an example the pattern address is for a visual pattern and that pattern also has associated with it a different sensory input, say an audio pattern, then at the visual pattern address would be stored the address representing the audio pattern associated with it. Also since the visual and audio were simultaneously happening patterns, at the address representing the audio pattern would be stored the address that represents the visual pattern. As a straightforward example of this, consider a child who is learning the various kinds of animals of the Real World and the various sounds that each animal can make. When the child sees an image of a Cow and has learned that a Cow makes the sound Moo, at the address that represents the image of the Cow will be stored the address of sound memory where the pattern that represents the sound Moo is located. And, at the address that represents the pattern that is the sound Moo will be stored the address of the pattern that represents the image of the Cow. This Cross Sensory Address Linking is the powerful way that one single sensory input that represents a known pattern, can instantly bring to mind any learned and associated other sensory pattern. This is why the simple sniff of the scent of perfume lingering in the air can immediately bring to mind the image of the person, who in our memory is associated with that perfume.

Here I have been alternating the descriptions of the described mechanisms between the terms of the Creature in a One Dimensional Universe with some discussion of the Real World interlaced. I will try to keep them enough separated that, which is which is apparent.

For our mechanical Creature of the One-Dimensional Universe, we would be required to store whole addresses that would point to the patterns associated by Cross Sensory Address Linking. In the Real World of biological Creatures, a single or a few connections between neurons originating at the associated memory locations for the different senses could accomplish this Cross Sensory Address Linking.

There are times, other than those were some trauma takes place, where more than two senses are strongly involved in the simultaneous association of their patterns. In this case, the Cross Sensory Address Linking scheme that we just discussed for two sensory patterns is simply repeated, thus linking the related sensory data to each other within the Long Term Memory.

By the method of Cross Sensory Address Linking we are able to build a large repertoire of remembered complex patterns.

Cross Address Linking

There are other linkings of addresses that takes place within the structures of Long Term Memory. Patterns that are detected by an individual sensory organ (Detector) can also be address linked in the same way as we described for the linking that can take place between different Senses. As an example the patterns stored within the area of the Long Term Memory that is associated with hearing can be Cross Address Linked. In this way the memories of the individual patterns that taken together represent a musical melody can be connected so that the melody is remembered as flowing in time, instead of it being remembered as individual unconnected chunks. I think musical artists will have some strong feelings about this type of linking. They often learn their musical scores in sections, one section at a time. As they learn each section, those patterns that make it up are Cross Address Linked. If at some time they are required to perform a particular section solely from memory, they will often discover they can only perform it, if they can start at the discrete starting points that represent the beginning of the Cross Address Linking. This same starting point problem exist for all learned activities that are made of long sequential strings of patterns in time, where the complex pattern is formed by means of Cross Address Linking or Cross Sensory Address Linking.

THREE CROSS SENSORY ADDRESS LINKS WITH ONE MISSING REVERSE LINKING

Here we see three cross sensory address links for four different pattern sensory inputs. The links for sight (visual) and hearing are bidirectional links, but the link to the memory for the sense of taste has only been established in one direction. This leads to the situation where if a known taste is tasted, but the tasted object has not been seen or the name of the object has not been spoken or read, then the individual is sure they know the taste but cannot name the taste.

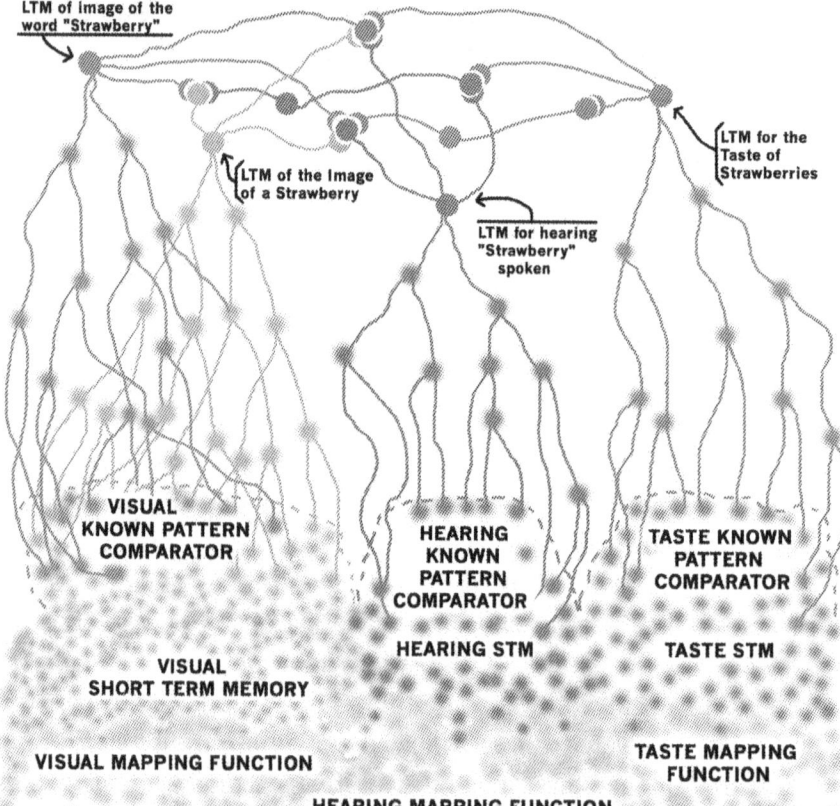

LTM of image of the word "Strawberry"

LTM of the Image of a Strawberry

LTM for the Taste of Strawberries

LTM for hearing "Strawberry" spoken

VISUAL KNOWN PATTERN COMPARATOR

HEARING KNOWN PATTERN COMPARATOR

TASTE KNOWN PATTERN COMPARATOR

HEARING STM

TASTE STM

VISUAL SHORT TERM MEMORY

VISUAL MAPPING FUNCTION

TASTE MAPPING FUNCTION

HEARING MAPPING FUNCTION

NRP
©

Here is it is time to note that both Cross Address Linking and Cross Sensory Address Linking are by necessity directional linkings. This is what we should reasonably expect for biological Creatures, since the flow of information in the basic neural structures is directional. It is the fact that these linkings are directional, that when we remember a piece of music, we do not remember it as being played backwards. And when we remember happenings within our lives, we do not remember them in a backwards order.

This directional linking leaves some important things to be considered about learning in general. When I first mentioned these linkings, the example presented was a child learning the pattern that represents the visual image of a Cow and learning the patterns of the sound that a Cow makes, Moo. But, because the physical mechanisms for biological creatures that accomplish the linking of the two different sensory patterns within the Long Term Memory are directional, once the child has learned that the Cow makes the sound Moo, the child must also learn separately that the Moo is the sound the Cow makes. This is the only way that the presentation of either the Moo or the Cow's image can lead to the bi-directional memory recall that associates the two patterns.

Further, all kinds of complex actions or movements that are executed by the body's muscles are orchestrated and sometimes are even timed by learned Cross Address Linkings. The only exceptions to this statement are those actions, which in a very primitive sense might be considered as executed as a result of instinctive mechanisms. Within this group of exceptions are those inherited and most primitive actions that are named "Reflex Actions." and those other instinctive actions whose primary place of residence is within the brain.

EXAMPLES OF LONG TERM MEMORY
ADDRESSES FOR CHANGING VISUAL IMAGES

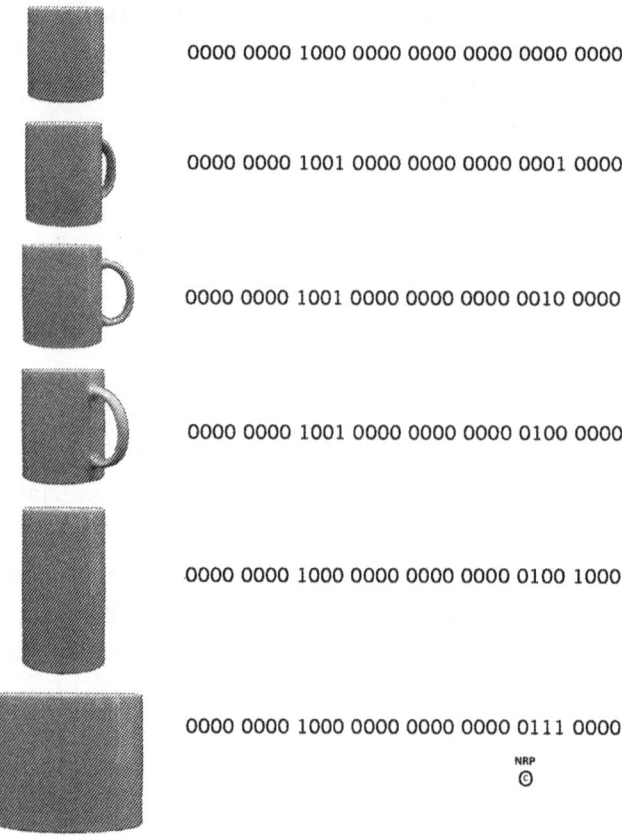

0000 0000 1000 0000 0000 0000 0000 0000

0000 0000 1001 0000 0000 0000 0001 0000

0000 0000 1001 0000 0000 0000 0010 0000

0000 0000 1001 0000 0000 0000 0100 0000

0000 0000 1000 0000 0000 0000 0100 1000

0000 0000 1000 0000 0000 0000 0111 0000

NRP
☉

Once a sequence of Cross Address Links has been learned for the control of a set of muscle movements, if the sequence is initiated then the muscle movements of the sequence follow one after another until the sequence has been completed. This situation is true without variation to sequences that are both short and quickly executed. You can witness the obvious truth to this axiom by carefully watching a boxing match. You will see the boxers use specific learned sequences for multiple blows even when the object of their blows has moved out of range of those blows. Once the boxer has started the learned sequence, the sequence moves through its entire course independent of any changes in the situation that makes the remainder of the sequence inappropriate.

The most astute athletic couches seem to sense the truth of this axiom and by carefully examining the specific movements of their potential competitors are able to devise strategies that make good use of this knowledge

I hope it is becoming apparent that our Long Term Memory is physically divided into areas that contain the pattern addresses associated with each of the discrete Organs of Sense. I believe this discrete separation adds credence to my speculation about the evolutionary prioritizing of the development of the senses.

It would seem that the mechanisms of Intelligence, as we have so far discussed them, exist intact and distinct for each of a Creature's sensory organs and that the mechanism that so powerfully links them is the Cross Sensory Address Linking Scheme and the Cross Address Linking which operate within the Long Term Memory. It is not important that we investigate the details of how the Cross Sensory Address Linking is accomplished. As far as the engineering of the process is concerned, it is a simple and straightforward procedure, but with no consequence to our consideration here.

It should be easy to understand that memory patterns that have many cross linking addresses to other sensory Long Term Memory areas are memories that are easily recallable as they have a maximum number of points to gain access to the whole memory of the event. By the same reasoning, it is understandable that memories with extensive sensory associated cross linked addresses have a longevity of the memory associated with them that is greater than memories that have no cross linked sensory addresses associated with them. You can consider it this way, if for some reason (stroke, a cosmic ray direct hit, etc.) one of the sensory long term memory address is totally lost, then there are still memory areas of the other senses related to the memory of the event where access to the memory of the event can be initiated. Thus the loss of one sensory cross linked memory address still leaves the other cross linked addresses and most of the memory of the event intact.

There are obvious arguments that could be made here about the more you learn, the longer in life you may retain you're learning, but we need to save those for the section on education.

We do need to note, that the scheme of the linking of pattern addresses within the Long Term Memory is not exclusively reserved to the cross linking of simultaneous occurring patterns from different senses. Any patterns that are strongly associated can be Cross Address Linked or Cross Sensory Address Linked. Also it is evident that merely thinking about unassociated patterns can cause them to be linked.

We might also note, that so called verbal slips of the tongue, that usually involve somewhat sound alike words are a testimony to the correctness of the coding and storage schemes of the Long Term Memory presented here.

It is the dual scheme of the pattern actually being the Long Term Memory address that represents it, and the Cross Linking of Long Term Memory patterns that give intelligent Creatures their wonderfully smooth interface with the Real World that surrounds them. It makes the Creature's interactions with their environment a harmonious happening, where the patterns detected within the environment resonate with the patterns within their brains and their responses echo back to the Real Natural World.

CHARACTERIZING PATTERNS

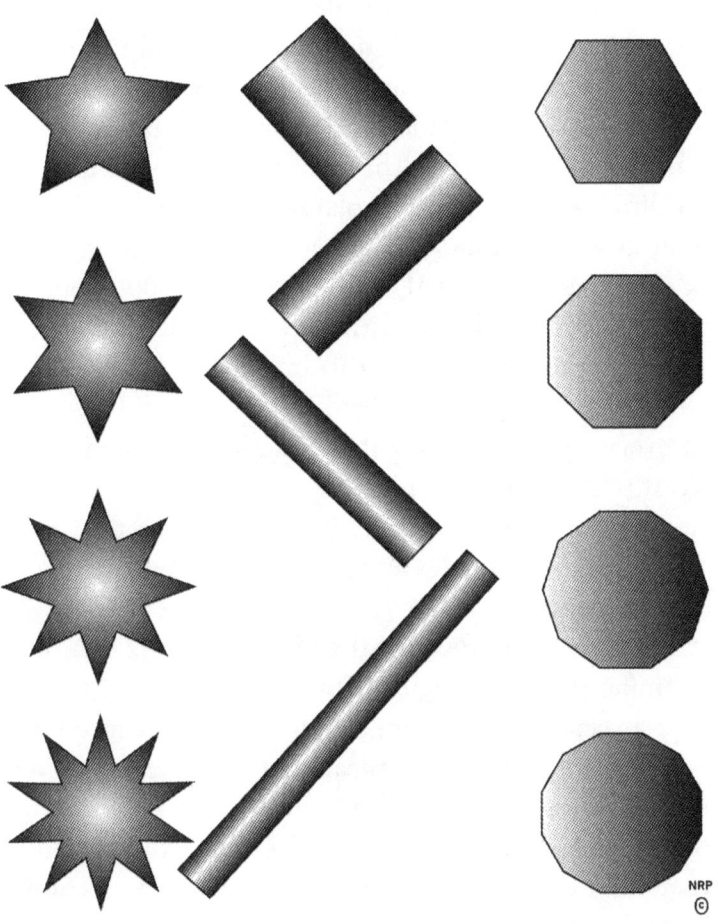

CHARACTERIZING PATTERNS

Let's examine how known patterns are characterized. First, let's consider patterns whose source is visual. The Filtering and Coding or Mapping Function associated with the visual field is able to produce codes representing the information contained within the visual field; these codes are represented as nearby memory addresses for images that in the Real World have nearly identical geometric shapes.

Let's examine in detail what this means. If for example we have a simple two dimensional square displayed in the visual field, then lets consider that as an example, that the Mapping Function produces an output code such as: 0000 0101 0000 0000 0000 0000 0000 0000 this code would then be the address within the Long Term Memory where the Threshold Marker would be set to indicate that this was a known pattern. This address in the Long Term Memory would always correlate to any and every square that might appear within the visual field. We might suggest that the first 1 within the code would represent that the visual image contained four right angles. And the second 1 would indicate that the four right angles were connected by four equal length straight-line segments.

Now lets consider what might be the Mapping Function's output for a somewhat similar geometric figure. This time within the visual field we will examine a rectangle, a rectangle whose length is in a sense represented by a square that has been linearly stretched in one direction. So the Mapping Functions output code might be 0000 0100 1000 0000 0000 0000 0000 0000. Where the first 1 within the code would again represent that the visual image contained four right angles. The second 1 would indicated that the four right angles were connected by four straight line segments, made up of two parallel line segments of equal length and two other parallel line segments of equal length but longer or shorter than the first two line segments, or if you would prefer the second 1 in the code could simply indicate that this was a linearly stretched square.

EFFECTS OF ROTATIONAL TRANSFORMATIONS

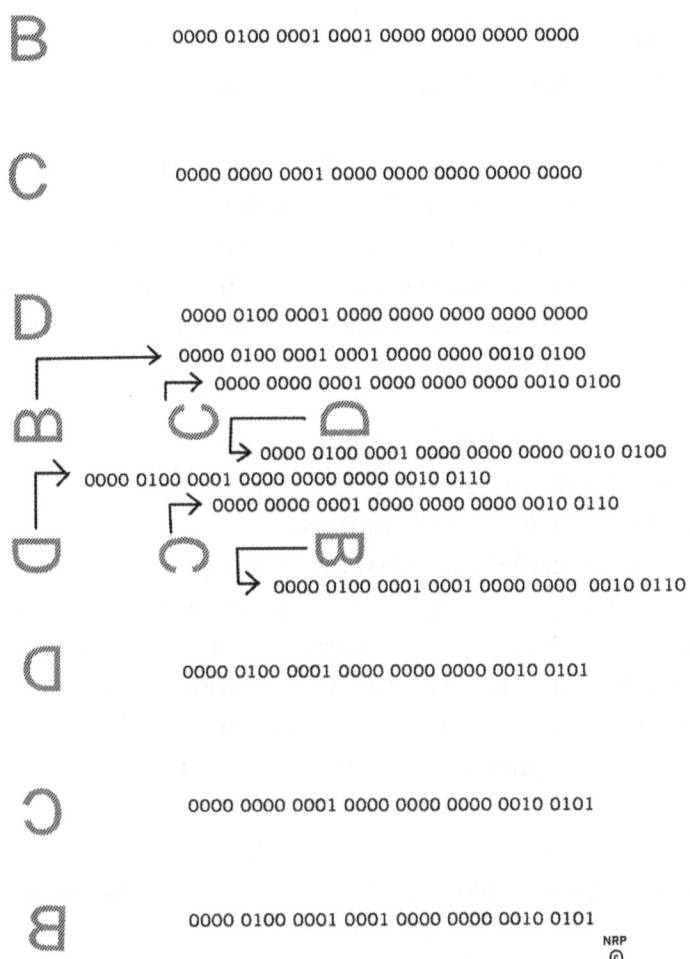

B   0000 0100 0001 0001 0000 0000 0000 0000

C   0000 0000 0001 0000 0000 0000 0000 0000

D   0000 0100 0001 0000 0000 0000 0000 0000
     0000 0100 0001 0001 0000 0000 0010 0100
     0000 0000 0001 0000 0000 0000 0010 0100
     0000 0100 0001 0000 0000 0000 0010 0100
     0000 0100 0001 0000 0000 0000 0010 0110
     0000 0000 0001 0000 0000 0000 0010 0110
     0000 0100 0001 0001 0000 0000 0010 0110

D   0000 0100 0001 0000 0000 0000 0010 0101

C   1010 0000 0001 0000 0000 0000 0010 0101

B   0000 0100 0001 0001 0000 0000 0010 0101

NRP
©

As a further example let's consider what the Mapping Function's output codes might look like for a Red Square, A Green Square, and a Blue Square. Here are the examples of the codes that the Mapping Function might give for each of these cases.

First 0000 0101 0000 0000 0000 0100 0000 0000 for the Red Square,
Next 0000 0101 0000 0000 0000 0011 0000 0000 for the Green Square,
Next 0000 0101 0000 0000 0000 0010 1000 0000 for the Blue Square.

The point to be seen here is that the most significant part of the Mapping Function's code is definitive of the most significant identifiable features of the visual object. And, that the nuances that are associated with the image, color, texture and such features that modify the overall image but do not essentially change the primary factors that determine the image are therefore relegated to the least significant part of the code.

Of course the most left hand part of the code is what is considered to be the most significant part and the right hand part of the code is considered to be the least significant part.

The point to be made here is that the Mapping function outputs codes (addresses) that are topographically near by each other, if in fact the geometric relationships of the images are similar. The more similar the images, then the closer to each other their Mapping Function Codes will be, and the closer they will be stored to each other within the Long Term Memory. Yes, their physical proximity will be topographically nearby each other within the Long Term Memory structures of the Brain.

Imagine for a moment these visual images: a short cylinder, a short section of tubing, a drinking glass, and a coffee mug. Because of the close visual similarity of the geometry's of these objects, they will all be found as memories stored within the same neighborhood of the Long Term Memory.

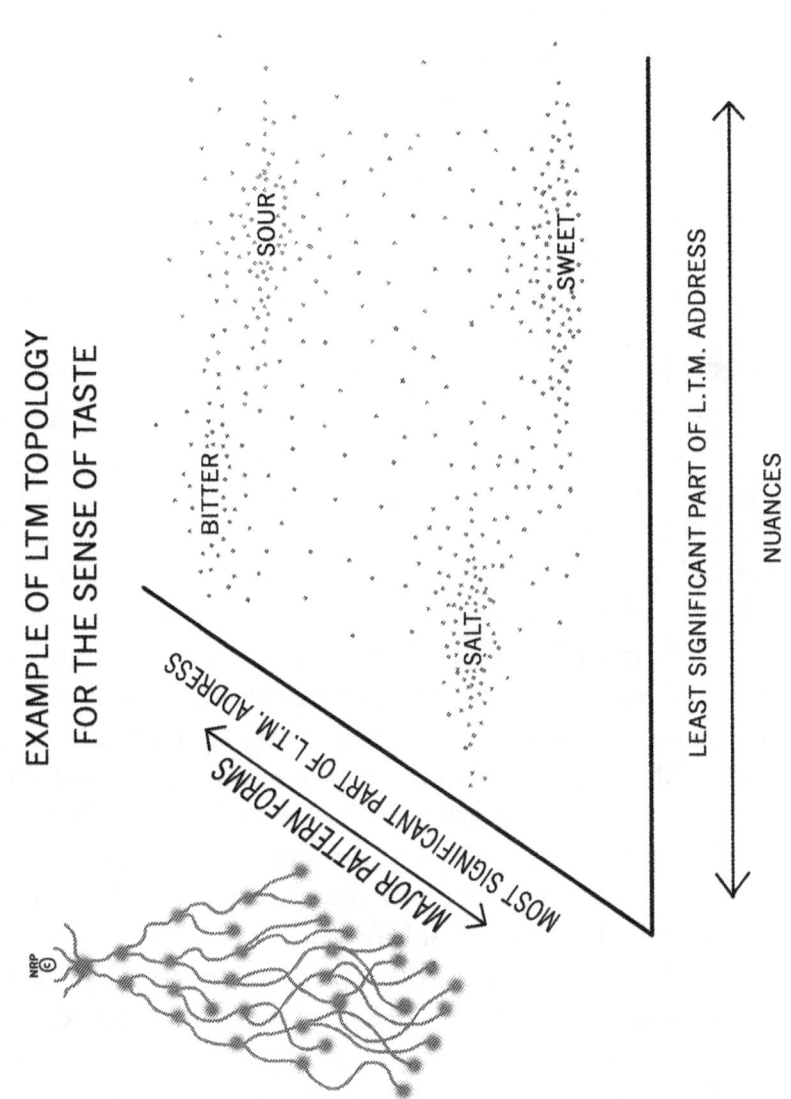

EXAMPLE OF LTM TOPOLOGY
FOR THE SENSE OF TASTE

MAJOR PATTERN FORMS

MOST SIGNIFICANT PART OF L.T.M. ADDRESS

BITTER

SOUR

SALT

SWEET

LEAST SIGNIFICANT PART OF L.T.M. ADDRESS

NUANCES

The Mapping Function maps similar visual patterns in to nearby neighborhoods of the Long Term Memory. In this way the images presented to the visual field are automatically characterized by the Mapping Function. Similar object patterns relating to visual images lay next to each other in the Long Term Memory.

Let's consider just one more example relating to the Sense of Taste. Although it might be true that the Alphabet of Patterns that represent the distinct patterns detectable by the Sense of Taste might be quite small, we should realize that the basic Alphabet of Heredity is limited to just four letters, four basic patterns. But with just those four basic patterns Nature is able to specify the exacting details of every feature of all life. So too, the proportional mixing of the Alphabet of Taste gives us the ability to detect a nearly infinite variety of delicate flavors. For the Mapping Function associated with the sense of Taste, we can imagine that it has only four distinct codes that are relatable to the most signifi-cant part of the code. These distinct codes would be relatable to the distinct tastes of salt, bitter, sweet and sour. But, the least significant part of the Mapping Function's Code would define the proportions of how much of each of the four primary elements of the Alphabet were present. We can imagine that within the Long Term Memory that was associated with the Sense of Taste, we would find four distinct sites that would relate directly to the primary elements of the Alphabet of Taste. The areas existing between these four sites would represent, by the distance that separated them from the four primary sites, all of the distinct flavors that were detectable by taste.

I hope I haven't overly worked these explanations of how the Mapping Function for some of the Senses is able to effectively charac-terize the patterns that it processes. For the remaining Senses that we have not discussed here, I am sure you can yourself visualize what their Mapping Function might do and how the Long Term Memory areas associated with them might be topographically related.

PREDICTING PATTERNS

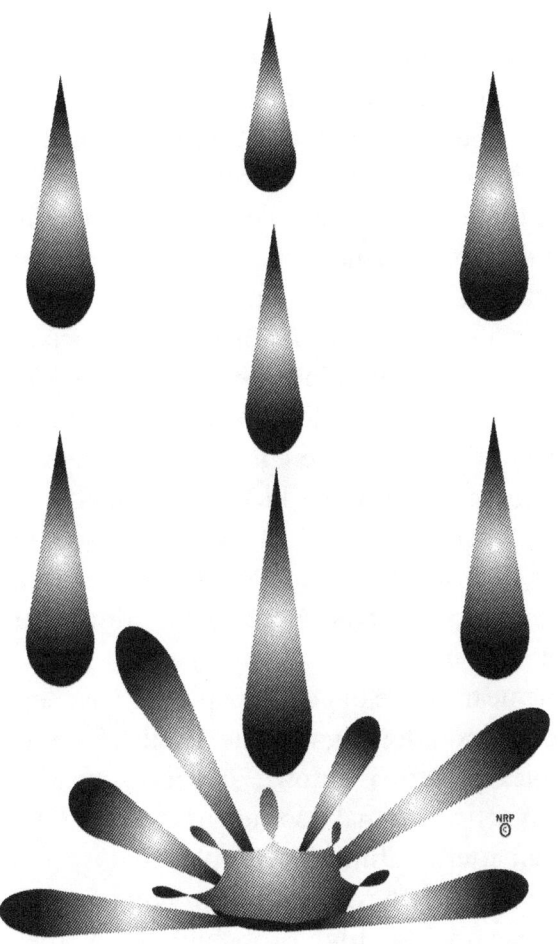

PREDICTING PATTERNS

We have more or less seen that there is no means within any of the mechanisms we have been discussing to predict the future in the manner of fortunetellers. But, what an intelligent Creature becomes very accomplished at doing is predicting in advance of the conclusion of a complex pattern that is evolving in time, just what that conclusion is likely to be, and to be able to predict it long before the pattern has run its course. This kind of prediction is only accomplished by a substantial familiarity with the particular complex pattern, a familiarity that must be patiently gained only through the experience of learning all of the details of the pattern's evolution in time.

It is certainly true that if the major logical associating elements of two different complex patterns in time are strongly related that intelligent Creatures can and do infer the consequences of one known complex pattern to the other. There is nothing really spectacular about this kind of inference. It is much like the Chimpanzee we had previously discussed, where by means of using the extremely generalized memory of the stick it allowed him to find and use a different, but equivalently substitutable stick to solve for himself the problem of knocking down the fruit.

Predicting the near future of complex patterns as they unfold in time is implemented by first knowing well the details of the complex pattern. Once the complex pattern is known and its parts are Cross Address Linked, it's a minor trick to make some direct Cross Address Link, from some part of the pattern within the complex that is an inflection point, directly to the complex pattern's end within Long Term Memory. In this way the Creature can with a high probability know the end of the real time complex pattern before it has run to its completion in real time.

A word about Intuition: Sometimes it appears that some persons are able to successfully predict some pattern, maybe one that represents the solution to some problem. They claim to have no familiarity with the problem and yet, they do sometime accomplish a successful prediction. We must be a bit suspicious about Intuition, because in thinking about the complexity and great numbers of patterns and the web of Cross Linking that might exist between them within the Long Term Memory, there may well be strong but unconscious relationships that exist, relationships that in fact tie the Intuitive insight directly to the solution. So we should admit that Intuition does exist, but that there is no magic to be found there.

RESPONDING TO PATTERNS

There are a few more kinds of data that need to be stored at the address or, in the case of complex patterns, "addresses" representing a known pattern. This is to implement what we referred to at the beginning of the paper in the definition of Intelligence as "responding to patterns" and also meets our requirement that the response be appropriate and significant to the Creature that detected the pattern. These other kinds of data might be pointers or Cross Linkings at the ending address of a complex pattern, which would point to a memory address that would initiate a complex Instinctive Reaction or to a simple or complicated learned reaction that would be an appropriate response to the detected pattern. It is most likely that some Cross Linkings are located at the earliest definitive inflection point of a complex pattern and from there they link directly to areas within the brain that will activate special preparedness or Instinctive reactions, that might initiate such things as the raising of the hair on one's neck, or begin a flow of adrenaline into the blood stream, or lead to patterns for the body's sexual arousal, or cause the Creature to turn and run, or to stand fast and fight.

The complexity of the appropriate responses that a Creature is able to make to learned patterns is unlimited. The responses range through all of those that are defined by Instinctive Reactions to the great long strings of learned reactions that even represent a musician's performance.

OUR LITTLE CREATURE'S INTELLIGENT ACTIVITY

We now know, that within the scheme we are developing, that, a pattern once detected, is remembered as being detected by a simple marker a Known Pattern Marker (a Threshold Number) stored within the Long Term Memory at a storage address that is simply the bits of the pattern itself. So now, we can take a look at what happens during a normal day to the data being detected that is coming to our Little Creature from our One-Dimensional Universe.

We need to note here that we have already pointed out, that because the patterns coming from the One-Dimensional Universe are so simple, they cannot be further reduced by the Mapping Function. Therefore our Little Creature does not use the Mapping Function to further reduce the incoming data to a simpler code, but uses it to apply the Mapping Rhythm to the data coming from its sensory Detector to give a sampling rate to those bits. The Mapping Rhythm for our Little Creature we will assume is the time necessary to accumulate thirty-two bits of data from the One-Dimensional Universe. In a Three Dimensional Universe this Mapping Rhythm would be the equivalent of how long a Creature's Detectors were focused and scanning on a pattern to resolve the basic identifiable parts of the pattern.

SIMPLIFIED INTELLIGENT SYSTEM

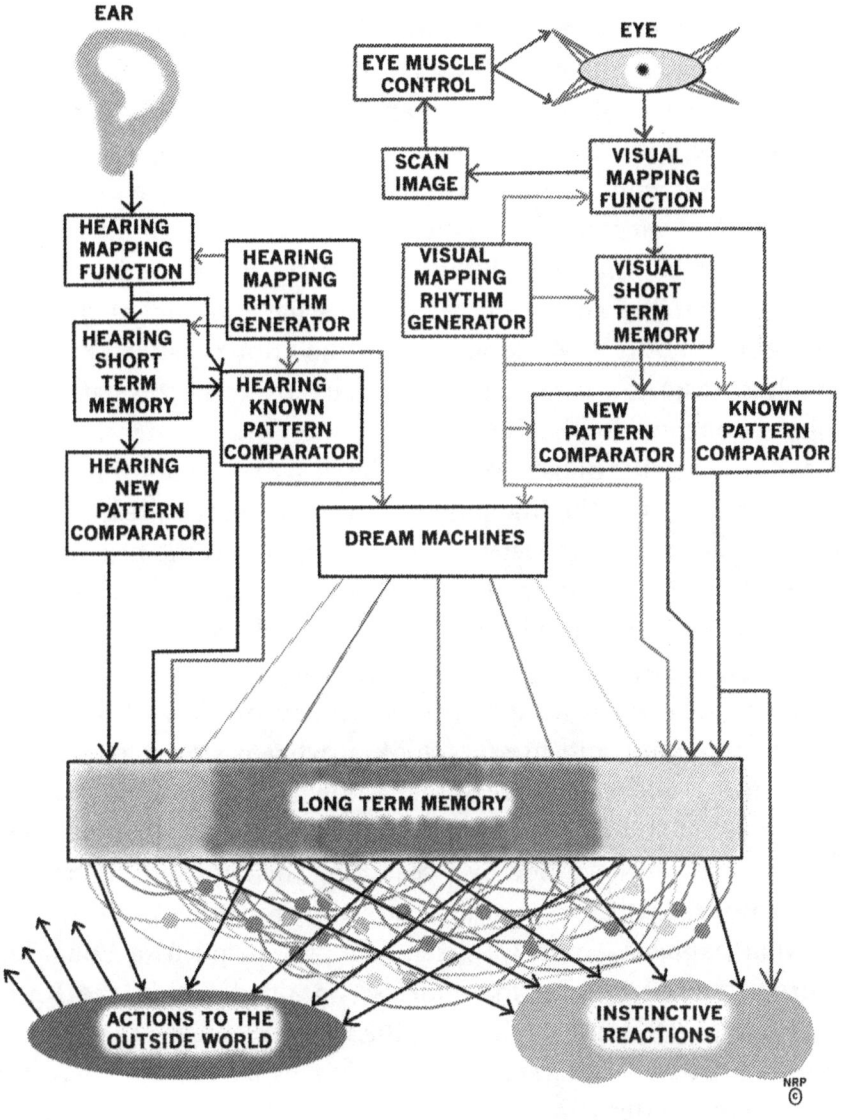

Imagine that we are looking at the Short Term Memory and as the first bit of data comes into the Short Term Memory, it is stored at the first storage address within the Short Term Memory, but we also store that identical data bit at the first storage location of a different memory (Exactly thirty two bits in size) which we know as the Known Pattern Comparator. Then after the Mapping Rhythm has completed one rhythmic cycle both the Short Term Memory and the Known Pattern Comparator will contain thirty-two bits of data that were sequentially received by the Detector. During the next periodic cycle of the Mapping Function, we take whatever data is in the thirty-two bits of the Known Pattern Comparator and use it to look at what is stored at that Long Term Memory address. We look to see if the known pattern marker at that address is set, if it is set, it tells us we already know this pattern that has just happened in the Real World (our One- Dimensional Real World). If the marker bit isn't set, then the system does nothing but wait for the next period of the Mapping Rhythm that allows the next thirty-two bits of data from the Detector to be loaded into the next available Short Term Memory storage locations and also simultaneously over-writing the old and used thirty-two bits of the Known Pattern Comparator. During the next period of the Mapping Function we again immediately take whatever data is in the thirty-two bits of the Known Pattern Comparator and use it to look at what is stored at that Long Term Memory address to see if the Known Pattern Marker at that address is set. If the Known Pattern Marker is not set, then we repeat these same routines over and over searching the data coming from the Little Creature's Detector for any already known patterns.

So what happens, when we are finally able to go to a Long Term Memory address by using the address contained within the Known Pattern Comparator and we find that the Known Pattern Marker at that address is set, that set marker immediately tells us, the Little Creature, "You know this pattern."

A SIMPLIFIED DREAM MACHINE

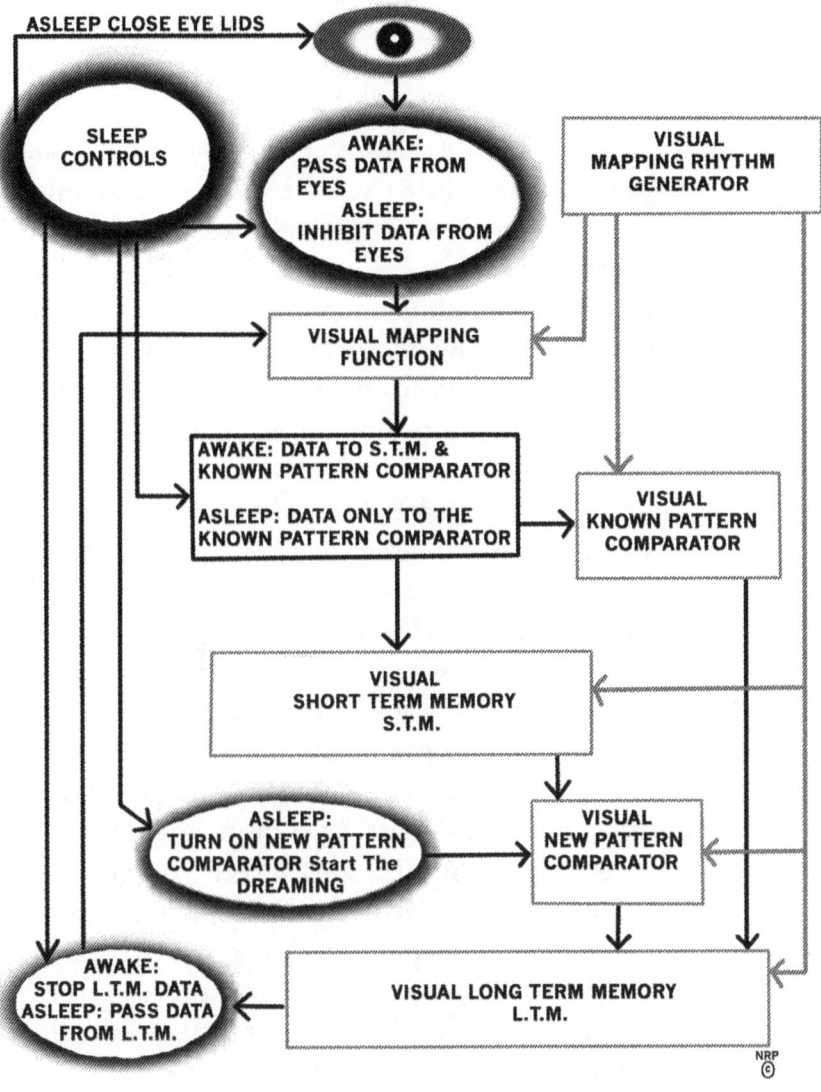

Also if there are any Cross Address Linkings or Cross Sensory Address Linkings that are tied to this Address of the known pattern then the associated memories indicated by those linkings are immediately remembered. And, if there were any linkings that tie this known pattern address to an address that would initiate some response from the Little Creature, then that response would be initiated.

Keep in mind here, that while this search of the incoming data from the Detector is going on, our Little Creature has been building within Short Term Memory a complete history of what bits were detected during the day's activity. When the day is finished and our Little Creature goes to bed for a restful sleep, something interesting now happens. Our Little Creature, now safe and away from the dangers of the outside World and isolated from the brutal bombardment of data upon its Detector, sleeps as a means for escaping from the World.

Our Little Creature within its sleep begins an involuntary dream, a dream that in our Three Dimensional World we call REM Dreaming. It's a dream whose direction and design is determined by the contents within the Little Creature's Short Term Memory. This dreaming is instigated and directed by the functioning that was described in the previous section "First Time Discovering of Patterns" and particularly on page 49 and as illustrated on pages 50 and 51.

After a good night's sleep with its dreaming, the Short Term Memory has been cleared of yesterday's data and any newly discovered patterns that were embedded within that data have been stored as memories within the Long Term Memory, also any known patterns that were within the Short Term Memory have had their threshold number set to a higher value. Our Little Creature is now ready to bravely face a new day armed with the new learning that has safely been stored away within its Long Term Memory. Each day the Little Creature discovers and learns more and more intelligible patterns from the World, and each day is better prepared to deal with whatever might exist there.

SIMPLIFIED LTM ADDRESS BIT FUNCTIONING

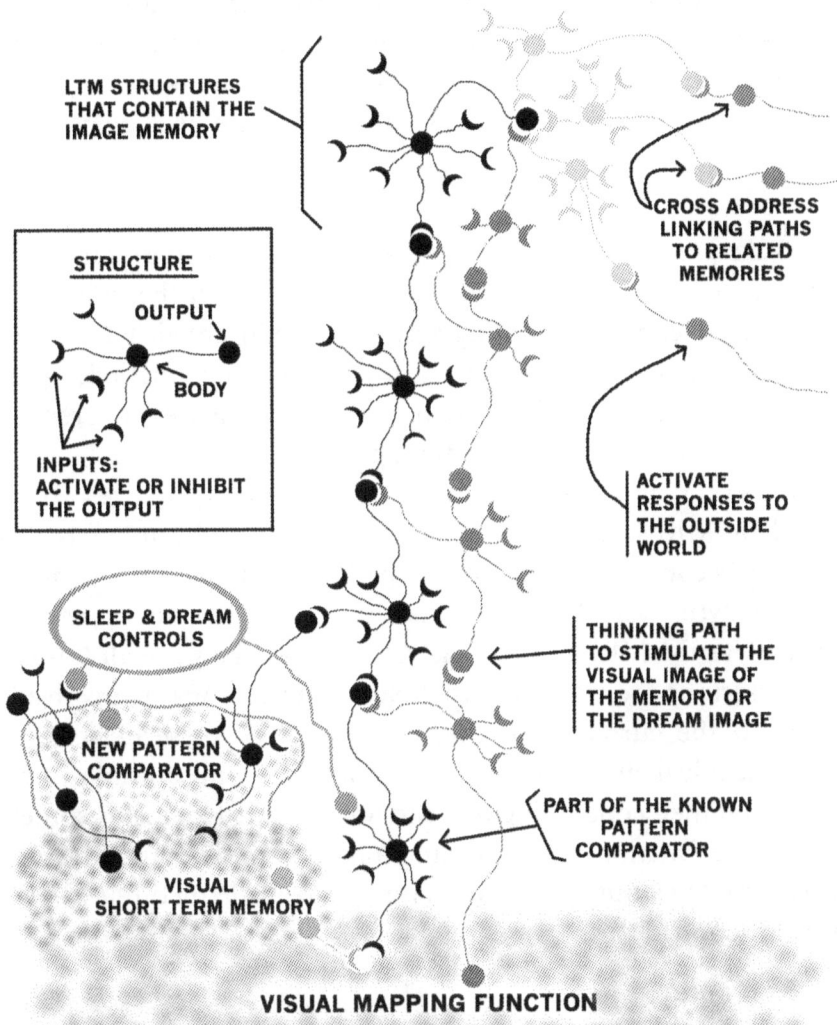

LTM STRUCTURES
THAT CONTAIN THE
IMAGE MEMORY

CROSS ADDRESS
LINKING PATHS
TO RELATED
MEMORIES

STRUCTURE

OUTPUT

BODY

INPUTS:
ACTIVATE OR INHIBIT
THE OUTPUT

ACTIVATE
RESPONSES TO
THE OUTSIDE
WORLD

SLEEP & DREAM
CONTROLS

THINKING PATH
TO STIMULATE THE
VISUAL IMAGE OF
THE MEMORY OR
THE DREAM IMAGE

NEW PATTERN
COMPARATOR

PART OF THE KNOWN
PATTERN
COMPARATOR

VISUAL
SHORT TERM MEMORY

VISUAL MAPPING FUNCTION

NRP
©

SOME CONCLUSIONS

The Mechanisms of Intelligence most likely came into existence at first, as simple modifications of the primitive Instinctive Mechanisms that existed in association with the Senses and allowed Creatures to react to their environment with responses that were fixed by heredity.

*   *   *   *   *

A word of caution: There was a time when investigators searching for the mechanisms of Intelligence were delighted when the first Electro-Mechanical Telephone Switching Systems were invented. They believed they had a new great insight in to the mysteries of the functioning of the Brain. Many speculative ideas about brain functions were referenced to the marvels of the Telephone Switching System.

In today's World everyone is excited about the images that are revealed by MRI and PET Scanners which can indicate areas of the brain that become activated when a patient is asked to perform some simple analytic task. I believe this excitement should hopefully be restrained, as the MRI and PET Scans are of such a generalized nature that conclusions about exactly what particular neurons are involved are far beyond the current resolving capabilities of these devices. Such scans are equivalent to viewing an Automobile with a crude Infrared Scanner and then concluding that the Automobile Exhaust is somehow related to the functioning or nonfunctioning of the Automobile Engine. This is surly true, but it just doesn't give a realistic picture of how the engine functions.

*   *   *   *   *

When you are forming a visual mental image of the structures of the Human Brain it might be helpful to think of the Brain's Structures as laying within the following general boundaries. Think in terms of two separate Three Dimensional Geometries:

One, the most primitive and most directly relatable to other Creatures, is an area of masses of nerve cells that are tightly clustered and whose functioning's are both Primitive and Dedicated. Dedicated to the most Rudimentary Interactions with the Physical and Chemical parts of the Anatomy.

For the second part: Think of it as a Vast Volume of Nerve Cells. A volume of cells where the greatest part of them are undedicated to any specific purpose. There, like some great warehouse of material waiting to be formed are the unused building blocks that the **Mechanisms of Intelligence can use to Construct the Wondrous Structures whose Coded Logic Mimics the Real World.**

Within this second part is distributed, the Newest Evolutionary Mechanisms of Intelligence, but they reside within a Vast Sea of Unused Neurons that await their enslavement to represent the patterns of the Real World.

So, It is true that we do not use much of our Brain, because much of our Brain is simply waiting to be commanded, to tell it, what it should become.

*   *   *   *   *

There are many speculations that could be made about how this rudimentary Theory of Intelligence, might cast some light upon the problems relating to learning deficiencies. The reader is left to their own devices in this area of speculation.

*   *   *   *   *

I would suspect that the Mechanisms of Intelligence considered here could lead to the construction of very effective and efficient electronic foreign language translators. Such translators could allow two persons with different native languages to speak directly with each other by means of automatic and instantaneous verbal translation from one language to the other language.

*   *   *   *   *

When we recall from memory some of the simplest patterns of the Visual Alphabet, we find we can visualize them in exacting detail irrespective of their spatial orientation within the visual field. When we try to recall the simplest visual words made up from the Visual Alphabet, we also discover that we can recall their image in exact detail irrespective of their spatial orientation. When we try to recall an even mildly complicated visual paragraph, we find we cannot form a complete visual image and we must resort to making up the image from the individual words that make up its overall structure.

I would like to emphasize that visual images recalled from the Long Term Memory are at best something like a slide show. They are a kind of still slide show and at best can only allude to motion by means of a crude juxtaposition of elements from one image to the next. Also, if images we try to recall from visual memory are too complicated, then we are only able to recall the memory with some pieces of it missing and we must then concentrate on the area of the missing pieces to bring them into the image, usually in doing so some other part of the image will vanish from out mind's view. For very complex visual memories they are always made up from many independent images that must be recalled separately to be examined.

There is something that would seem, at least at first consideration, to be an exception to what we have just said about the recall of complicated visual images. We are able to recall in what seems to be exacting detail, the images of the faces of family and friends, or any person that we have been associated with for a long period of time. I think we need to be a bit suspicious here, about just how complex or simple might be the patterns that make up the determining images of a known face. I would suspect that number of patterns from the Visual Alphabet that can define a face as unique might be quite small. You should keep in mind that most of the features of a face are probably just nuances that surround the few actual features that define one face from another. For this reason, strangers identifying other strangers in Eye Witness situations are highly likely to be incorrect in their identification, no matter how sure the identifier might believe themselves to be correct.

*   *   *   *   *

It is frequently said that when people are considering anything new that "People see what they want to see". The truth of the matter is people only see what they can understand based on the patterns they already have stored within their Long Term Memories. A more succinct statement might be: All people see everything in terms of what they already know.

*   *   *   *   *

The Sense of Taste for many creatures has been isolated to those objects that are plucked from the immediate environment and delivered by the creature's physical extremities to their mouth. Because of this kind of isolation of the Sense of Taste from the continuous real world environment, most creatures only know the world of tastes as they relate to isolated distinct objects. Imagine for a moment that all of your Senses, other than the Sense of Taste became nonfunctional, then your only way of knowing the world would be by means of continually tasting your changing position within it. Over a long period of time the mechanisms of intelligence would build up a topographical map within your Long Term Memory that would represent the connected geography of the real world in terms of a continuous mapping of tastes. You would know the real world in quite a different way than you know it by means of your other senses. For some Creatures in nature this way of knowing the real world is their primary way of knowing it.

When we think about how creatures other than humans might exercise their mechanisms of Intelligence or Instinct to accomplish those extraordinary feats we see them perform as rituals of survival, we always think in terms of our own understandings of things. To be successful in understanding how creatures other than humans function within nature we must realize that each of the mechanisms of intelligence are exceeding powerful at knowing the real world. As just an example when considering how migratory creatures are able to learn their migratory routes, we think in terms of how we are able to travel from one place to another and we usually do not do it by our noses. But, creatures other than us may well make their migrations using primarily maps of smells and almost completely ignoring the geography.

Other than proposing strange and unusual mechanisms for explaining the behaviors of creatures other than humans, we should first consider how the enhanced mechanisms of Intelligence for one or more Senses might explain a particular behavior.

*   *   *   *   *

There exists a special situation that is detrimental to our ability to accept newly formulated ideas. Whenever a new idea lies considerably outside of our current repertoire of known patterns, we are always more than willing to reject the idea without any concern for examining in detail its basic elements. In many instances the parent of the new idea has carefully and over a long period of time built up within their memories step-by-step the trail of new patterns that finally resulted in the discovery of the new idea. Consider the work of Mendel concerning the inherited traits of Beans. Consider the recent work of the discoverer of Helicobacter Pylori as a primary cause of Stomach Ulcers. Consider Alfred Wegener's proposals about Continental Drift. Consider J Harlen

Bretz's theory of Catastrophic Ice Age Floods. Even when Galileo said the Moon had mountains much like those of the Earth his idea was rejected even though anyone who looked through his telescope could see it was true.

Not only are new ideas that are distant from our current understandings most times rejected, but people especially those who consider themselves experts of the subject, usually go to great lengths to castigate in every way at their civilized disposal, those who were the parent of the new idea.

It takes much extra work to follow step-by-step in the footsteps of the parent of a new idea. We, all of us, are too willing to ignore anything that lays beyond our own comfortable repertoire of known patterns and this laziness will always extract its price upon our future hopes for discovery.

GEOLOGICAL KNOWLEDGE BASE

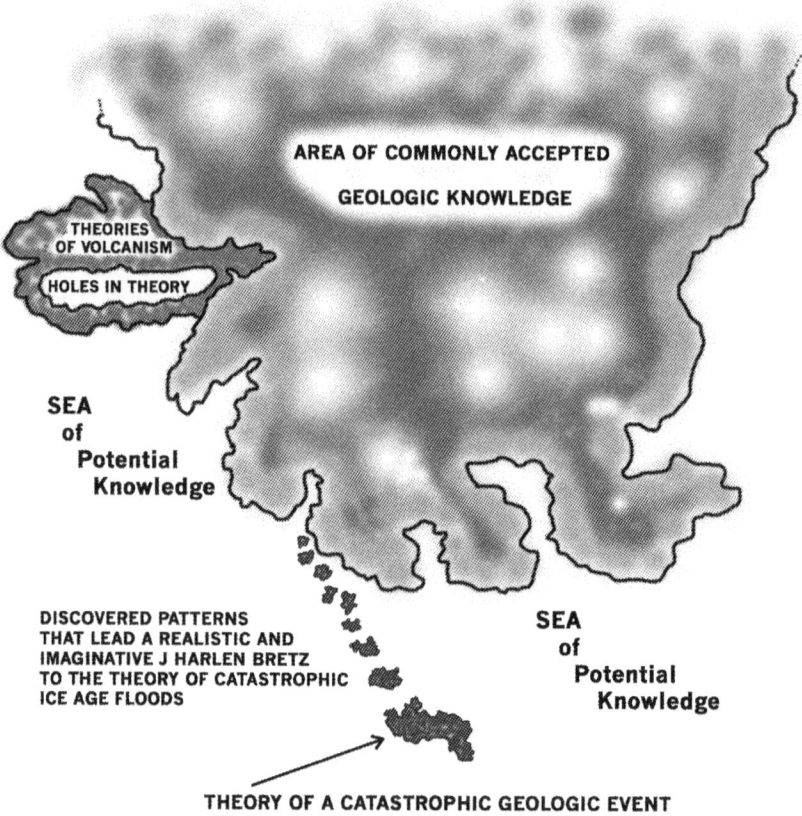

For those of us who have lived for a significant amount of time, we have learned that within a profession, those who have had both the longest history of experience and the most diversified experience are the most likely to be able to identify and pinpoint the solution to a problem. We consider such persons as Experts, but we must understand that their expertise is there because they have learned from previous experience the patterns associated with many problems. But in truthfulness, we must also admit, that when a totally new problem, a problem that is unrelated to any previous problem comes upon the scene, then even the acknowledged Expert comes to a sudden stop, and in a matter of fact, is back in school. It is the truth that whenever we face a totally new problem we are all reduced to poking, testing, trying and all matter of primitive means to get an understanding of how it might be understood and solved.

*   *   *   *   *

The collective patterns of our Long Term Memory, define very much about who we are in terms of what we know. If you have a lifetime that is mostly submerged within a world of family and friends, then your memory is abundantly filled with those patterns and they represent in a sense very much about whom you are. Whatever parts of life you are mostly involved with, such as your work, hobbies, sports, or the arts, these activities lay down the Long Term Memory patterns proportionately to how much you have learned about these things and these memories represent who you are and how you are able to see reality. We all love to allow our thoughts to swim within the lakes that are rich with our favorite memory patterns. This is especially apparent for politicians. You can see politicians swimming within their favorite pattern lakes, and no matter how hard you try to get them over to a different area, they will continually return to the same lakes where their patterns are well rehearsed and defined and where they feel safe.

*   *   *   *   *

PREVAILING MEDICAL KNOWLEDGE

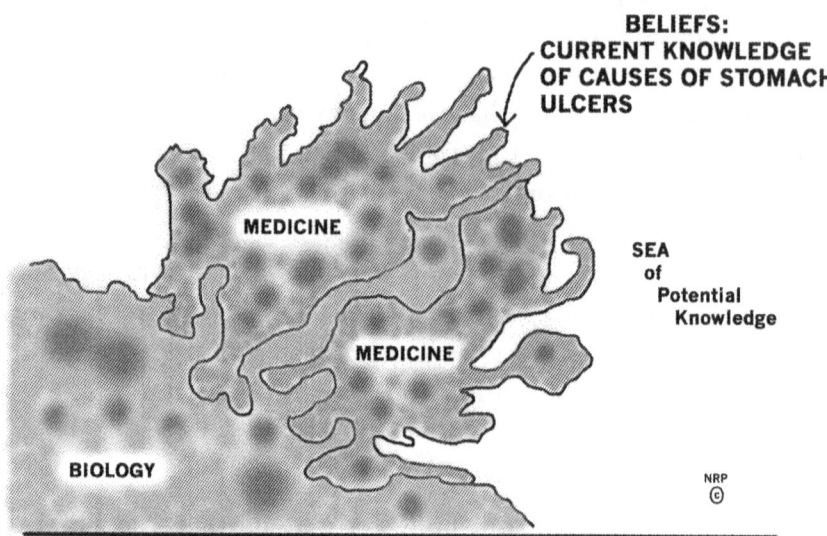

BELIEFS:
CURRENT KNOWLEDGE
OF CAUSES OF STOMACH
ULCERS

MEDICINE

MEDICINE

SEA
of
Potential
Knowledge

BIOLOGY

NRP
ⓒ

INDIVIDUAL'S NEW PATTERN TRACK
TO A NEW DISCOVERY

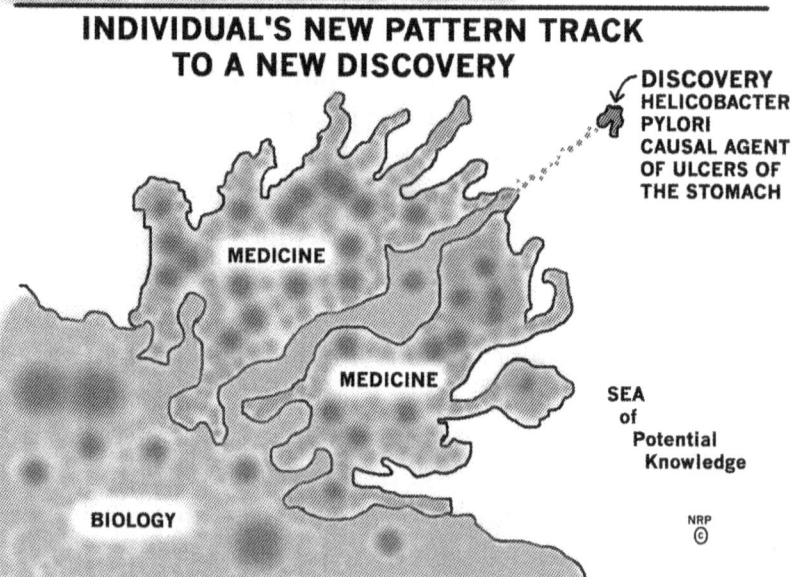

DISCOVERY
HELICOBACTER
PYLORI
CAUSAL AGENT
OF ULCERS OF
THE STOMACH

MEDICINE

MEDICINE

SEA
of
Potential
Knowledge

BIOLOGY

NRP
ⓒ

The more diverse is your repertoire of patterns, the more varied a person you are, and the more easily varied you can further become.

*　　　*　　　*　　　*　　　*

You have surely seen a pianist performing, where literally a long stream of music producing motion pours from their fingers. A good musician can execute from memory a very long and complicated musical structure with a nearly flawless performance. I would hope then you would not be surprised to consider that we as individuals execute the actions of our daily lives as a similar performance, as just interpreting complicated strings of patterns that we have learned by heart, and responding to them with complicated strings of actions. We all spend a lifetime in learning a repertoire of patterns and actions that we can and do string together as needed to meet the individual require-ments of getting through each day's activities. As adults during a day's activities, our senses are busy testing the situations of the environment around us, and to each perceived need, we respond with a set of learned patterns and actions to satisfy the perceived need. From day's beginning to day's end, we literally do nothing new or exceptional. Because for most people the repertoire of learned patterns is so extensive and because we have an ability to mix and link learned patterns and actions in a nearly endless manner, we sail through each day, oblivious to the truly mechanical Nature of our dealing with the day's activities.

*　　　*　　　*　　　*　　　*

All of Human progress has been laid on the false Shrine of Intelligence. We are further lead in this deception of how wonderful Intelligence is by the complexity of the modern World of Automobiles, Telephones, Television, Medical Wonders and all the other Wonders of the Modern World. In the strongest sense, we are mesmerized by the wonderful dazzle from the Human Made World that surrounds us. We let it all; make us believe in the wondrous power of our own Intelligence. We never take the time to stop and realize that the glories that surround us, those made by Humankind, were purchased at a cost of multimillions of lives, lives spent in the slow processes of search and discovery for every and any new scrap of insight. It has been a painfully long search that has lasted for tens of thousands of years. A time during which Our Kind, by means of poking and testing, trying and failing, and trying and failing again, suffered this method of trial and error for learning each new thing. No great inspiring God of Intelligence handed us insights in to understanding new things. By all historical evidence we have paid a great price for what we have attained.

With these thoughts in mind it is important that we can begin to admit that Intelligence is the mechanism that carries the Creatures through their daily routines of survival in a World of diversities. Intelligence is not the Great Lord of our mastery of Nature. It is the straightforward part of all Creatures that allows them to learn the patterns of Nature and to learn responses to those patterns, which lead to their survival on a day-to-day basis. It is not the forceful insight that allows a Creature to change Nature. The laurels of our spectacular successes in modifying Nature are not due to Intelligence. That success is due instead to Humankind's curious abundant Creativity, which will not be easily finished. It is a Creativity that searches forth, recombining, manipulating, destroying and rebuilding, even in places where Society or Culture forbids. **It is a Creativity that Delights in its own Surprising Direction. A Creativity who's Kernel is Thinking.**

I believe that this Creativity must have been spawned by some evolutionary modification of the Mechanisms of Dreaming. We Humans have the ability to Dream in many ways. One of these ways of Dreaming is by our own free will. We are able to Day Dream ourselves into a World that does not exist in reality, a World of our own making. It's a World where we put together the pieces of patterns in any combination we choose. **There is a very special kind of Day Dreaming that we call Thinking.**

It is of the most importance, that we give careful consideration to how these traits, which have severely benefited Our Kind's survival and contributed immensely to the quality of our lives can best be understood, encouraged, and enhanced within the general population.

*   *   *   *   *

Note:

We should consider that minor evolutionary modifications of the Mechanisms of Dreaming or any other mechanism involved in mental functioning, like their counterparts of the strictly physical body are subject to continued evolutionary modification.

INSTINCTS

INSTINCTS

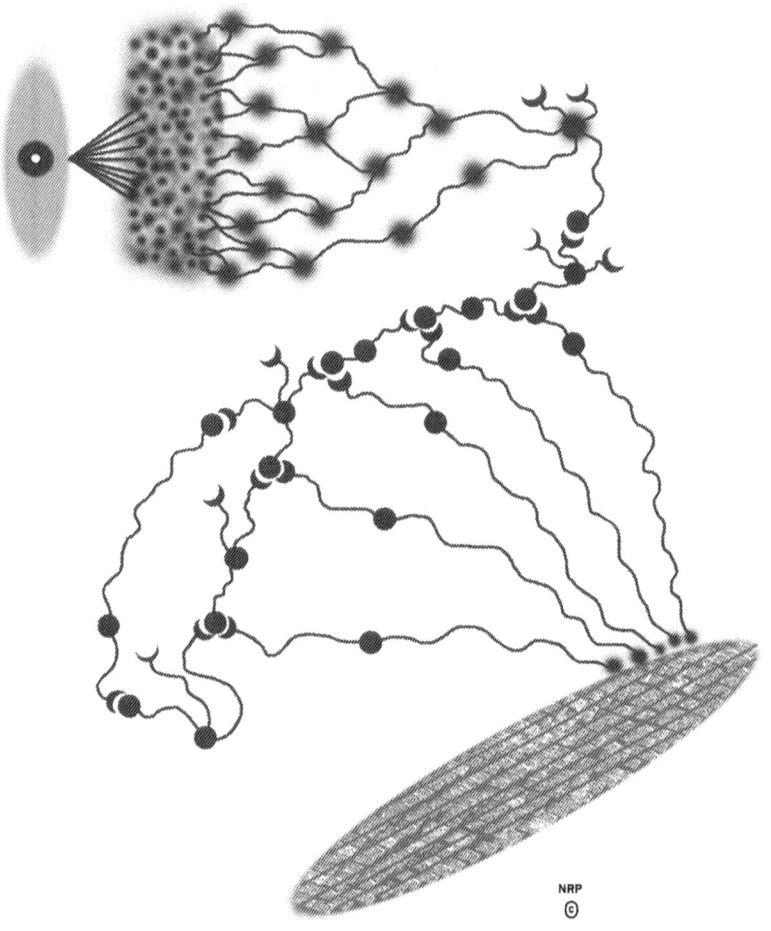

NRP
©

INSTINCTS

(Instinct: Inherited, essentially unalterable, tendency of an organism to give a specific response to an environmental stimuli without requiring analytic thought.)

*   *   *   *   *

Instincts like all inherited traits always exhibit a broad range of intensity in their manifestation across the whole section of the population that inherited the trait. Even inherited physical characteristics, such as blue eyes, are represented by a broad ranging intensity of blue from being barely detectable as blue, to ice blue, to dark blue. Even the inheritable diseases are represented by a broad range of how each particular individual manifests the characteristics of the disease. In some cases the disease may take a swift course and completely ravage the individual, while in other persons the same disease may proceed along its course very slowly and never reach a catastrophic intensity.

So with Instincts, we must remain aware that their expression, within an individual, lays within some spectrum of possibilities that exists for the overall population.

*   *   *   *   *

Separate from the mechanisms of the Brain that make up its functions of Intelligence are the inherited Neural and Chemical mechanisms that exhibit themselves as Instinctive Actions.

We need to consider the complex characteristics of Instinct in the light of what we can see about the physical characteristics of the Creature's of Nature, including ourselves. Consider the wondrous complex material features of our physical nature, the Eye, the Hand, the Ear, the Foot, the Mouth and all the marvelous complex organs that make up our bodies. Each of them was worked against the fabric of the environment over millions of years, molded by Master Mother Nature to give us, each Creature, a magnificent physical harmony within the complex material environment of Nature. It is easy to look at the Human Hand and marvel at its wondrous subtle physical complexities. Just by visual observation we can see with ease the hand's structures. By means of medical dissection we can reveal the hidden physical mechanisms that allow the hand to mechanically perform its functions.

All of the physical features that make up our bodies are so easy to see, but the features that make up the mechanisms that identify our Instincts are invisible to the eye. They lay almost totally hidden. All are nearly ethereal things, whose presence is embedded within the subtle connections of Nerves and the Chemistry that bathes them. Instincts are real things, but their invisibility allows them to escape counting. They are powerful things in their own way. They are as powerful as any physical extremity. They are as much a physical and permanent part of every creature as is any Hoof, Trunk, Eye or Arm. Instincts are as powerful in guiding the activities of a Creature as the muscles and structures of a leg are in predetermining how a Creature will walk and run. We must always be careful in analyzing the actions of any Creature and ignorantly attributing those actions to free choice, when in fact they may be totally driven by Instinct.

I would propose that Nature's Evolution has endowed each and every Creature with a repertoire of Instincts, which if countable would approximate in number the distinct countable physical features of each Creature. It should not be too difficult to believe that during the millions of years of evolution of the physical features of Nature's

Creatures, that the evolution of each Creature's Instincts was also taking place at a comparable pace. For many of the more simple Creatures it is easy to see that most all of their life functions are controlled by Instincts. It is maybe easiest to believe that this might be true, when we observe some insect going about its daily activities. It is nearly beyond belief to see a tiny Creature like an Ant, whose central nervous system's cells are countable in the hundreds, performing exceedingly complex functions. The Ant has had no schooling. No fellow Creature taught the Ant how to fulfill its mission of being a functional Ant. The Ant's life long dance across the environment and its complex interactions with that environment are determined by the fate of its birth, by its Inherited Instincts. And with a bit of reasonable suspicion, we should be willing to consider that the Human Creature is also heavily cloaked with multitudes of major and minor Inherited Instincts. These Instincts move Our Kind, and us as individuals, down pathways that were determined for us by a past hidden in the Ancient Prehistory of Evolution. Although the Ant cannot look at it's own actions and see them as Instinctive, as deterministic, you would think that we as Creatures of a higher reasoning power might be capable of examining our own actions and seeing the truth of what is there. But it is more to the truth that we see within ourselves the forest of our actions, but cannot see the trees that make that forest. In many cases it is true that we see what we want to see, nothing more, because we refuse to look in detail.

SIMPLE VISUAL INSTINCT

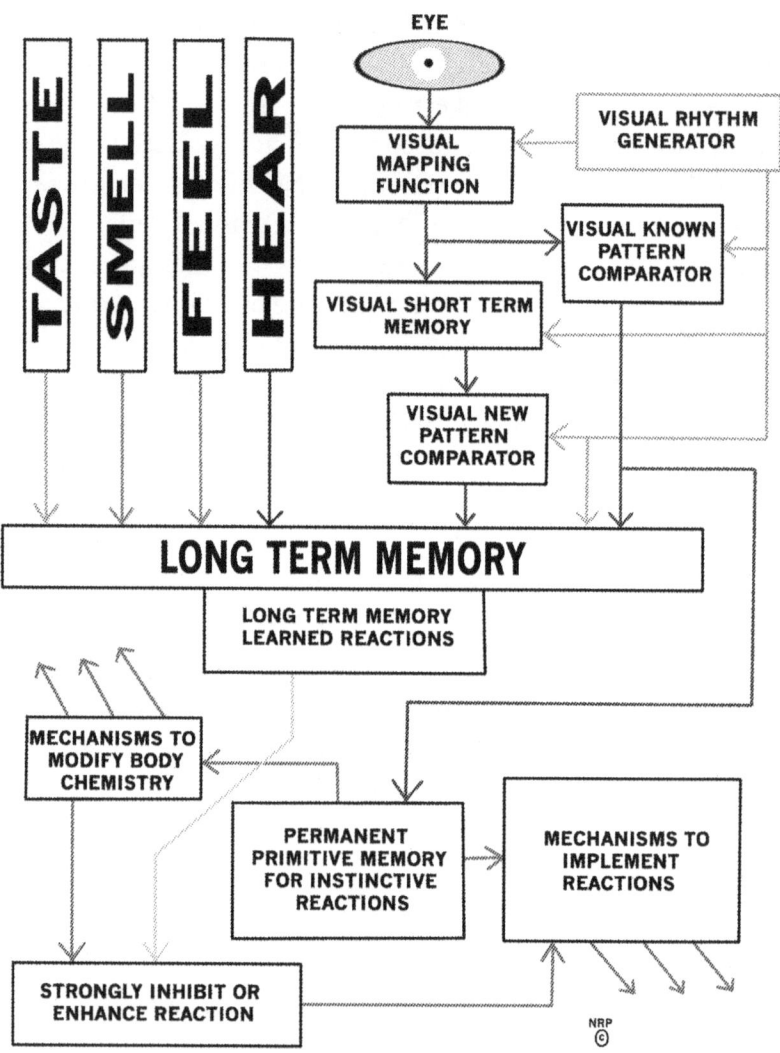

We often hear that we as humans have not been present in the environment for more than maybe a few million years. This might be true but we and those Creatures who are our relatives, our direct relatives, have been evolving in the environment since the very beginning of life on this Earth. Our direct relatives form a continuous sacred chain of life that leads from life's earliest beginnings to connect directly with each of us. I believe that we should try to understand, that most all of our Instinctive Nature was determined long before we became Homo Sapiens, that our Instinctive Nature is mostly concerned with mechanisms that gave our ancestral predecessors some advantage for survival within an environment that was savagely hostile, and that today, we are Creatures wearing a New Thin Skin of Civilization, which we wrap around us as a camouflage of the Animal that lies beneath that skin and certain aspects of the Nature of that Animal, which we ourselves do not want to see or admit is there.

There is no way to understand the nature of a problem and seek a reasonable solution if we are unwilling to admit to the existence of the problem.

THE SAVAGE INSTINCT

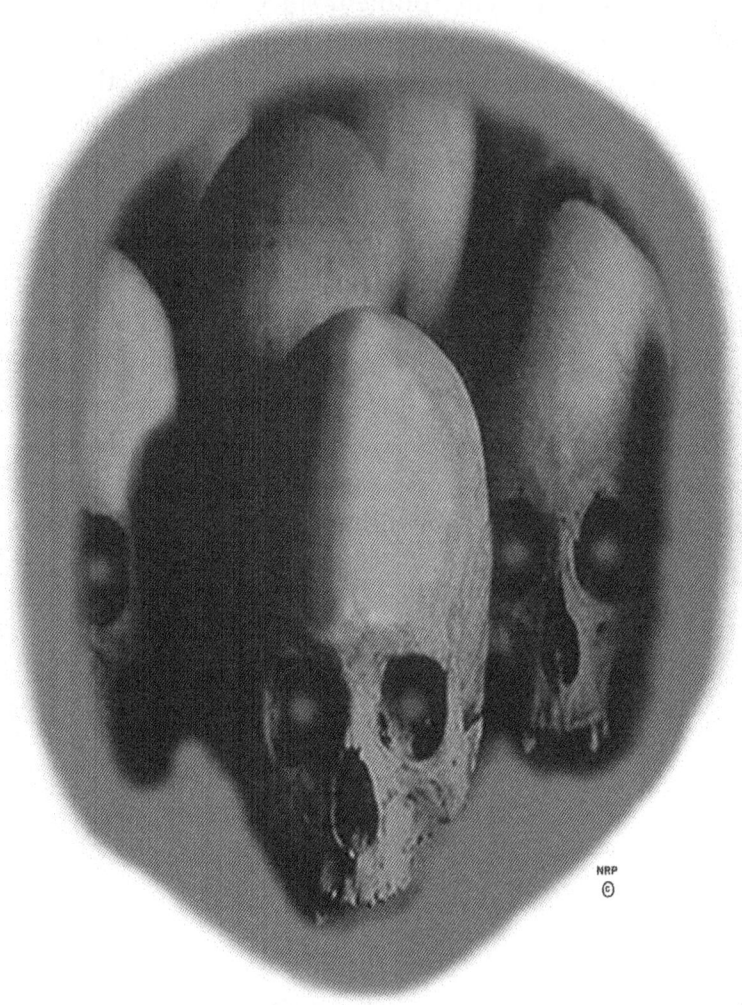

THE SAVAGE INSTINCT

And so, let's peek beneath the skin here and there and see what might be hidden. We are Creatures of a weak physical design, no great Teeth for Biting and Tearing of Flesh. No Razor Sharp Claws with which to hold an opponent at a distance. No swift Legs to carry us faster than the Leopard. Not even a powerful Sense of Smell to tell us the faintest hint of what is drifting in the wind. It would seem that physically we were at a great disadvantage, as compared to many Creatures, for surviving in a Primitive World. It would seem that in a Primitive World of physical struggling, we didn't have a chance for surviving. But here we are, Supreme Survivors of it All, Survivors who now sit atop the heap of time, wearing the Thin and Gentle Skin of Civilization as the Badge of our Success. How can this be? We are taught, that we are near descended from angels, but we as Creatures of Nature's Universe unlike the Angels of Myth are the most Dangerous, Most Potentially Vicious and Most Deceitful Creatures in Existence. We have at our very core a Savage Instinct. Our own-recorded History bears truthful testimony to this fact of our Nature. This truth is found in the piles of tortured and mutilated bodies that are stuffed into and dangle from the pages of the books that record our History. It is there in our History, from our earliest records and continues to the present day. It is our Instinctive Nature and it accompanies us through all of time ready to be called on at a moment's notice to release its power in the Name of Survival. Scholars and others go to the greatest extremes in their attempts to convince us that we are not savage at all, but Gentle Social Creatures. Many people would like to believe that these powerful mean traits are only in others, whom they can point their fingers at, while denying that they are present within themselves. There are those, who would like to believe that only others can commit atrocities and they themselves could never do such things. There are those, who like to believe that a good civilized education can calm the beast inside, that an educated person is more reasonable and can by reason free themselves from their Savage Instincts. But the fact is such that many of those persons who have committed the most terribly vicious crimes against their fellow Human Beings have been highly educated people, who loved and patronized the fine arts. It may be true that in some, the Nature of the Vicious Creature sleeps so deep as to not be easily awakened, while in others it lies nearer to the surface of their Nature and is ready to jump out at the slightest provocation. The Savage Instinct is most likely controlled by Chemistry and by Triggering Patterns from the environment and bows little if any to Intellect. The fact of the matter is that for most of us, who live in mostly reasonable and secure environments, we never encounter those events or strings of events that would trigger our Primitive Savage Instincts. But for those who meet face to face, again and again with unbearable fear, humiliation, inescapable threats, or are in any way physically or mentally terrorized, then if there is anyway possible the Beast that is the Savage Instinct will always rise up in vengeance. During times of war, we can most easily see in many individuals, that the Savage Instinctive Beast has been fully unleashed. After each war's end, it is usual to ask how could any group of people have participated in the atrocities that were committed during the war? It should be more to the point to ask, given the orchestrated arena of fear and hated that institutions propagated against certain groups, how could the people not have participated?

We sometimes see the Savage Instinct raging in individuals living in an otherwise peaceful society. Once the Savage Instinct has been released within an individual, the vicious acts performed sometimes become self-reinforcing. It is always the case that when an individual exhibits these Vicious Instinctive Tendencies, everyone is asking the same questions. How can this be? What caused them to do this? Was it their parent's fault? Was it because they didn't go to church? Did they have a bad childhood? Was it because they were a loner? And on and on the same questions are asked over and over. It is in the act of asking these questions, that the askers are distancing themselves from any probability that they could have done such a thing. Their reasoning is that it was some most exceptional cause, which drove the other person to commit the vicious act. It is the way of continually denying the Basic Nature of what is actually behind the vicious act. It is how the individual says, without actually stating so, that nothing could possibly drive them to committing such savage acts.

It is the custom of Societies to work at keeping the Savage Instinct subdued. They attempt to accomplish this goal by making heavy penalties for violent actions. The method is successful in the general case and because it is generally successful, we might be led to falsely believe that the Instinct is not a basic part of the entire population. But, now consider the interesting situation, where there are no strong penalties or taboos against a certain kind of antisocial savage violence that takes place vicariously in the playing of certain video games. The players of these games enthusiastically engage in committing what most would consider to be the most repulsive acts of violence. The very large numbers of people who willingly play these violent games, is an undeniable testimony to the fact that the Savage Instinct is alive and well within the general population.

Good economic times within a Society are a balm that tends to hide the Savage Instinct by never allowing it to be called to the surface of our personalities. Even captive Tigers are contented and docile Creatures when they are well feed and sheltered. But, when that economy that provides so well for them fails, and they become hungry, the Savage Instinct comes immediately to the surface of their personality. So also for humans in times that are economically difficult, or because of war, or other stresses, the Savage Instinct is on a short trigger for being released. In the best of economic times it is natural that crimes, of all kinds, including crimes of violence decrease. The simple truth is, this is equivalent to the times when the Tiger is well feed and cared for.

When the worst of economic times are at hand, all crimes including crimes of violence will increase. There are no numbers of police or other forces that can change that situation. Attempts at using excessive force to control this rise in violence many times, might just help in aggravating the situation. Such times, when the Savage Instinct is running strongly within the population, are times that are ripe for violent social unrest and even political revolution.

The fact that Society is willing to allow their governments to implement the death penalty is itself a testimony to the existence of the Savage Instinct. For Society, it is their way of exercising the Savage Instinct while believing their hands are clean and that they are just Simple Gentle Creatures. It is of course government officials, who are too weak and unwilling to stand up against this example of the most Savage Will of the People that allows it all to continue.

As long as we, as a people, continue to deny what is really a part to one degree or another of each of us, we will never find success in understanding our Nature or in finding some reasonable controls of it. We will continue on into the future, wringing our hands in futility trying to understand how such Savageness can continue to Stock a Civilized People.

*   *   *   *   *

I surely do not mean to give the impression that all of our Primitive Instincts are of a Savage Nature. We have many complex Instincts that served us well in the distant past, and that serve us joyously to the present time. But we should also admit that we did not pass through the Savage and Primitive Past Ages riding solely upon the Wagon of Smiles and Song and Dance.

*   *   *   *   *

THE PROJECTILE INSTINCT

It seems, it would be reasonable to wonder at a rather strange situation. In modern Society, we all have witnessed that certain games of sport are able to command the attendance of remarkably large crowds that come to observe their playing. Many sports can once in a while draw a large audience, but there are some sports that consistently draw huge crowds. All of these sports are involved in the control of some projectile, usually a ball. If you were an alien visitor to our world, and you were witness to these sporting events, I'm sure you would be puzzled as to how the apparently simple manipulation of a projectile could be of such great interest to all of those people. I believe it can only be explained by remembering that the Instinctive ability to throw and accurately control a projectile was an important primary mechanism for our survival during primitive times. You might think of it this way: If in the prehistoric past, Michael Jordan was a member of your tribe, you had meat on the table every day! Your whole tribe was one that was sure to survive!

There is something Primitive and Instinctive inside of us that worships at the Shrine of the Controlled Projectile and we love to see it exhibited. We pay our highest and special worship to those within the team who are appointed to execute the most accurate control of the projectile. Children at a very early age delight in their personal discovery of the throwing of things. We all delight in the exhibition of it being done with great accuracy. We seem to especially enjoy seeing it done by teams representing our tribe.

THE HERD INSTINCT

There is an Instinct that in the past served us as well as the more Fierce Instincts. Today that Instinct, in many cases, works against our best hopes. I speak of the Instinct that is Our Kind's natural attraction to be a part of a Herd. Herds are of many types and sizes, there are the small ones that you might like to call a group; there are the largest ones that are called nations. Herds exist in every size and variety: the family, the tribe, the city, the religious group, the police, the professional associations, the teams of sport and all special interests groups. You may prefer to use the expression "Social Group or Social Animal" because it has a gentler, a more civilized sound. But, I think it is more to the point to use the cruder "Herd" as it is more to the point of what, in modern times, is really going on within this Social Structure.

Every Herd is made up of a group of individuals together with a body of knowledge or myth. The group of individuals that makes up any Herd considers themselves to have become a part of the larger organism that is the Herd. When an individual joins a particular Herd, they assume the mantle of the myth that belongs to the Herd. That mantle of myth (or knowledge) in many cases is something that the Herd has acquired at great cost over long periods of time. It is always necessary, that to belong to any Herd, the individual must meet the entry requirements of the Herd. The Herd Instinct drives each individual towards belonging to the most powerful and prestigious Herd to which they can gain entry. In belonging to the most powerful Herd, each individual member gets a feeling of maximum security and maximum worth. But, individuals are driven by their instinct to some kind of Herd, even if it is only the immediate family, or the minimal next step up, some religion, or maybe a gang.

Being individuals that belonged to a Herd served us well during the Prehistoric and early Historic Times. Much of what Our Kind was able to accomplish could only be done with groups laboring together at hunting or building. During recent Historic Times much of what could only be accomplished by a large group of persons laboring together is now accomplished by machines.

Now, in our present world, the Herd Instinct, which we cannot escape from, is making much of life more and more unbearable. Throughout the world our cities are bursting to hold the Great Herd of People inside of them. For most cities, the people continue to spill out into the surrounding areas. Some Herds are so large that individuals no longer can identify with them in a manner that is satisfying to their needs. Instead of the individual feeling a part of the herd, they feel lost, smothered and neglected by it. Most individuals, needing desperately to belong to some Herd, join smaller herds that they can more personally identify with. Too often in our present world, too many of Our Kind, because of educational or economic reasons, are only equipped to join Herds that are at the bottom of the social ranking and so gangs proliferate.

Of all of the modern problems related to the Herd Instinct, the problem of gangs is perhaps the easiest to solve. Almost any alternative that gives the individual a feeling of strong bonding to a Herd together with the feeling that the individual feels needed is sufficient to solve this problem. Such a Herd must be of a complexity that the individual members can find a place where their contribution to the Herd is noticeable and relevant.

It probably is a good time that a new Herd is established, a Herd that is more sophisticated than the present day Boy and Girl Scouts. It needs to be a Herd where the diversity of our society is accepted and honored, a Herd that has appeal for the young persons of both the urban and rural environments.

Individuals, who feel insecure in their individuality, need the strength of the Herd to give them a feeling of worth. Herds are important structures within society in that they can be powerful bonding agents that contribute to stability.

But Herds also have in this modern world a darker side. It is sad to note that it is a serious major fault of the Herd and particularly of the individuals who are members of the Herd, that they work at making individuals that are not members feel fear for their individuality. Members of many Herds work relentlessly at putting down any person who is not a member and with whom they come into contact on a daily or frequent basis. Also, members of Herds are fiercely protective of the Mythology of the Herd. They are protective of the Herd's Mythology to the point of being both unreasonable and cruel to any who would challenge it. You can see this to be true even within what most consider as being the nobler Herds of Medicine, Religion and Science. It is only necessary to look at what is happening within Nations, between Nations, within Religions, between Religions, within the institutions of Medicine, Science and Schools to see the defining evidence of the Herd's conflict with different Herds and with the individuals that desire to be different. In almost every field of human endeavor, we see the Herd Instinct leading almost all down some common trail with joyful willingness to trample any who would deviate from the path. Even if the leader of the Herd has some fruitful insight to where they are leading, it is a disaster that all should follow without seriously questioning or searching for alternative paths. In our society, we preach the value of the individual, but if anyone really dares to be that, then the Herd tries to enthusiastically trample that individual underfoot. Such a Herd mentality costs Humankind a great and unreasonable price in every field of discovery. We cannot change the underlying cause of the Herd Instinct, but we must modify its damaging results on modern civilization. The Herd always rushes to trample any that dare to be different. It is not, in recent times, to the Herd Instinct that we owe any Salute for our Civilized Successes. It is to the very few, who have risked and escaped being trampled, that we owe our Salutes and Gratitude.

BODY LANGUAGE INSTINCT

Communication by means of merely assuming a certain pose of the body or by simple or complex movements of the body is certainly the most primitive form of communicating desires or intentions. The origins, of this most primitive means of communicating, must lie in the most distant past. Because of the long time separation of the origins of this Instinct, it is very difficult to even detect or understand all of its ramifications to our own kind, but surely they are many and of great consequence to our everyday actions.

Throughout every part of the Animal Kingdom, we can see Creatures who make complicated or subtle movements of their bodies to communicate with their own kind or with totally different Creatures. Many times the most beautiful and complex body motions are directed towards obtaining sexual favors. Watching very complicated mating dances, we might find it difficult to believe that such a complex string of patterns capable of directing the motions of their bodies could be hereditary. But, we are quite willing to believe that the equally complex physical designs and color patterns of a bird's plumage are inherited.

There are certainly body language patterns that can communicate between species. The intent of the crouch that predators, including Humans, take when sneaking up on their pray, is easily understood. Also the mere lifting of the arm as if to claw or strike is a body language sign that communicates easily between species.

The sudden up lifting of arms with the fingers of the hands spread to symbolize claws is commonly used and accompanied with a growl as a means for humans to frighten each other. There are many motions within the human face that can communicate with great accuracy various emotional conditions. There are static facial states that are clues about physical health.

There is a very general problem in not being able to identify all of the instinctive body language communications that are common to Our

Kind and also those that are common to other species. Remembering that reactions to body language can be Instinctive and Powerful, understanding them can only be to our great advantage.

Consider the situation we oft times hear, when some Human in dealing with another Creature who has been their long time friend and then, for no apparent reason the Human is suddenly and without warning attacked and killed. There is certainly the possibility that the Human made some Body Language Sign, a sign whose meaning was unknown to the Human, yet it was a sign that was so powerful as to trigger the Savage Instinct within the Creature that consequently lead to the death of their long time friend.

Much of the overall nature of all animals is their Instinctive Reactions that assist in their survival. Therefore, a major component of these Instinctive Reactions might be associated with sexual activity. We should be willing to consider that body language that is of a most primitive origin must have many signals that are concerned with communicating sexual interest, desire, willingness or rejection. These body language signals might also be able to communicate the magnitude associated with these feelings. There is the distinct possibility that these signals are too strong to be overridden by spoken language symbols. A situation could arise when a spoken no is overridden by a more powerful body language sign that is saying yes. Herein, we can see a further need for understanding what this instinct is all about.

THE SEXUAL INSTINCT

There can be little doubt that within the Animal Kingdom the Nature of each Creature's Sexuality is Instinctively Determined.

The instincts involved in sexual attraction are highly driven by visual cues about the overall condition of the body and specific features about the body. The appearance of the hips, waist, buttock and breast seem to be very important Instinctive Stimulators. That the facial image is symmetrical, for some strange reason seems to have great importance. This image being symmetrical is what is usually meant about being beautiful. It has been suggested and is conceivable that this is taken as an indication that the individual's head and what is inside of the head is genetically OK.

In general in determining sexual desirability, there always seems to be a quick visual scanning of the overall body. If the body looks generally symmetrical it is a powerful indication that it was derived from a good and complete set of genetic instructions. Both men and woman look for these indicators in each other. If all of the correct physical parts are signaling sexual attraction, but some body movement tells a negative story, or there is discovered some physical damage, or the appearance of sickness, then all of the sense of attraction can be immediately canceled.

I would doubt that age by itself has any negative affect on an individual being sexually attractive. It is more likely that it is only those physical features often associated with age, that tell the tale of the individual not being in good physical condition.

Each of us is born with a predetermined sexual preference, which certainly must be determined by hereditary factors. It does not take very much investigation to understand that individuals from their earliest years have strong feelings concerning the direction of their sexual orientation. They did not have to be schooled to know it. They did not have to be brainwashed to know it. Their sexual orientation was upon them naturally from the time of their earliest feeling for others within their species. It is quite clear from listening to many individual testimonies that whatever their sexual orientation is, that it was there as a natural condition of their being and that it remains the same unchanged throughout their lifetime as does any inherited trait.

When we consider sexual preference for persons of the same sex, we come upon some rather unusual circumstances. We are forced to wonder about the genetic nature of this Instinct. It would seem highly unusual if its source was genetic in nature, since in present society it is thought that members of this group do not reproduce themselves.

It is an undeniable fact of nature that if a kind does not reproduce itself, that its kind dies and becomes extinct. Also, you simply do not get Elephants by breading Rabbits. If in fact you should like to believe that this trait, this Instinct, is not inherited, then you are faced with a Miracle in Nature that is equivalent to a Virgin Birth.

Careful consideration might leads us to believe, that because of the extreme pressures of the Herd, many in this group are socially forced into acting against their real sexual preference. Because of unbearable Herd pressures they marry and reproduce themselves. It is in this way that their genes for this Instinct are passed on to some of their offspring. This seems the most reasonable way for this Instinctive trait to have survived throughout all of time.

There is the slightest possibility, that the Instinct that drives sexual preference is in such a fine state of neurological and chemical balance, that for some reason not understood, it can be easily swayed by subtle changes in chemical balances to determine the direction of sexual preference. I believe this last supposition must be ruled out of reasonable consideration, as we know of no such simple means that can effect a change of sexual preference in any individual. It would seem the best bet is, that Sexual Preference is Instinctive in essentially all cases. This then must lead us to some further unusual speculations. Within the general population estimates for the percentages of the population that profess to a sexual preference for the same sex is in a low percentage range of around five to ten percent. I believe that based on the assumption that this Instinct is most likely an inherited Instinct, we have to consider that it exists in a much larger percentage of the population. Just considering the proportions of a normal bell curve and that many within this group are forced by Herd pressures to disavow themselves, we can be very suspicious of the numbers. It is more likely true, that somewhere near 5% are in manner as the whole group is characterized and it is somewhat easy to identify them. Just keeping in mind the normal bell curve as applied to this group, but speaking of percentages as applied to the general population, it is reasonable to believe that there is another 5% that are mannered like alpha males or alpha females, and they simply exist in society totally unsuspected of their preference. We are still left to consider the middle of the curve. At the middle some 10 to15% must lay somewhere with characteristics between these two extremes. Those in the middle also have traits that are relatively undetectable. Within this population of the middle and upper percentages most must be married with families, a fact that might be reflected in part by the high divorce rate and serious unhappiness with those who stay married, either because of duty to their children or other less noble reasons, such as a financial situation. Many of those who stay married certainly have a life with some happiness, but it must be certain, because of the most powerful nature of this Sexual Instinctive Drive, that they surely have a chronic feeling of dissatisfaction and of their life being unfulfilled. Based on these considerations we might be suspicious of the reasons for the high rate of suicide among teenagers. It is sad to note that the teen suicide rate appears to be the highest in those areas where religious influence is most dominant and religious intolerance toward this group is strongest. Within this population and because of the Instinctive Herd Mentality and coupled with Institutionalized Persecution, there are many hidden within the group that use the age-old adage that "the best defense is a powerful offense."

They therefore, to hide their own Instinctive Nature, wage a vengeful and unforgiving war against their own kind. Not being open, they usually hide behind some mythical righteous fortress from which they hurl their insults and condemnations. Any non-bigoted and serious religious scholar of the Bible will tell you, that just because something is written in the Bible it does not mean that it is the word of god. The Bible is a collection of writings, written by men, and as such they had their own personal and social axes to grind. During the period of history that the Bible spans, any sexual act that did not result in the bearing of children had to be forbidden. Each tribe's survival was dependent on women producing the greatest numbers of children, simply as a means of trying to balance out a Nature that took them as sacrifice. In ancient times, an average mother was lucky to have only two or three children survive to the time of their sexual maturity. To encourage the family to "be fruitful and reproduce" and to damn any sexual activity that did not produce children was a tribes main philosophy for survival, and not just survival, but growth in numbers and therefore in a World of Herds to grow in power. Even a casual examination of societies and their culture's throughout history indicates conclusively that there does not exist any natural instinctive bias against members of this group. It is clear that all biases against members of this group are perpetrated by various Institutions of the Herds that feel they have something special to gain for themselves by condemning members of this group.

The time may not be too far off before we might be able to identify specific genes that govern the Instinct for Sexual Preference. I believe it would be the gravest error if we tried to vary the gene structure of any individual to change their sexual preference to opposite sex preference. Nature has, in its time tested wisdom, given us this Instinctive Preference. It surely is there for a good purpose even if we in our ignorance do not exactly understand. As a society by meddling with this Instinct, we could suffer a great loss of creative talent. Our History bares witness to the greatly disproportionate high number of contributions made by members of this group. They have been some of the World's Greatest Political Leaders, Military Leaders, Philosophers, Teachers, Scientists, Artist and Athletes. It would seem that coupled with this Instinct, is a different way of seeing the World, and therefore allowing insights that others rarely find.

DIFFERENTIAL HEARING INSTINCT

The senses are basic and exclusive mechanisms for detecting the patterns of the Real World. Each of the senses must have associated with them a long list of Instincts that have evolved along with their physical structures.

The Sense of Hearing and the mechanisms that make sound patterns storable in Long Term Memory have an exceptional Instinct embedded within them for certain kinds of differential hearing. I would guess that parts of this Instinct are at least as old as are the first Creatures, who were able to utter sounds as grunts or groans.

The Mapping Function for Hearing is very much concerned with discerning the finest detail of any nuances imbedded within sounds. (You should here be remembering, that what you might believe to be the most significant components of a sounds may not be the most significant components for the Mapping Function) The major parts of any communication with sound must fall upon the Sense of Hearing and the Mapping Function like a ton of Rocks. There is little if any ambiguity in the distinct patterns. It is within the even most minor nuances of the sounds where complex Creatures have hidden their subtler meanings. We might think of the major sounds of language, as attention getters for the subtler sounds that lay nestled among their rocks. The major sounds are oft times the crier that points the general direction to the sweeter meats.

We need to note here, that there are strong differences between the methods of communicating a language that is both spoken and written. There are accompanying great differences in how a person understands and reacts to these two different ways of communicating.

Seeing a written word and reading that word with the Eyes, because of the immediate exclusivity of the senses causes the pattern's information to reach the Long Term Memory storage area reserved for patterns detected by the Sense of Sight. Hearing the same written word, as a spoken word, causes the patterns representing the spoken sound to reach a different Long Term Memory area associated with Sense of Hearing.

I propose that Creatures that have even a minimal spoken language, or any way of communicating by sound, have associated with their Sense of Hearing an Instinct that is exceptionally powerful at detecting the most minor nuances within the sounds of their language. They are capable of detecting the slightest dialect or accent, which displaces the sound patterns away from the strict core meanings of the common language. Each individual intelligible word of a spoken language has sound characteristics attached to it, when spoken by an individual, that allows it to be identified with a strict objective core meaning, allows it to be identified as some displacement from the core meaning, allows it to be identified as to the individual who speaks the words, allows it to be identified as to the speaker being within the group of the family, or within a group of friends, allows it to be identified as being a member of the tribe, or identifiable as being a member of a nearby tribe, or as being foreign to all of these. There are also many other nuances associated within the sounds that embody the spoken word. These other nuances can stimulate sexual arousal or can color the word to stimulate many other varied emotional conditions within the listener.

We can understand from our own memories of sounds, that the voices of the members of our families and friends or any persons are stored there in exacting detail, and most importantly that the nuances associated with each of them and causes them to be discrete individual voices are preserved in great detail. When we recall from memory any words spoken by a familiar person, we recall that memory as if the person was actually speaking. We hear their voice within our mind. This is a strong testimony that the Differential Hearing Instinct is very much concerned with the sweeter meats hidden amongst the burden of rocks. We should be sure that this Differential Hearing Instinct allows for the pinpointing of powerful messages for all creatures. We can be sure that when the Lady Frog listens to the choruses of Male Frogs singing their songs into the night, she hears within one individual's voice the subtle sounds different from all the others that commands her to find that one, the one who has rang all of her hormonal bells and filled her with delightful yearnings.

So, it is also true that for Our Kind the simple sound of a voice from an unseen person can trigger strong reactions about the desirability or undesirability of that unseen person.

We cannot here consider all of the Instincts that might be associated with language when it is communicated by sound. What we do want to consider is how this Differential Instinct of Hearing might give some insight into an important social problem of our time and in fact through all of time. We need to consider some aspects of how and why this Instinct is so important to our own kind. It is surely as important in similar ways to other Creatures.

The main differences of real importance that separates individuals within or between races are not the Color of their Skin, Facial Features, Hair Color or any other physical features that persons normally associate with marking an individual as different from them. These features, which many tout as making the differences between so-called races and as being the main identifying features that allow individuals the grounds on which to discriminate against each other, are not what I believe underlies the basic Nature of discrimination. The fact is, that within any group we find that these individual physical features exist as a continuous morphing across the group. Also, as a whole, these features are pretty well common to us all. There is no feature among them that makes them grossly abhorrent. There is no feature among them that inherently should cause anxiety, hatred or fear.

The Absolute Single Greatest Difference that Exists Between Humans is Language!

If we consider the Nature of the spoken language there are some interesting considerations that might help us understand both the Nature and reason for the biases that lead to discrimination against certain groups within a society. Consider that as Primitive Creatures one of our prime fears must have been a fear of being destroyed by our Own Kind. To attack and destroy a nearby group was a relatively easy means of acquiring both their material goods and more importantly to acquire their territory. Many other Creatures in the Animal Kingdom strongly guard against these intrusions by members of their own species. For Humans this was most certainly true during those most primitive times, when different factions were becoming more and more successful, therefore allowing the size of their groups to grow. It seems to be the case, that groups living in relatively close proximity are groups that have the most similarities in a common spoken language. But it is the Nature of a spoken language, that it is learned by children from the adults. It is this kind of learning that gives each group their special dialect or identifying accent. This dialect remains a mark on their language as long as they stay generally separated from other groups that speak the same language. Some groups that foraged over areas that were adjacent to territories of a nearby group, because of restraints upon food supplies, encountered each other for only brief periods during a year. Remaining separated for most of the year, probably allowed them to maintain distinct spoken language nuances. It must have been from the most primitive times that the distant sound of a different dialect was an early warning of a possible impending attack. When hearing your own spoken language even from a far distance, you are able to identify the speaker as being a member of your group. It is not difficult to believe that an important condition for survival was to be able to distinguish these dialectical nuances of the language. This must have been the case over a very long period of our primitive history, a period long enough that we have an instinctive uneasiness whenever we detect the dialect that seems to be close enough to our own primary language and different enough to alert us to the dangers of a possible attack from a neighboring tribe or group. It was probably true that during times when food supplies were sufficient that nearby groups had infrequent but good relationships with each other. On the other hand, when food supplies were in very short supply for very long periods of time, it was the nearby groups that must have been the main competition, a competition that was about life and death, about the survival of the families and friends within the group. The result is, even now, when we hear such dialects of our common language, the instinctive bias raises an automatic prejudice as a sense of anxiety, an uneasiness that seems to reside as some ghostly feeling deep down in the gut.

We might wonder why we don't have strong Instinctual Biases, prejudices, against groups that speak languages that are totally foreign. It is simply because for most all of time, we never had any contact whatsoever with such groups. They were so separated from us by great distances, that there was no contact with them. There was no means by which to develop an Instinctual Bias. They were not a threat. We had no fears associated directly with any such sound patterns that lay completely outside of our known language patterns. We also have no bias against the songs of Birds, the crowing of the Cock, the call of Frogs, or the communications of other Creatures that have not regularly posed a dangerous threat to us. We do have biases against those Creatures, who make sounds of communication that we can identify with threats to us, as individuals, or to our group. If you are alone in the wilderness, the sound of the Hiss of a Snake, or the Roar of a Lion, I assure you will raise within you an Instinctive Fear that rattles uncontrolled within your guts. It is easy to see in other animals, how they respond instinctively to sounds that for ages of time have denoted the presence of a nearby threat.

Consider an interesting thought experiment and see what conclusions we might draw about these propositions. Imagine the situation where by coincidence, two individuals who are previously unacquainted with each other come into verbal contact by telephone. Imagine they are separated by such distances as to not allow them to meet or see each other. We put on them the single condition that they do not ask questions about to which ethnic group they belong. And I tell you, as an observer of this situation, that it is the condition of these two persons that they each have strong historical prejudices against the ethnic group to which the other belongs. In such a situation, where they can only learn about the other individual by what is said, by voice tonal qualities, by linguistic style and all of the nuances that are possible to convey by the human voice, these two individuals are able to begin knowing each other. These communicable voice qualities are all controlled by the learned patterns that are stored in the individual's Long Term Memories. As the contact between them continues, both of the individuals are simply revealing to each other patterns from their Long Term Memories and also exhibiting their learned reactions to those patterns, which are also stored in their Long Term Memory. They also have Instinctive Reactions to their communications. If the contact between them persists for enough time, the individuals, as we say, get to know each other and so to understand to what degree they believe they are similar or different.

Such a contact which only can involve the exchange of Long Term Memory patterns with no knowledge of physical characteristics of the individuals is enough and a primary way of establishing a relationship between individuals. The relationship that develops can range across the entire spectrum of Human acceptance or non-acceptance of another individual. But it can only be based on what they have communicated by voice.

It is not too difficult to believe, that as long as the information contained in the tonal qualities of the communication does not alert either of these two to the fact that they each belong to an ethnic group that they are prejudiced against, then they could become friends, especially if the general information that the two exchange indicates that they are enthusiastic about the same interests in life; they might become strongly bonded as friends.

What should be said about this situation, if after these two become strongly bonded friends, then they are allowed to meet face to face?

I cannot say that the Differential Hearing Instinct is the only element that contributes to and prolongs the unreasonable prejudice that exists between groups in a society. But I do believe that it is the primary one, the one that clearly connects our Instinctive Fears from the Primitive Past to the Modern World. Of course there are all of the unreasonable unjustified hatreds that institutions and individuals work at attaching to this prejudice, and it is interesting that they do become attached, but all of these can easily be shown to be without merit. They are things that are testable and rationally verifiable. But the curse of the Instinct is that its strength is in not being controllable by means of logic, and so as long as the conditions persist that trigger the Instinctive Reaction, the biases associated with it will survive.

Babies and very young children sometimes are very fearful and cry when they are in a safe environment and are introduced to a stranger. We usually think that the child is upset because they visually recognize the person as a stranger and are therefore afraid of the new face. It is more likely that the stranger has spoken, and the child immediately recognizes that the voice is coming from an outsider to their known group of family and friends.

It is very probable that this Instinct began originating far, far back in our history, to times when those relatives that were eventually to become Our Kind used it as a great advantage for surviving.

This Instinct is very strong within communities of other Creatures that span a great range of evolutionary complexity. It is very strong in Humans, Whales and even Birds. These other Creatures will many times gang up and attack any individuals who, by means of simply communicating by sound, have alerted them, that they are an intruder.

Humans have at times demonstrated their willingness to flock together and rain terror onto individuals who are outsiders in a like manner to the other wild Creatures.

I think we can see that many times in the modern world that individuals, who belong to groups that have strong social prejudices against them, are able to integrate and be both successful and accepted if their spoken language and its nuances correspond to those of the dominant group. I would further suggest that, no matter what may be the outwardly visible physical characteristics of an individual, if we observe that their vocal speech patterns seem to be identical to ours, and we detect no accent or dialect, we feel at ease with them, and feel that they are one of us.

We can also note that if a speaker has the physical characteristics of one ethnic group, but speaks with the accent of a different ethnic group, we have a tendency to identify them with the group associated with their accent and not necessarily with the group whose physical features they represent. Many times in observing such a situation we find ourselves with an uneasy confusion within us.

It is curious that biases are so attachable to this Differential Hearing Instinct. There can be biases that contain either negative or positive feelings towards an individual or group. It appears generally that the biases that give a positive feeling are associated with those accents that originate from a foreign language and that biases associated with local accents are almost always negative.

You might be more willing to accept how the Differential Hearing Instinct is tied directly to the hidden strings that affect us, by considering how deeply the sounds of a musical score can touch and arouse our deepest emotions.

If it is true, as I believe that it is, that strongly negative Instinctive Feelings are associated with the sounds of dialects and accents within a common language, then to overcome these unreasonable biases, a nation must educate its population to speak a common language. A common spoken language that is recognizable by the ear as friendly, because its subtle sounds are those of the national group.

MORBID CURIOSITY INSTINCT

There seems to be an Instinctive Morbid Curiosity that draws us like a magnetic force to all kinds of things and events that are Morbid in Nature. The more morbid the condition, the more strongly we are drawn to dote over it. This Instinctive drawing to scenes of morbid attraction can be seen every day in such simple events as the extreme slowing of traffic as it approaches the site of a vehicle accident. The traffic always slows so people can gawk at the accident even though the accident is in no way physically blocking the roadway.

Stories that are of the most extreme Morbid Nature are always the top sellers for Newspapers and other News Media. There are Newspapers whose main stay for profit is their dedication to exploiting the Public's Morbid Curiosity. Stories that are considered to be a high watermark of Morbidity, such as, the Jack the Ripper story, are repeated over and over throughout near History. The story of Dr. Frankenstein has been a Morbid Delight ever since its creation. Any examination of stories that have been the greatest monetary successes of our times will reveal that a great number of them are steeped in a Morbid Tale.

Consider Frankenstein, Dracula, The Mummy, Aliens, and even the story of the sinking of the Titanic, which many would consider to be a love story. If the same love story were told without the morbid back-drop of the multitude of lives that were lost in the dramatic sinking, then the story would have only been mediocre at best. Young persons swarm to movies that are bathed in bloodshed and horrible deaths. We are hopefully curious about what primitive mechanism might be beneath this Instinct of Morbid Curiosity. It must have in some way been a strong factor in contributing to our survival. Most likely it is this morbid curiosity that drew Our Kind to the scenes of the dying and death, where we could as scavengers find food. We couldn't smell the distant scent of blood or battle in the air like many other scavengers. But whenever, we heard the chaotic sounds of a distant struggle, we must have surely been drawn nearby to await the outcome and the scrapes it might provide.

Since we are, most of us, quite well fed, we no longer attempt to feast at the Morbid Sites that have drawn our attention.

Many animals that are carnivores also harbor an Instinctive Morbid Curiosity. This simple attraction to a site of a chaotic struggle and death has contributed to their survival.

We should not be too upset by the fact that we are drawn to Morbid Scenes. The magnet that draws us is probably within our genes. It is something that we cannot escape. It does not mean that by this Morbid Attraction, this curiosity, we are susceptible to committing Morbid Atrocities. It is the Savage Instinct that we must be concerned about in that respect. Morbid Curiosity is itself a Benign Instinct.

MYSTIC ATTRACTION INSTINCT

The Instinct of Mystic Attraction is very curious in that, in the general sense, it seems to have no specific benefit. It would seem to have no benefit for either the individual or the tribe or a modern society. It is within itself, almost mystical that it exists. But it does exist, and it reveals itself in our love from an early age of Fairy Tales and all kinds of Magic and the beliefs in things that are beyond verification by using any tests involving logical means. It is a powerfully strong Instinct, which is resident even within those persons who are well educated. It is reveled in a multitude of stories and beliefs originating in ancient times and also in the present day.

The Mystic Instinct ranges to include: Fairy Tales, Creatures of Make-believe, All kinds of Magic and Magical Tales, Flying Saucers, Telepathy, Teleportation, Religion, Miracles, Fortune Tellers, Psychics, Astrology, Prophesy, Ritualistic Behaviors, and others. The only commonalties, between the various manifestations of this Instinct are that the basic elements are not verifiable in Nature and seem to be creations of a creative imagination. Such an Instinct would seem not to be survivable within an environment that is all about selecting traits that contribute to survivability.

What we might guess that we have going here, is an Instinct that is a minor consequence of some other Human Characteristic that is itself a strong contributor to our survival. It would seem likely that the primary element that secondarily spawns this Instinct is our Creative Thinking, which has been a most powerful instrument for our survival. Creative Thinking leads naturally to all kinds of creations, creations that are applicable to the real world, that are applicable to the pleasures of the Arts and to creations that do not necessarily make any contributions to either. It would be, I think, a good bet that the Mystic Instinct survives because of the power of its primary source.

We should be somewhat amazed, at the high position some of the elements of this Instinct have assumed within the present society.

PATTERN INSTINCTS

Our instincts that are associated with simple and complex static patterns that exist in Nature are in many cases simple and obvious, but surely there are many that have not been recognized. It is interesting that for the most simple of these Pattern Instincts, we can see many, of what are essentially the same instincts, exhibited in Creatures that are of an entirely different species.

Here I will list only a few instincts as a means of giving a cursory idea about them, as most everyone has some familiarity with them:

Shiny

There is an Instinct that attracts us to objects in the Natural World that are Shiny, and to others that are unusually colored compared to the general background color. The general Nature of this Instinct seems to be that we are attracted to anything that is an inflection point as compared to the general environment that surrounds us.

Simple Geometry

We seem to be Instinctively attracted to investigating objects of all kinds that show a great regularity to their structure, including uncomplicated geometric objects like straight lines, perpendicular lines, triangles, squares, simple circles, etc. It seems not unreasonable to believe that this instinct has strong connections to the most basic structures within the brain, that are involved in the pattern coding in preparation for pattern information storage into memory.

Regular 3D Geometry

We are also drawn instinctively to investigate other more complicated but regular geometries, particularly the three dimensional geometry's of inorganic crystals and the regular organic geometries that are the immediate representation of all living things.

Holes

We are Instinctively drawn to investigate, with some reluctance, Holes. The whole ranges of Holes seems to be on our Instinctive Menu, Little Holes and Large Holes, even Dark Holes, are a sweet attraction. It is not difficult to imagine how well this instinct has served us through the ages.

General

Just as speculation we might consider that there may be multitudes of simple visual static patterns that to us as Homo sapiens and to other Creatures, Instinctively Communicate Information that is of great importance for Survival, patterns that upon their detection, rise up great fears, or beckon towards safety, or call powerfully in some unknown way.

Here we have considered a very few of the Instinctive Static Patterns that are detected by the Sense of Sight. We of course realize that patterns detectable by each of the other senses must necessarily have many Instinctive Reactions associated with them.

Smell

The Sense of Smell detects patterns that represent chemical agents that are drifting in the air or in the water or are resident in the ground. We are beginning to understand in detail just how very important the Sense of Smell is at Instinctively controlling the actions of many of Nature's Creatures. We must assume that it has powerful affects on Our Own Kind.

Taste

An Instinct associated with the Sense of Taste, and is known to everyone, was surely a powerful influence in contributing to our survival. This is the Instinctive Scowl that spreads across the Human Face at the taste of anything that is particularly bitter. Even the smallest children can exhibit this Instinct. The scowl is a powerful nonverbal warning to others that the substance is not desirable. Bitter taste in Nature is the usual warning of a poisonous substance.

MOVING PATTERN INSTINCTS

Music

The detection of sounds especially those sounds that we associate with music are a kind of moving pattern. They exist as a condition that flows through time. We seem to have an attraction to those tonal conditions that in their atomic form make a pattern whose structure exhibits a gracefully extended regularity in time. These patterns in time are sounds, such as the sound produced by the vibration of a string or the tones from some wind instrument. We are also attracted to those sounds in Nature that are a singular pattern repeated in time, such as the beat of some instrument of percussion. We can only guess at some of the reasons behind our clearly Instinctual Attraction to Music. It might be, as suggested by others, associated to our bonding with the rhythmic sound of our mother's heart beat. I suggest that it probably also has much to do, about the sounds of those Creatures of Nature that were never threatening within themselves, those Creatures whose sounds were a kind of Song to our ears that all was safe and well within the near vicinity.

The journey through the patterns in time that we make, when we hear any piece of music is quite an unusual journey. It is a most unusual journey as compared to the journey through time, which we make when our sense of sight is taking a journey through the patterns of the visual landscape. On the journey of the sense of sight through the visual landscape, we can in a sense, see into the future. As we travel, we can see distant objects and watch as they slowly move closer and closer. As those first distant objects draw ever nearer, they reveal more and more the details of their structure. On the other hand a musical journey is like traveling or moving, where you are facing backwards to the direction of your movement in time. You cannot detect any musical sounds in the future, because they have not yet been born. At every instant in time, each and every note within the musical journey is born fresh and new. Their image, their musical structure appears instantaneously and develops to its fullness like some phoenix arising from nothingness. The sound images construct their evolving forms within your memory, but they slowly fade into the receding landscape of sounds, where their structures dim and disappear in time and ever-new tonal patterns are born instant to instant.

It is often said that "A picture is worth a thousand words", but for the human ear a piece of music is a thousand pictures in glorious sounds.

Overhead

Patterns represented as shadows that suddenly appear above the heads of a Creature seem to bring a sudden fearful Instinctive Alertness.

Peripheral

Any pattern that moves unexpectedly in the peripheral vision brings a sudden fearful Instinctive Alertness.

THE PECKING ORDER INSTINCT

It would seem that for many of the more complex Creatures there is a well-established instinct within Herds of any and every size to establish the individual members in some ranking of position within the group. This is common even within the smallest social group, the immediate family.

Pecking Orders are probably most clearly delineated in the smallest groups within a Herd. Within small groups, Pecking Orders that have been in place for long periods of time are usually very strongly established. They can lead to serious unrest, if an outsider tries to become a member of the group. Only if the outsider is clearly seen by all members of the group as fitting into the lowest Pecking Order, will they then be easily accepted by the group, as this in a sense, moves everyone within the group, one notch up in the Pecking Order Ladder.

Pecking Orders are a Natural Primitive way of establishing Order within a Group, an Order that excludes the Chaos that would result from Anarchy.

SELF CENTERED INSTINCT

Every individual Creature that is Conscious of their Living Existence, Instinctively and naturally believes that they are the Center of the Universe. It is clearly the result of a simple and powerful logic. All of their senses clearly and unambiguously communicate that everything in existence is spread evenly across a landscape in which they are at the Center.

TERRITORIAL INSTINCT

The Territorial Instinct exists and is strong in many of Nature's Creatures and is no less so within Our Kind. It is an Instinct that has served each Creature well. It is directed in the most general case to the protection of a territory, where a Creature gathers or stores food, where it might have a Safe Sanctuary for Protection against the Elements of the Weather, and a place of Protection for the Raising of Their Young. It is this area of territory that Creatures see as belonging to them, and leads them to attempt to exclude other Creatures of their own kind, and any other Creatures that might infringe upon their perceived rights of ownership.

For Humans all of these reasons for exhibiting a Territorial Instinct are also valid, but for us the Territorial Instinct is extended to include those territories that exist only within our minds. We are ready to defend our perceived territories within our work environment. We are ready to defend those territories that involve the properties that we directly own. We are ready to defend those territories that we embrace as theories with which we feel closely associated. We are ready to especially defend those territories that enclose our religious beliefs.

Our greatest problems, involving physical conflict and social violence, come about when we are involved in defending the territories that only exist within the mind, and we falsely relate them to territories of the geography.

OWNERSHIP INSTINCT

It is obvious that for Humans, from our earliest infancy, that we instinctively try to establish our rights to ownership of physical objects. Even before infants can use spoken language, they are capable of communicating their strong feelings for personal ownership of objects. When children are first developing their use of spoken language one of their primary and most powerful communications is "Mine".

NURTURING INSTINCT

Probably one of the most important Instincts that have contributed to the survival of any Creature is the Instinct of parents to supply the most basic requirements of life for their young until they are somewhat able survive on their own. This Instinct is widely spread across many species, but is most highly developed in the most advanced Creatures. In some mammals the Instinct has evolved to such an extent as to include Nurturing that exceeds the most basic requirements for surviving. This Nurturing includes the guidance of the young to discovering patterns in Nature that are known by their adult populations.

INSTINCT TO BRING HOME FOOD

The instinct to bring food from the place it was obtained to a more secure environment has surely had important benefits for all those creatures that exhibit this instinct, including humans. You can observe even today, that those wild creatures who attempt to consume the food that they have obtained without first bring it to a safer place often have their meals stolen from them by some fiercer creatures. The simple act of bring food to the surroundings of the home provides two very important ingredients for survival. Firstly, a large friendly group can then protect the food and secondly it allows for the sharing of the food among the members of the group and in this way substantially contributes to the inter-bonding between members of the group. We could believe that the sharing of food within a common group is the primary force for strongly bonding with other members of the group and is an even more powerful mechanism for bonding than are sexual relationships between the members of the group. Sexual relations between group members are probably the second most important element in establishing strong bonding between individuals.

Subconsciously we seem to realize the great importance to the bonding between individuals within the group of the family and or friends that is played by get-togethers for consuming food within the safety of the home. In more distant times this sharing of food within the tribal group was certainly the single most important method of unifying the group towards common purposes. In today's world it is sometimes difficult for families to share this still most important ritual for bonding. The single most important ritual for establishing and maintaining strong bonds between the members of a family or groups of friends is the sharing of food within a safe environment. It is an ancient ritual that surely precedes even Our Kind's becoming human. To not honor this Instinctual force, weakens nature's basic fabric that binds relationships. This Instinct is one that should be honored at every possible opportunity.

IDEAS AS AN APPENDAGE INSTINCT

There is a strong possibility that for Humans, we Instinctively treat our long held beliefs, as if they were some Physical Appendage of our Material Bodies.

Consider what the situation is, when anyone makes a challenge to one of your long held beliefs. If the belief is strongly held, you fight against any attempt to change it. No matter how logical is the argument for changing the belief, many people will mount a fight against changing. They will even mount a fight that is totally without supporting logic. They may become so emotionally aroused that even the Savage Instinct might be activated. It is the kind of struggle that we might expected to be mounted, if someone were trying to remove by amputation their Hand, or their Arm, or Leg. This Instinct is one that is basic to some of the most serious problems of conflict within and between Herds and among the individuals that are their members.

HOARDING INSTINCT

The hoarding of material goods is an Instinct that is common across a broad spectrum of species. We see it in Insects like Ants and Bees. We see it exhibited by Birds, by Squirrels, and it is most highly developed and exhibited by Humans.

In some the Instinct is so powerful that they Hoard every kind of physical object and are mentally unable to Part Company with any of them.

In others it is exhibited by the Hoarding of certain selective types of objects and we kindly refer to those persons as Collectors instead of Hoarders.

In many the Hoarding is specifically oriented towards those items that might be required for a comfortable long-term survival. Usually the primary items in this group are Moneys and/or Food.

This is an Instinct that has served us well through difficult times, and generally serves us well at the present time.

PUT-DOWN INSTINCT

We can see, with some sadness, this strange condition flourishing in Societies throughout the World. We sometimes over-emphasize it in the philosophy of most Team Sports. Simply put, if you cannot win, then stop the other team from winning. Team Sports are partly exercising the philosophy of War, so in a sense it is an understandable part of the game of War. But Our Kind also exemplifies it as: if you can't succeed, then try to stop anyone else from succeeding. It is an antisocial Instinct that needs to be controlled and spoken out against at every possibility. People become very cleaver at instituting this Instinct against their friends and associates. Sometimes people use a straight on attack. But usually, they implement the attack indirectly, behind another person's back, or by means of making use of persons other than themselves. Quite often, they will slip little barbs into their conversation with the person they are trying to put down. Sometimes they will implement the Instinct by means of obviously overly praising someone.

It is a situation that is rampant within the Society and usually is considered just part of life. But, it is a most foolish practice in that it tries to continually pull Our Own Kind down from attaining good things.

It might be more appropriate to call this Instinct, the Selfish Instinct. It probably is strongly connected to the Ownership Instinct, or Pecking Order Instinct, or the Territorial Instinct, or maybe to all of them.

INSTINCT TO PERSECUTE TO ESCAPE PERSECUTION

Within the framework of deeds that surround this instinct are some of humankind's most regrettable injustices.

The mechanics that underlie this instinct start as weak and simple seeds that can easily be recognized as detrimental and evil and these could quickly and easily be shattered and thereby stop the development of this instinct into the full-grown terror that it can become. Both the water and fertilizer that nourish this instinct during its early beginnings is fearful silence. This instinct almost always starts it seed as one individual or a very small group of individuals who begin the persecution of an individual or a small group of individuals. The persecutors discover that they are generally unopposed in their persecutions and so then other members of the society join with them. They join with them simply out of a fear, that by not actually belong to the group of persecutors, they might somehow be seen by those persecutors as silently opposing them. With time the ranks of those who are the persecutors grow more and more by the simple means of fearing that if you are not one with that group, that you might be identified as a de facto member to the persecuted group. The momentum of this instinct can grow until the persecuting group has become a major social herd were all nonmembers are so fearful, that they remain silent even when they see the most inhumane injustices committed by those persecutors.

You can witness this instinct's beginning signs of awakening and its attempt at survival on any primary school yard within the world, and if it is not summarily stopped in its infant beginnings, it surely becomes a full-grown monster of injustice that is then difficult or impossible to stop.

You can witness this instinct in a yard of domesticated chickens where its consequences quickly become bloody and an individual is pecked to death by a mob of their brothers and sisters.

There is only one hope of stopping the cruel injustices that this instinct always brings and that is to stop it at its very beginning otherwise fear will become its powerful shield and its mechanism for survival.

INSTINCT TO LIE

It would appear that it is for some Creatures, an important part of their Instinctive Nature to Lie. This does seem to be the case for Humans; it clearly has specific advantages that aid a Creature's tactics for survival. To be able to deceive another Creature, or even your Own Kind, is a most basic means of escaping from a situation that might be of severe consequence. Lying exists at almost every level of the Animal and Plant Kingdom. Lying can involve the physical presentation of fixed patterns, that do not naturally couple to those associated characteristics normally belonging to the individual that would exhibit them. It can involve the release of chemical patterns that drift through the air or water and convey a lie about the identity of the individual that originated them. In Nature there is pretty much a set of lies that are appropriate for confusing one or many of the senses of another Creature. For Humans, lying is involved with the use of body muscles usually facial expressions or faked direction of movement. But, it reaches its crowning glory by use of the written and spoken language.

SYMPATHETIC INSTINCT

At least in Humans and to some degree in other Mammals there exists an unusual Instinct, the Sympathetic Instinct, whose strength or weakness seems to vary almost as a chemical concentration might vary. It seems that an individual's degree of sensitivity to having a Sympathetic Reaction to the emotional state of another individual is a result of some Instinctive Mechanisms that are exhibited from the time of their birth.

We can sometimes see the Sympathetic Instinct being exhibited by mammals that are quite different from humans. These mammals usually exhibit the Sympathetic Instinct by showing their sympathy for other individuals of their Own Kind, who have suffered physical wounds or death. These Creatures display their sympathy by using physical actions that unambiguously communicate their sympathetic meaning to their Own Kind and are powerful enough to communicate their meaning across the barriers that separate species. Their clear signs of sympathy are obvious and touching, and are strong enough visual and or vocal patterns to evoke a sympathetic understanding in humans.

Within the extremes of this Instinct in the Human population are those individuals, who are so sensitive; we might name them Sympathetic Resonators. These are persons, whose extreme sensitivity causes them to actually feel within their own bodies the emotional experience that another person is feeling. They can actually feel within themselves, the physical conditions of pain or joy that they detect within another person.

At the opposite end of the Sympathetic Spectrum are those individuals who have no sympathy at all for another individual's emotional state. We might call such persons Sympathetic Duds. These are persons who are unable in anyway to empathize with the emotional condition of another individual of their own species or of any other species. These Sympathetic Duds, if they happen to cause physical or emotional suffering to another individual, are unable to feel any remorse for their actions or for the sufferings of the other individual. Luckily the general population lies within the bounds of these two extremes and most persons exhibit a mid-range of Sympathetic Reactions to the emotional state of other Creatures.

The Sympathetic Instinct surely is an element that springs from the sense that individuals within a group are emotionally bonded. In the truest sense it is an Instinct that strives to be a kind of self-protection, where an individual is able to see others as part of their image of self. Surely this Instinct has been an important contributor to both the survival of groups within a species and therefore survival for the individuals that exhibit this Instinct.

DESTRUCTIVE INSTINCT

There seems to be an Instinctive part of us that is interested in discovering the consequences of the destruction of real objects within the world. Even in small children, you many times see that when one child has constructed some object of their desire, another child will joyfully destroy that object. It might seem inappropriate to some that there is a feeling of joy in the act of destroying. It is probably this feeling of joy that is the Instinct's driving force.

The Destructive Instinct, within a modern society, is an Instinct that needs to be placed under the strongest restraints, if only because the machines and other instruments we have to implement destruction are awesome in comparison to those of our ancient ancestors. In warfare, we can see the Destructive Instinct freed to work its most terrible results.

This is an Instinct that is not a completely negative situation. Many things can only reveal their inner structure and any treasures that might be hidden there, if they are broken open or destroyed. The mere destruction of objects must have led us to the discovery of hidden sources of food. Also, the attempted destruction of small rocks must have been insightfully revealing, when it sometimes produced useful rock scraps with their sharp cutting edges.

The smashing together of rocks during the nighttime or in the darkness of a cave must have reveled a sight of wonderment as the bright sparks from those impacts streaked through the darkness.

The attempted destruction by burning might have been our first introduction to the cooking of foods.

The attempt at destroying by the smashing of seeds, nuts and shellfish was surely our beginning of food processing. Destruction by the methods of smashing or burning surely has contributed to many discoveries that have served us admirably. Destruction is a process that we still use today for attempting to discover of what things are made.

Creatures other than us use the destruction of objects as a means of getting at certain foods.

THE INSTINCT TO SUCK

The instinct to suck is an instinct that is incorporated within the basic nature of many creatures other than just mammals. In mammals and particularly in humans, the instinct to suck, like other instincts, is one that lasts for a lifetime. Small children even after the time they have finished nursing for mother's milk like to have a pacifier to satisfy this instinct. If pressures from various Herds did not condemn this instinct, it would be the normal situation to find pacifiers in common use within the adult human population.

Many times individuals who have the strongest inclination for this instinct are thumb suckers even after they have become adults. Since thumb sucking is essentially condemned by the mythology of some Herds, those individual adults who perform thumb sucking, usually automatically resort to it only during sleep or during very private times.

Adults many times resort to instinctive sucking rituals during various sexual activities that take place at private times, and they consider these actions as very adult and separate from the more primitive instinct, when in fact they are not separate.

The Instinctive desire to suck is so basic and so much in need of some regular satisfaction that many persons find joy beyond the sweetness and flavorings of hard candies in the sucking actions that are usually used to consume these types of candies.

The Instinct to Suck is such a benign Instinct and yet gives such personal pleasure that people should regularly satisfy this desire.

THE INSTINCT TO SLEEP

We usually think of sleeping as something that we consciously decide to undertake. For most persons, who perform regular routine daily schedules, have significant mental stimulations and some minimal physical activities, after they have decided to retire for sleeping, sleep comes to them relatively easy. We normally do not think of sleeping as an instinctive condition and the reason for this is because we usually retire for sleeping long before the Instinct to Sleep attempts to force the sleeping state upon us. The Instinct to Sleep is so strong when it becomes activated, that if we are then to remain awake, we must make monumental efforts to stay it off. We might be able to believe that the driving power behind the Instinct to Sleep is an attempt to shut down the sensory inputs to the Short Term Memory after it has somehow become over-burdened with sensory inputs. This Instinct's powerful attempt to shut down the sensory inputs to the Short Term Memory is most likely a Creature's way of protecting the Long Term Memory from a potential overflow of sensory data, that when not buffered by the Short Term Memory would flood directly into the Long Term Memory.

Sometimes while driving an automobile the Instinct to Sleep becomes so strong that it cannot be resisted. If at these times the automobile driver will stop and sleep for only ten or twenty minutes, the REM Dreaming's relief to the contents of the Short Term Memory will be sufficient to shut down the Instinct to Sleep and the driver can then continue with their driving. If the driver attempts to use stimulants such as caffeine instead of relieving the Burdens on the Short Term Memory and continues driving, when the caffeine finally wears off, the Instinct to Sleep will return with more powerful demands for sleep than were present before the caffeine was consumed. The only reasonable solution to shutting off the Instinct to Sleep is to in fact sleep, and thereby allow the Short Term Memory to relieve itself of its memory burdens.

INSTINCT TO BUILD

The Instinct to Build is strangely common throughout much of the Animal Kingdom. The structures that animals build range from the most simple burrowing structures to the towering buildings, homes, roads and other structures that are constructed by Humans.

This Instinct is really most amazing, when we consider the very complex structures that are produced by the Creatures that exhibit this Instinct.

Creatures other than Humans are able to build marvelously complex structures that fit their needs to near perfection. This is an Instinct that bears true testimony to the nearly unbelievable complexity of the Mechanisms of Instinct and to the astonishing results that they can deliver.

OPTIMISTIC INSTINCT

Without much doubt, for Humans, there seems to exist an Instinct that leads us to believe that the future is pregnant with some kind of mystical hope of a better time to come. This Instinct is very much involved with our willingness to struggle for survival against all odds. It is surely what has led us to believe that we can survive, even against death itself.

CONCLUSIONS

Here we have touched upon a trivial number of the Instincts that guide our daily existence. The most Primitive Senses, we should suspect, have Instincts associated with them that share a common connection with other Creatures, even those who are our most distant relatives.

*   *   *   *   *

There should be some suspicions, that at least for Humans, there are Instinctive Biases that appear to be within us from our birth. These are biases that seem to affect our lifetime interests and in some strange and fateful way to guide us along a path that we follow with joy. Sometimes, it seems, some people, from the time of their birth, were meant to be an Artist, a Naturalist, a Teacher, a Dancer, an Athlete, a Joyous Person, or a Person without Joy. Sometimes, we feel that a person has become misdirected, and then we see the Doctor who works as a Soldier, a Dentist who works at Manual Labor, the Actor who is a Fireman, and in this world of maladaptation, we have people unhappily wandering through life trying to survive in a profession where they find no real joy or happiness. Some people seem to be without any bias that directs their personal desires. It is obvious that children of the same parents can be markedly different in their personalities and their attractions and interests.

*   *   *   *   *

Sometimes things that at first observation seem to be the most obvious, simple and without underlying depth, are things that can subtly connect to a much larger meaning. I suspect this is true for all of the Instincts that are associated with the simplest patterns that are detectable by the Senses.

*   *   *   *   *

It is of considerable importance, that we make a major effort to discover those parts of our actions as Humans that are truly Instinctive as separate from those that are learned.

*   *   *   *   *

With some small consideration, we can understand why Economic Systems are the most stable, long lasting and successful, if they include within the tenants of their structures those elements that both respect and feed upon our Natural Instincts.

*   *   *   *   *

For Our Kind we can hopefully realize that in the truest sense, throughout the brief history of life, all of the Creatures of life are the wind beneath our wings and we share so much in common with them. We must ultimately make our understanding to be the triumph of all of life. And pray, that humankind is increasingly successful in its hopeful search for survival against the Forces of Chaos and the Hidden Spirits that Drive Us.

We should be suspicious that very much of what we are, as Creatures within Nature, is defined within the boundaries of Intelligence and Instincts.

DREAMS

DREAMS

THE MOTHER OF INSIGHT, CREATIVITY AND INVENTION IS DREAMING

Some Types of Dreaming

There are many discrete kinds of dreaming that take place within the human brain. Some of them are:

1. The **REM Dream** which is associated with an observable rapid movement of the dreamer's eyes, as if the dreamer were scanning the dreamed scene. REM Sleep Dreaming is an involuntary dreaming.

2. There is a type of dreaming, we might name **SIND. The Solve It Now Dream.** This is a quite different dream from REM Sleep Dreaming. In this dream, the dreamer actually believes they are awake. It's a dream where the dreamer is close to a wakeful state, but is actually in a light sleep, and is able to work out a detailed solution to some rather complex problem or steps of a sequential procedure. It's a kind of Thinking Dream.

3. There is the infamous **Day Dream**, where an apparently totally conscious person, is able in a wakeful state, to ignore all sensory stimuli and escape into a Dream World of their own rational design.

4. There is **The Reader's Dream** that the reader of a story creates, allowing them the sense of seeing the story visually unfold within their mind.

5. There is **The Listener's Dream**. A visual Dream, created in the mind of the person who is listening to the Storyteller, as they tell the story.

6. There is **The Dream of Sounds,** in which the Dreamer can recreate in their minds sounds from their memory.

7. There is the **Ultimate Dream of All Dreams. The Dreaming we call THINKING.**

Dreams of Other Senses

There probably are dreams associated exclusively with each of the individual senses. But, as we know the more subtle senses convey messages to the mind that are difficult to describe. We should be quite certain that Dreams solely involving the senses of Touch, Smell and Taste do exist.

It is possible that the awakening morning-time erection for males may be the result of a discrete dream initiated solely by the Sense of Touch or Feeling.

REM DREAMS

The first kind of dreaming associated with deep sleep and Rapid Eye Movements (REM) is a very primitive dream that is common to most complex creatures. It is an involuntary kind of dreaming that seems to take its own direction, where the dreamer wanders without control through a Dream World. You can observe your own household pets experiencing this kind of dreaming and understand some clues about what might be going on within their dreams.

We now need to think back to the earlier information about how we originally discover new patterns in Nature. This is clearly equivalent to what we call the learning process. There is no simple or easy way to learn new patterns from our Universe of Intelligible Patterns that are mixed in with a background of Chaos. The only way to learn these new patterns is through a complete, exacting, and exhaustive search of the last day's, or last few days, data stored in the Short Term Memory. This sequential searching, through every possible pattern combination, is something a Creature cannot accomplish while carrying out a normal daily routine of survival against the threats of Nature; this is at least true for the more complex Creatures of Nature. The daily routines, necessary to simply survive within a hostile environment, require much attention to all that is taking place within the environment. This means that Creatures must give much attention to already learned patterns and reacting to those patterns, if they are to survive.

The routine of actually learning new patterns, patterns previously unknown, is a routine that requires a kind of escape from the World's daily barrage of incoming data. It must be an escape that allows time for the slow, tedious, and exacting search of the Short Term Memory, an escape that must completely isolate the Creature from the distractions of the Real World. The mechanism that provides this escape is Sleep. I suggest that the process of sorting through the Short Term Memory data, to discover any patterns and particularly any new patterns that are there, is what we call REM Dreaming. **The associations that are triggered while the Short Term Memory is being sorted and tested against the patterns already stored in the Long Term Memory is both the cause and body of the REM Dream.**

We are all familiar with the sometimes very strange Nature of Dreams. We often refer to surreal things as dream-like, meaning they do not quite conform to the structures of the logical World. In reality dreams probably conform exactly to the logic contained within the web-like structures of the Cross Address Linkings and Cross Sensory Address Linkings of the Long Term Memory. REM Dreams are disturbances within the Long Term Memory, and are caused by the testing and the movement of patterns from the Short Term Memory and the processes involved while they are being stored into the Long Term Memory.

Remember how similar coding of related patterns might exist in close address proximity to each other in the Long Term Memory, and might also be Cross Sensory Address Linked to some other sensory storage locations in the Long Term Memory. Well, when the brain is sifting throughout the Short Term Memory, and testing what is there against what is in the Long Term Memory, it can stimulate these related memories that give rise to a Strange Dream, a dream that is difficult for the dreamer to associate with anything that they might have stored in their Short Term Memory during the past few days. Many times, the most abundant elements of a dream may be those from Cross Sensory Address Linkings or simple Cross Address Linkings, while the elements that came directly from the Short Term Memory are few, but are the causal agents of the whole dream. **We should realize that simply** thinking of different memories or new patterns during our normal daytime activities can introduce those thoughts and patterns into our **Short Term Memories.** It would seem that the patterns stored in the Short Term Memory are sorted out of the Short Term Memory on a first in, first out basis. Meaning by this that during dreaming, the patterns within the Short Term Memory that are the oldest time wise, are the first patterns to be processed and tested against those patterns, which are permanently resident in the Long Term Memory. Also the most recent patterns stored in the Short Term Memory are the last to be processed out during REM Dreaming. There are of course exceptions to this general rule. The exceptions are for those patterns within the Short Term Memory that were stored there and were associated with a very high pattern intensity or during a very emotional state of mind. Very emotional states affect the body's chemistry and somehow put a high priority on the associated pattern as being prioritized for immediate processing from the Short Term Memory during REM Dreaming.

Let's consider a real example of a real dream. Here is how the dreamer described the dream: " I dreamed, I was in a place like a Zoo. There was this most strange creature there. It looked like a pig, but had the tail of a Raccoon. The tail was standing up vertically and it was flipping from side to side like a Cat does with its tail when it is nervously watching some prey. The creature's face had one large Eye in the middle of its forehead, and the Eye was black. Someone was talking, but I couldn't see whom it was. They were saying, "This Creature is the last one of its kind on Earth, because the rest of them were hunted down because they had Electrifying Eyes." I felt sad that there was only one creature of this kind left on Earth. Next to this strange creature was a farmer preparing to slaughter a Cow." The dream ended and the dreamer woke up.

The dreamer confessed that there was nothing in the dream that made any sense to them, and that nothing had happened the previous day that they could relate to the dream. But, the dreamer's son, a smart boy, who had been listening to his father's and my conversation about dreams, filled in the details. The facts were, the previous day they had watched together the video "The Lion King II". The Raccoon-like tail, within the dream, was Pumba's tail. The Big Eye came from a Daffy Duck Cartoon they had also watched together during the day. In that cartoon, there was a short hairy monster with one eye in the middle of its forehead. As to the last part of the dream, they had together read that day, a magazine article about Meat Packing.

That dream was actually pretty much straight forward, involving mainly new unusual patterns from the Short Term Memory and these were incorporated in to the dream without too much morphing. It did include some complex additions probably generated by stimulation to the Long Term Memory and associated with Cross Address Linkings and Cross Sensory Address Linkings such as: The setting being Zoo-Like and also the not seen speaker, whose spoken words were heard and the feeling of sadness that they aroused.

There are some unusual things that sometime happen during REM Dreaming. Regardless of the fact that REM Dreaming takes place during a state of deep sleep, sometimes a Real World Pattern that happens in Real Time is strong enough to get the attention of the sense of hearing at the same time a REM Dream is taking place. If the pattern is not too unusual as to wake the dreamer, and it is a known pattern, the pattern gets incorporated directly and instantly into the dream in what seems to be a seamless inclusion.

Why is this so? It's because patterns as they come out of the Mapping Function are themselves their own Long Term Memory address, the address where they are known, and so the dream includes that memory as soon as it is stimulated and the dream goes on from there. **Any known sensory patterns of the real world that happen during a REM Dream, and are strong enough to get the dreamer's sensory attention, and are not threatening enough to wake the dreamer, must always get immediately included into the dream.**

THE DREAM

"THIS IS THE LAST CREATURE OF ITS KIND ON EARTH"

© NRP

This automatic inclusion of **a Real-Time Real World Sensory Pattern** into an actively unfolding REM Dream is a particular problem for those who are young bed wetters. They are asleep and dreaming when a feeling from within their bladder gets their attention, but is not a strong enough feeling to wake them from the dream. They instantly get incorporated directly in to their dream that they are going to the toilet to relieve themselves, and suddenly discover that they have actually urinated while sleeping. This is a very easy problem to correct. It only takes a commitment from the child to solve this problem. The setting of an alarm clock that wakes the child before their bladder is full will allow them to get out of bed and relieve their bladder. If the child is willing to commit to this routine, the problem will be summarily solved.

It was previously mentioned that probably patterns stored in the Short Term Memory are processed for new patterns and stored into the Long Term Memory during REM Dreaming and that these patterns within the Short Term Memory are processed on a first-in, first-out basis with the exception that those patterns which were associated with a high emotional state have the first priority for processing. In the general case this would mean as an example, that a student doing late night studying, would have those newest patterns stored into the most recent areas of the Short Term Memory; if they did not get sufficient sleep that same night with its REM Dreaming, then it is possible that those newly studied patterns may not get processed into their Long Term Memory and this would leave these newly studied patterns in the vulnerable position of remaining in the Short Term Memory and prone to being easily forgotten.

One thing that is important to consider about this is, that the learning of any new information is not an easy process, it takes time, much effort and Sleep with Dreaming.

There is an unusual kind of REM Sleep Dreaming that is difficult to reconcile directly to the processing of the patterns from the Short Term Memory. This is the dream where the theme of the dream is repeated over a time of days, weeks, months or even years. In this case, all of the major patterns within the dream are kinds of stand-ins for what would be the patterns representing the Real World situation that stimulated them. You might believe the dream is likely to be repeated because the problem it represents cannot be resolved using representative patterns. Sometimes by listing all of the attributes of the representative patterns, one or more of the attributes will contain enough information to understand the nature of the Real World situation that is actually triggering the repeated dream.

Even this repeated REM Dream, and its apparently irresolvable meanings, must originate from the daily dumping of the Short Term Memory. A situation might well exist were Cross Address Linkings are so strong, that the Real World Patterns stored in the Short Term Memory always activate some pattern related to them by means of Cross Address Linkings. This would not only explain why the dream is difficult to relate to the actual happenings of recent experiences, but also why the dream is a repeating dream. It is often the case that the patterns of the actual REM Dream are there because of strong Cross Address Linkings. This means that the patterns actually visualized within the REM Dream might be patterns that have strong Cross Address Linkings or even patterns that reside topologically nearby to the address within the Long Term Memory of the actual Short Term Memory pattern. It is also quite possible that in some instances because of over working of some Memory areas within the Long Term Memory, that they become sensitized to being an easily triggered memory. It is clear that some drugs, particularly those that are able to cause hallucinations, have this kind of effect on the sensitizing of specific Long Term Memory areas.

*   *   *   *   *

All of the types of dreaming, other than REM Dreaming, are dreams where the dream's content and direction are more or less under the control of the dreamer.

SIND DREAMS

SIND Dreaming, unlike the most primitive REM Dreaming, is not an involuntary kind of dreaming. It is one of those types of dreaming that has as its core essence, direction by desire.

There are many persons having unresolved problems particularly problems that involve some kind of organizing or sequencing of tasks, who work at solving them while in a dreaming state of mind. While working on the problems, they believe themselves to be quite awake, when in fact they are in a shallow sleep of SIND Dreaming that continually alternates to deeper states of REM dreaming. They consider that they have worked on the problem all night long, and have not had any normal sleep. But on rising from the bed in the morning they find themselves to be quite rested. Also, many times a bedroom partner may tell them that when they awoke during the night, that the other appeared to be sleeping naturally, maybe even snoring. SIND Dreamers insists that they didn't get a wink of sleep the whole nightlong. They many times discover, that they have pretty much solved the details of their problem.

DAY DREAMS

The Day Dream is much like the SIND Dream, except it takes place while the dreamer is fully awake. Day Dreaming is also a type of dreaming that is separated, from the primitive REM Dreaming, by the fact that it is a dream that is pretty much under the dreamer's control. Day Dreaming can be triggered by the individual's need to escape from sensory information that is boring, or the strong desire for some wish fulfillment. During the time the dreamer is dreaming, they are more or less oblivious to any sensory information from their surroundings.

We should be very appreciative that the ability to Day Dream is a relatively new talent for Our Kind. In the distant past to be out in the Wild Environment and actively involved in a Day Dream was pretty much certain to be your downfall. During those savage primitive times when alertness to all that was around you was a primary condition for survival, Day Dreaming would have been a severe impediment. But the time would come, when there was enough safety from life's dangers that the luxury of the Day Dream was able to flourish.

Day Dreaming is most probably the result of some evolutionary modification of the mechanisms of REM Dreaming, which itself is totally involuntary. It is not unreasonable to guess that Day Dreaming is a relatively recent evolutionary development, probably within the last few tens of thousands of years.

When people are recalling memories of past happenings, this is certainly a kind of Day Dreaming. It is interesting to note that evidence for strongly Cross Sensory Address Linking can be found within these kinds of Day Dreams. If you are a person who is multi-lingual and multi-cultural, your visual memories associated with either culture are directly tied to the language associated with that particular visual memory. Whenever you recall a memory that contains both visual information and sound, they come up into your mind together attached and inseparable.

Day Dreaming is strongly related to another kind of dreaming, a kind that I believe is one of humankind's greatest attributes and is comparable in importance to bipedal walking and the intricate freedom of our hands to manipulate objects. It probably has some fundamentally basic association to our discovery and use of Art, Symbols and our

Written Languages. Day Dreaming probably is, the elementary basis of the Master of all Dreaming, the Dreaming we call Thinking.

When primitive Hominids went carrying torches into a dark cave to paint an image of an Animal onto the walls, they did not have to drag the Animal into the cave to see its image, and in that way recopy its image onto the walls. Clearly instead, they wakefully Dreamed the Image into their Minds, and seeing it in their Mind's Eye, they painted it, as they saw it in their Day Dream. They painted it, as if it was vitally alive. They painted it, as it might be seen galloping across the landscape. They painted it, in its fullest glory, as they beheld it in their best and most desirable Dreams. **The act of drawing the image of some animal upon a cave's wall is certainly the act of creating a Symbolic Representation of something that exists in the Real World. It is the immediate beginning of symbolic representations whose ultimate metamorphosis would become written language.**

It is a part of our not uncommon misunderstanding of things, that for all of civilized time, adults and even teachers have warned children and students against Day Dreaming. Luckily for Our Kind, there have always been some who ignored the warnings.

READER'S DREAM

The Reader's Dream is the unfolding within the reader's mind of a set of visual images that represents for them the essence of the written story.

The Reader's Dream is especially interesting because the visual images that come forth to make up the dream must come directly from Cross Address Linkings and/or Cross Sensory Address Linkings. Here we can understand, that the written words upon the page are only images of the symbols, in the sense that the patterns they directly represent have a distinct location in the Long Term Memory. But, the patterns of the corresponding visual images that they refer to are only relatable to them by Cross Address Linkings. As an example: The written word "COW" has a direct address location in the visual part of the Long Term Memory, but the visual image that represents what people see when they actually see a Cow in the Real World is located at a different Long Term Memory address. These two different visual Long Term Memory addresses can only be associated by the use of Cross Address Linking.

A most important consideration about the Reader's Dream is that for each individual reader of the same written story, both their visual imagery, and their understanding of the story are necessarily different. These differences are solely rooted within their known pattern repertoire residing in their Long Term Memories and the Cross Address Linkings associated with those patterns. From this we should understand that the same written material for some, can paint a most lavish and interesting dream, while for others, it may be dull, boring and colorless. For some, the story material is understandable, while others find it clueless, **but for everyone the written story, and the story they find there, is different.**

It should be quite clear without any doubt, that certain written material can only be fully appreciated by those individuals who have known pattern memories and Cross Sensory Address Linkings and Cross Address Linkings that can match up with the information contained in the written material. We really don't try to force the reading of Shakespeare onto small children. We do oft times try to force it on to High School students, many of whom are not prepared to receive it, and find neither joy nor inspiration in it. In such a case, the experience can end as an unpleasant waste of time for all, and a kind of poisoning for any possible future interest in such material.

LISTENER'S DREAM

The Listener's Dream is the visual imagery that unfolds within the listener's mind, while listening to the telling of a story.

The Listener's Dream's, sole source of imagery is from Cross Sensory Address Linking. All of the other considerations made for the Reader's Dream apply to the Listener's Dream.

SOUND'S DREAM

The Sound's Dream is that dream whose essential elements are all sounds.

The Sound Dream is usually a dream that takes place during a wakeful state of mind and it is a kind of Day Dream consisting of the memories solely associated with the Sense of Hearing. It is possible that the Sound's Dream may also take place during sleep and REM Dreaming. In the Sound's Dream wakeful dreaming, the dreamer can recall directly from their Long Term Memory an individual sound or strings of sounds. There is essentially no Cross Sensory Address Linking involved, at least between distinct senses in this kind of dreaming. The linking that is involved is Cross Address Linking; it is linking between different areas dedicated to the same sense, the Sense of Hearing.

We could suspect that this kind of dreaming is important and frequent for those who are musical composers, musicians and the many persons who love music.

We often hear persons say, "What images do you get in your mind when you hear a certain piece of music". If people get some visual images in their mind, when they hear a piece of music, then they were not put there solely by the music. They can only be there, because of some previous Cross Sensory Address Linking that was constructed at an earlier time. **The Sense of Hearing is within itself independent of the Visual Sense.** Therefore, associations with the patterns derived from the Sense of Hearing and the Sense of Seeing must have Cross Sensory Address Linking to associate them. It might help to realize the situation this way. **No one ever asks, "What do you smell when you hear a certain piece of music?" or "What do you taste when you hear a certain piece of music?" They somehow seem to know that these questions are inappropriate.** But because such things as musical sounds and visual images are purposefully linked in artistic musical creations, people tend to believe that they are a naturally related, when in fact they are not.

In Nature some sounds are naturally linked with the image of their creator, and this establishes the Cross Sensory Address Linking that relates them. The call of a bird and its visual image, the roar of the lion and its visual image, understandably can get naturally linked. The sounds made by a Violin may get naturally linked to the image of a Violin. When we link the sound of a Violin to the image of a Flying Bird, we are forcing a linkage that does not exist in nature.

I here reminded you, that it might be interesting to reread the section of Instincts under the heading " Moving Patterns – Music."

LACK OF SLEEP and REM DREAMING

If sleep and its associated primitive REM Dreaming are not sufficient for the Short Term Memory to be completely searched for the discovering of new patterns and other patterns that exist there, and in that way cleared of its old data, then a Creature's response to new incoming data during the next day may become impaired. To what extent the new day's incoming data is affected is surely proportional to how much clearing of the old data was accomplished. It is most probable that the capacity (pattern storage capacity) of the Short Term Memory is greater than what is normally required to store an average day's incoming data. This must be true, as the amount of incoming data during any day must be quite variable. A Creature needs a Short Term Memory capacity that can match a maximum worst-case day's data. I make this suggestion, as we know that persons, who have had no chance for Sleep and REM Dreaming for more than one day, are able to function for quite some-time greater than one day. In fact even missing Sleep and REM Dreaming for several days leaves individuals as somewhat functional, at least as long as they are dealing with well known patterns coming in from the Sensory World. By examining various REM Dreams reported by individuals, it seems that the dream content can be associated with the Short Term Memory content that is up to about three days old. This most likely means that the storage size of the Short Term Memory is large enough to store at least three average days of memories.

When persons are sleep deprived for a few days, and they must face a barrage of new patterns, as say for college students, the impairment of their functioning becomes apparent. We can see this same impairment in its most severe example during wartime. Soldiers who are severely sleep deprived and are in the midst of the battlefield become almost totally dysfunctional, when they are exposed over and over again to new powerful images of unexpected patterns, patterns that are literally exploding onto their senses. **We call this condition Extreme Battle Fatigue or Shell Shock.**

It is clear that when individuals are long deprived of Sleep and its REM Dreaming, the effects on their functioning is severe and notice-able. It is also quite clear that when Sleep and Dreaming are delayed for a sufficient amount of time, that individuals can and do drift in to a kind of involuntary dreaming while they are technically awake. This type of involuntary dreaming is not the general type of dreaming we normally call Day Dreaming. It is instead like REM Dreaming, but where the patterns of the dream are strongly disassociated, where the images float through the dream in unreasonable and unconnected pieces that do not make any systematic sense. It is a kind of dream, that is best described as severely fractured, and the patterns within the dream are not at all reasonably associated with each other. In the normal REM Dreaming there is a somewhat reasonable and connected flow that makes the dream like an unfolding story.

This kind of fractured dream can also happen during REM Dreaming when the dreamer is under the influence of alcohol or other drugs, which must somehow interfere with the systematic processing of the search through the Short Term Memory.

When persons have been deprived of sleep for even one night, they can appear to be functioning normally as long as they are reacting to situations that contain well-known patterns. They sometimes can perform complex functions such as driving their car to some distant place, even when the journey is topographically complex. They may even arrive at their destination unaware of exactly how they got there, not even remembering those strong landmarks, that they usually use as inflection points to make the trip. The problem is, that as long as the journey did not involve any new extraordinary situations, they can complete it safely, but if some unusual new situation should present itself, it most certainly means a disaster is at hand. Driving during times, when an individual has a severe lack of sleep is most likely as dangerous to other individuals on the road, as if the driver was intoxicated. Sadly there is no way to keep sleep-deprived drivers off from the roads, or to discover if they are sleep deprived at the time of an accident.

There are some historical cases, where extreme sleep deprivation, has led to tragic situations from which the individual has been unable to fully recover. We might guess as to the nature of such problems. If the Short Term Memory, which we see as one kind of resistive buffer against the flood of chaotic data impacting directly upon the Long Term Memory, is rendered completely nonfunctional, then this resistive barrier to the Long Term Memory is incapacitated. In such a situation all in-coming sensory data from all of the senses, known patterns, unknown patterns and purely chaotic noise, might be directed to the Long Term Memory. Over a period of time such an uncontrolled bombardment of data would lay down memories and Cross Sensory and Cross Address Linkings that would surely be disastrous for the individual to functioning normally in the Real World. The memories and the Cross Sensory and Cross Address Links created under such a situation could not have any rational relationship to any logic of the Real World. It would be a situation similar to what might happen, if some parts of the brain were physically scrambled.

There are a few more general observations we should make about Sleep and Dreaming. It is evident from observing the Real World, that persons whose senses are encountering vast numbers of new patterns require the greatest amount of Sleep and Dreaming. All complex mammal infants, because of their newness to the World, are exposed to a situation where nearly all things their senses detect are new patterns. These infants therefore require an exaggerated amount of Sleep and REM Dreaming to assimilate this flood of new information. This need for extensive periods of Sleep and Dreaming is especially apparent for the Human Infant.

Any persons that are in an intensive learning experience must also require sufficient Sleep and Dreaming to process out the flood of new patterns within their Short Term Memories. Also, persons who are unusually active creative or analytical thinkers may in fact require Catnaps as a means of unburdening their Short Term Memories. The need for extra sleep is certainly true for Collage Students, who always seem to feel they are not getting sufficient sleep. We should suspect that the greater their lack of sleep, the more effort must be required to learn new material.

We might wonder why it is that many older persons, who really are not facing the discovery of new patterns, require so much sleep. They often require naps during the day in the same way, as do many small children. In the case of small children we can equate the rest requirement to their abundant exposure to new patterns. So what condition is it that might require the older adult a need for frequent naps? Most likely it is because the Short Term Memory capacity of older persons has decreased in its storage capacity. The decrease in the pattern storage capacity of the Short Term Memory could mean that it fills to capacity sooner and needs to be sorted out frequently which requires Sleep and Dreaming. We might also understand from this, the reason why some older persons seem to be so forgetful of resent happenings.

We should also consider the very distinct possibility, at least for normally healthy persons, that for both the Short Term Memory and the Long Term Memory, that their size, (not meaning physical size, but the areas they are able to utilize) and ability to function are proportional to how much they are exercised. For the physical body we have clear evidence that mechanical exercise improves its functioning. Because of the obvious plastic nature of the brain and how its memory structures get organized we must conclude, that they are also prone to change by being exercised.

In this light we might attribute a decreased Short Term Memory Size to the very fact that it is not being sufficiently exercised.

You should not get the impression that the only function of Sleep is REM Dreaming and the process of sorting out and storing information from the Short Term Memory into the Long Term Memory. **Sleep is not a simple thing, it probably also has something to do with the re-establishing of the body's complex chemical balances, whose warehouse might be severely depleted during a normal day's wakeful activities.**

We should realize that sleep deprivation by itself is a Severe Kind of Torture, and it can lead directly to confessions that have no basis in reality. Severe sleep deprivation can cause an individual, who is being questioned about some event of which they have no knowledge, to incorporate some of the patterns proposed by the questioners into their Long Term Memory. With enough dwelling by the questioners upon a subject, an innocent person can become suspicious of their own innocents. Given enough time they can become confused, shaken in their own original beliefs and willing to make any statement as means of escaping the sever mental terror that is upon them.

THE DREAMING WE CALL THINKING

After we have now considered several different types of dreaming, we might wonder about what is going on inside of our minds when we are thinking.

We could almost believe that it is not very different from some kinds of dreaming. It would seem in fact, to be a kind of dreaming in images or spoken words or both. It might also include other patterns originating from other sensory origins.

The kind of thinking we do when we recall some past memories of our life seems in fact to be a kind of Day Dreaming, where the substance of the dream is a set of essentially sequential individual patterns recalled directly from our Long Term Memory. This is in fact, a straightforward Day Dream, with the special feature that the patterns are essentially set, fixed, and generally present the same dream whenever they are recalled. We like to call this thinking, but truly it is not. It is just a special type of Day Dreaming.

We need to set some bounds on what we mean by the term "Thinking." If we seriously consider most of what goes on within our minds, I think we can equate it to some kind of dreaming. So how should Thinking be considered so as to distinguish it from the kinds of dreaming we have already considered? The problem is that the basic elements of thinking have much in common with other types of dreaming and sometimes cannot be fully separated from them.

We need to be rather hard-nosed with our definition of Thinking. I propose that **the Dream that we call Thinking has just a few central** themes. It is a very special kind of dreaming that is directed towards Discovery. It is a dream where Discovery is sought by means of Creativity. These two elements are its sole components, but from them arises all of those new magical insights into the visible and invisible places in nature and to all of the wonderful creative inventions of Science, Art and Technology.

Thinking is a most Special Kind of Dreaming that is purposefully directed at new Discovery by means of Problem Solving. Thinking directed towards discovery is noticeably different from the Day Dream, which flows with ease and pleasure. Creative Thinking is best characterized as difficult work, and is usually not accompanied with pleasure. Pleasure comes with abundance at the end of the Thinking Process, if it has reached a successful conclusion.

When the Dream that is Creative Thinking is taking place, it involves the bringing of patterns from the Long Term Memory and creatively fitting them into sequences and then examining if these sequences lead to an unknown pattern, or if in fact they are themselves a new complex pattern of some interest. Here we must not mistakenly say "of some new value" for value is something that is related to the Real World, a relation that can only be established after Thinking is completed. If nothing of interest is found, the sequencing of the patterns can be rearranged and examined again, or some patterns can be removed, or replaced with other patterns. **In Thinking, the creative manipulation of patterns has essentially no limit.**

Here we need to take a moment to realize from our remembrance of how patterns are laid out in the Long Term Memory, that there arises a basic Natural Logic to where they are located and what might be located within their immediate neighborhood. It is by thinking that these logical relationships can lead to the discovery of associated patterns that are missing, unknown. For Thinking that involves patterns or the mechanisms of the Real World, any new discovered patterns can be tested against reality to see if in fact they exist there.

For a moment here, **I want to re-emphasize that Thinking never takes giant inspirational leaps to some great new idea.** Considering a simple Real World analogy should give us some insight. In Nature you cannot physically cross a great chasm in one leap, and you cannot wish your way across. If you are to get to the other side you must step by step build a bridge, whose construction brings you ever closer, and closer, until with one last final step you are there. You are reminded, that to build the bridge you must have at hand the physical materials necessary for its construction, wishes or desires have no substance from which you can construct a physical bridge.

When the Thinking Mind makes new discoveries, there is also no way to instantly span across the great chasms that exist between memory's areas of known patterns to areas of distantly unrelated and unknown patterns. It is by Thinking that we are slowly able to fit in, step-by-step, the pieces of missing patterns to bridge the chasm. Here again you are reminded that the pieces you need, to construct the bridge of thought, are the patterns that you must already have stored within your Long Term Memory. You must already have all of the pieces or must discover the missing ones from the Real World one at a time.

Having a great wealth of stored patterns within your Long Term Memory gives you a major benefit of having the materials ready for constructive Thinking. Consider for a moment Shakespeare. He was able to build a Magnificent Empire of Creative Writings, because he had, perhaps the world's greatest wealth of building materials stored within his Long Term Memory. He was a Creative Thinking Artist. He had a gold mine of resources, words, and was willing to experiment at combining them in ever-new ways to give us new and delightful insights in to Society and Human Nature.

You may now be wondering, how is it that this thing we call Thinking has any guidance as to where it is going with these pattern manipulations. It is because of the very fact that the memories we have acquired, like the building of a bridge to get across a chasm, contain within themselves

General Algorithms that we are able to use to guide the process of Thinking. Whenever we learn strings of logically connected patterns, contained beneath the substance of the information, are the connections that represent their logic of the path. As an example, when we learn some theorem in geometry the specific elements of the theorem might fade from memory and be totally forgotten. But, the logical path that was the underlying part of the theorem might have been useful and so was recalled many times as guidance for other logical determinations. All of the specifics elements of the theorem are gone, but the logic of the paths that connected them may remain, because they were of a general nature that could relate other elements to their original logic. Consider the general logic associated with $A + B = C$, the exact remembrance of what elements were the initial elements we first learned, may have faded from memory, but the logic of their relationship still survives as a general path, and we are able to apply this path to elements that are different from those first learned. In the most general sense, when we learn $A + B = C$ and we have had the time to learn strongly connected relationships that are associated with the original learning, then in the most generalized terms we understand that the original equation can represent any two groups that are separated and that they can in fact be brought together as a single group. This generalization of the original learning is much like the generalized memory of the stick that the Chimpanzee used to find an equivalent stick to knock down the fruit from the tree, as we discussed in the first section of the book.

When there are many complex patterns that Thinking is required to creatively manipulate, we are sometimes forced to ease the mental burden, by putting the patterns into the Real World. We do this by various means but mainly by copying the patterns, or symbols representing the patterns, on to some material object in the Real World. By this means we are able to visualize the patterns in a more stable form than that, which exists within the mind. By use of this method, we have been able to use Thinking's Creative Manipulation to control and develop patterns of enormous sizes. **In this way we have constructed complex pattern sizes that are far beyond any that could be assemble directly within the mind. But, it is still within the mind that the pieces of these giant complex patterns are creatively shuffled.**

Thinking is the primary means by which humans are able to establish new Long Term Memory Cross Address Linkings and by that means give fresh new insights, perspectives and understanding to the older memories that are stored there. Thinking is the means by which we are able to impart a deeper and more generalized meaning to memories that were once just isolated recollections.

Sometimes we refer to someone as being brilliant. How then do these characteristics that we clearly recognize as extraordinary brilliance come into existence within an individual. **Most members of any physically healthy population are as likely to have normal functional mechanisms that make up their intelligent systems, as they are likely to have normal healthy functional livers.** It would not seem unreasonable to believe that mental brilliance for an individual arises spontaneously as the result of the new Cross Address Linkings that are formed during the process of thinking. The more often and the more deeply we think about the patterns that are stored in our Long Term Memory and about their possible interrelationships, the more Cross Address Links are formed that then represent newly discovered associations and other relationships that didn't exist before the process of constructive thinking took place. It is by the activity of regularly thinking and learning new patterns that gives birth to this thing we see as mental brilliance.

Thinking can involve any creative manipulation of patterns, and much of it in the present day is involved in the Artistic Creation of New Patterns, Patterns that do not exist in the Natural World or that we have not explicitly observed there. You only have to observe the wonderfully complex patterns that are being generated by today's Artists to begin to understand how exciting and stimulating they are. We should begin to realize that these creations lead us to new ideas and speculations that come from the minds of the creators and are not necessarily found by us directly in Nature. **And so, we are led in searching for discovery, by manipulating the Real Patterns from Nature, and by the manipulation of our Dreams themselves.**

Thinking is certainly the most wonderful kind of Dreaming and the limits of its creativity and discovery seem pretty much boundless.

TRYING TO SUBDIVIDE THINKING

Here I have set the definition of thinking on rather minimal basic elements. There are those who would divide it in to parts and exemplify those parts by arguments relating to different paths of accomplishing the solution to a problem. So-called "Divergent" and "Convergent" thinking are often sited as different kinds of thinking. It would seem to me that they are not different kinds of thinking, but these are only different paths to the solution of a problem. What is actually portrayed here is a confusing of paths with the statement of the problem. As an example: they would say that convergent thinking produces only one correct answer, always the same and there was only one correct path to get there, whereas Divergent thinking has many possible correct answers. An example would be to solve the problem of how to get from one side of a river to the other side. Solving such a problem could give many solutions, like using a boat, building a bridge or flying across. But, here we are confusing path with the problem's logical end, which is "getting to the other side of the river". Any Thinking that takes us by any path to the end solution is just Thinking. Truly in many instances there may be only one path that will successfully get us to the problem's conclusion, but that condition is contained within the nature of the problem, not within any special kind of Thinking to get to the problems conclusion. Other kinds of problems have many different paths that will give the common end condition, but the Thinking that gets us there is no different.

OTHER CREATURE'S THINKING

It is pretty much evident, that almost any specific trait found within a species is to some extent also present within some other species. There is much evidence that Creatures other than Humans do in fact some quite limited kinds of Thinking. It is foolish to belabor by degrees whether or not what they do is actually Thinking. **Thinking is thinking, no matter how limited or extravagant are its results.**

OTHER GENERAL THOUGHTS ABOUT DREAMING

Mutli-Sensory Requirements

In REM Sleep Dreaming, there are sometimes situations that require the stimulation of multiple sensory inputs, stimulations that the Dreaming cannot simulate, this always leaves the Dreamer with a confused sense of failure. An example would be: In a Dream where the Dreamer is running as a means of escaping from some fearful Dream situation and the Dreamer fails at movement beyond a snails pace. The Dreamer seems to be running fast, but they find they are just nearly at a dead stop. The Dreamer tries harder to run, but just can't escape. What has happened here is that the Dream was unable to supply the normal sensory inputs that have always been associated with running. When we run in reality, we always have the strong feeling of our feet striking the ground and the strong visual imagery of the landscape moving past us.

But within the Dream World, even while the Dreaming urge to run is strong enough to cause us to make a running motion with our legs, we know we are not really running because the other sensory elements are missing. It is for this reason that in the Dream we are in a sense frozen, stopped, and cannot escape from the threatening situation.

Other Missing Feedback

Also in REM Sleep Dreaming we find that many dreamt of actions that require Real World Visual feedback to verify them are impossible for the Dreamer to fulfill. An example of this might be the need in a Dream to write something. The Dreamer always discovers that it just simply cannot be performed in the Dream. At most, even with the greatest Dream effort, the Dreamer might get one or two letters or a single digit of a number written, but nothing further. The Dreamer is usually not even able to accomplish that. The Dreamer is of course missing the sense of feeling from the fingers and hand and the hand to eye feedback that are always involved with writing in reality. There is one exception to this situation. If in the dream you are trying to write something as well rehearsed as your own signature, you will discover that it is easily and summarily accomplished in that you can see that the signature exists, but you will not see the actual script changing as the signature was being formed.

Dreams of Flying

It is interesting that in Dreams, we are capable of Dream Flying and can do it with great control after some practice of course. How is it that we can fly within the Dream World and yet find it difficult to run? It is simply because in the Real World, we do not fly by using our own body mechanisms and therefore have no burdens of sensory inputs that must be satisfied to justify our Flying within our Dreams. And so, we fly, we soar, and we love the complete freedom of it.

Twists and Turns of Dreaming

To help further complicate the landscape of Dreams and make them more difficult to understand in terms of direct cause and effect, which they in fact are, is the infamous Cross Sensory Address Linking, and each language's use of words that when spoken sound the same or nearly have the same sound, but have more than one meaning. Every language has many of these words. If we first just look at this from the point of Cross Sensory Address Linking, we must admit that no two people necessarily have the same linking between sensory patterns stored in their Long Term Memory. So right here we have a major obstacle to interpreting someone else's Dreams. This is a very big and major obstacle.

Let's consider the more easily understood multiple meaning situations. We can at least see, that here there are some defined limits. Just a few simple examples will show the kinds of paths a Dream might possibly split in to: A Dreamer who in the Dream recalls the spoken word "Drawer" might get cross linked to an image of a person who is drawing, or to a drawing, or to a chest of drawers, or get linked to underwear. We can with not much work find many such examples of multiple meanings: Drawers, Wine, Pick, Stick, Prick, and Fly. The potential size of such a list can be huge.

Dreams can also take unexpected turns, when they encounter very strong bonding between objects or situations that are pleasurable. The same is of course true for objects or situations that are strongly bonded with fears. In either case the main trend of the Dream may suddenly change. The Dreamer may find that there is a very strange mix of objects and situations that seem to fit together rather nicely, or the opposite situation could turn the dream into a real nightmare.

Some persons would like to make us believe that in dreams, the images of one object is substituted with the image of another object, because we just can't bare to face up to the situation that is represented by the real object. More likely the substituted image more closely represents the characteristics of the Real World situation. Dreaming of say, a big long smooth tree limb may in fact be representative of a Penis. But it is not necessarily because the Penis is an objectionable object within the dreamer's dream that it is substituted. It is more likely that the Dreamer is contemplating a really big one, and the only thing that best fits the bill, is a big tree limb. Also, big Tree Limbs and Penises probably have nearly the same address within the Long Term Memory.

I can see no mechanisms within the structures of Intelligence, that are involved in Dreaming that are tuned to wishfully substituting one image for another image to meet the needs of a Scrupled Society and its Taboos. The mechanisms that are the cause of REM Dreaming are deterministic, but also very complex, there is no evolutionary advantage for unnecessarily tying them in any way to moral judgments.

Herds within society many times systematically and repeatedly associate patterns, which are normal natural patterns within nature, with complex pattern constructs that portray them as bad or evil. In such cases, REM Dreams and the Dream we call Thinking have their natural direction corrupted by the Cross Address Linkings that have been associated by these so-called Moral Complex Pattern Constructs.

Children's Nightmares

The Nightmares of small children are probably much to do about the learning of new patterns that appear powerful and are not yet fully understood. Children are in a New World, at least for them, were they are faced with new patterns that are not a part of reality, so they cannot understand how these new patterns fit within the Real World. They come across many scary new images, from books, films, television and many other sources, that are not part of the Real World. Until these images are resolved as part of the Fictional World that exits within the Real World, they will affect a child's dreams.

Signal Errors

Probably an infrequent cause of changes in the path a Dream is taking might result from a neurological signal error. This does happen. We see it even in fully awake situations. We notice it in things, like the slip of the tongue, where a similarly sounding word is accidentally spoken in the place of a word that the speaker intended. From our proposition that similar patterns are stored in close proximity within the Long Term Memory, we can guess that a minor nerve misfiring could activate the memory for the wrong word. Words such as Bind, Find, Kind, and Mind probably reside at LTM addresses that are right next door to each other. So, even during dreaming, a single nerve misfiring could result in the change of direction the dream is taking. This must not be a very common occurrence for most people, or we would also notice it during their normal daytime activities.

Drugs of various kinds might have unexpected effects on dreaming.

Complex Landscapes

Most people are surprised at the seeming complexity of the landscapes that can appear within their Dreams. Those complex landscapes are camouflage, mere skeletons of their Real World Images. The brain has a nice trick it uses in both Dreams and in day-to-day wakefulness. It's as if we would feel too uncomfortable and insecure if we realized, we weren't really seeing all that was around us. So the brain puts up for our viewing, a backdrop of reality, that's barely hinged to a skeleton that takes the place of the Real World. It's all a simple matter of the real limits of just how much data the brain can process at anyone time.

Dreams and Thinking That Recall Motion

You might believe that within your memories you can recall exactly, as if viewing a motion picture, memories that are in motion. In fact you cannot recall memories of motion in that kind of detail. The reason is quite simple. The brain just cannot handle the vast amount of data required to simulate exact memories of motion. The best we can do about recalling memories that involve active motion is to recall isolated images of a few defining visual aspects that are representative of motion. If you examine your own thoughts carefully, you will see that this is true. If you try to recall images of motion that have other Cross Sensory Address Links tied to the visual image, you might falsely believe that you are really visualizing motion because it all seems so real. The reality is enhanced by the remembrances associated with the visual images, remembrances of the feelings within the gut, or feelings that were originally associated with the muscles, but the visual images even in these cases are only infrequent representative snap shots that define just enough detail to just barely indicate motion.

CONCLUSIONS

REM Dreaming is necessary for a complex Creature to examine the information collected by its Short Term Memory. The examination and storage of newly discovered patterns is facilitated by Sleep. Sleep is Nature's method of escaping from the sensory storm of a wakeful daily life. Sleep is a retreat to a place of solitude, to an inner World, where the mechanisms of Intelligence process data on their terms.

REM Dreams are directed by primitive mechanisms that work at their own purpose. The Dreams flow essentially uncontrolled by the Dreamer and do not necessarily visually represent any logic of the Real World. This does not mean that Dream is normally without any logical guidance, but the logic of the Dream's unfolding is hidden within the extremely complex net of associative connections within the Long Term Memory, and the stimulation of that memory by the processing of the data within the Short Term Memory.

Dreamers who desire some interpretative meaning of their Dreams are themselves the best source of any realistic interpretation. They only need to bear in mind, that the primary driving factor of their Dream is the contents of their Short Term Memory, but also remember that those contents most probably will be morphed by memories within the Long Term Memory. Also, they must keep in mind that equivalent substitutions of symbols or meanings might be present. Usually with a careful and critical analysis, a Dreamer can discover the full nature of their Dream.

Probably the most difficult Dream in which to discover its real world components is the recurring Dream. In the recurring Dream all major elements of the Dream are substitutions. It is the case that the recurring dream is made up from groupings of old memories, but remember that REM Dreams are stimulated by recent happenings. It is those recent happening patterns that are the direct cause of the Dream. It is those patterns that have reoccurred in the Real World within the day before the Dream that trigger the repeat of the Dream. Those triggering Real World patterns are immediately substituted for other patterns and the substitution is always invariant. This makes the Dream appear to be old patterns that are again and again repeated. The dream is in fact made up from old memories, but its real causal origin is within a very few days of the dreams happening.

The only hope for any person other than the Dreamer to interpret the Dreamer's Dream is when the other person knows the details of those events stored within the Dreamer's Short Term Memory. That person must also know how patterns stored within the Dreamer's Long Term Memory are connected by association. You can understand, this leaves the Dreamer as the best hope for the interpretation of their Dreams.

Such stories of Dreams as the famous, seven fat ears of corn being consumed by seven lean ears of corn, are evidently contrived to meet the needs of the storyteller. There is no supportable evidence that dreams are a method of realistic prophecy, but only unrealistic prophecy.

EDUCATION

EDUCATION

EDUCATION

Many a Fish shall Perish, Many a Machine shall Rust,
Many a Howl of Nature Stilled, Many a Garden shall become Dust,
Until People can Speak Together and
Understand.

Near to the heart of humankind sits,
Like some Dinosaur from a landscape of times past,
Our cherished Educational System.
Draped in modern buildings and wearing flashy instruments and bangles and beads,
The body of modern education still speaks with half the voice of ancient Egypt.
Translated Egyptian Hieroglyphs have a child pleading with his teacher,
"Don't beat me master, for I have learned my lessons well".
Every culture's God of learning is rote memorization.
It together with the whip make a time-tested duality of power,
For forcing children to become women and men of culture's desired mold.

It's a simple system of monotonous repetition and fear,
Whose final product is a most stunning reflection of the
method itself.
It's a system that mechanically tramples,
Strangles,
And mutilates the most human of human traits,
The desire to seek, discover and learn.
The desire for learning in the young human child is the
bubbling fountain of their youth.
Its water, pure curiosity.
Its forceful drive far exceeds all else in the animal kingdom.
But in every culture we see the child's sparkling enthusi-
asm for learning systematically
Crushed,
Crushed
And Crushed.
Until learning is changed from joy to drudgery,
From seeking to accepting
And from understanding to parroting.
The educational system which we hypocritically call
modern is the ancient system,
Where the whip has been replaced by other fears.
It all results in the same end and speaks with an archaic
hollow voice,
Lacking in understanding,
Echoing up from the distant dark past,
Out of cadence with time's demands.

*   *   *   *   *

Conservative, Conservative, Conservative
Will you please give that bird a cracker!

*   *   *   *   *

INTRODUCTORY COMMENT

In this section, I am not going to bombard you with endless statistics. Statistics have always been used to prop-up any argument anyone wants to make.

I am not going to mull through the tons upon tons of written material in existence concerning education.

What I will attempt to do is look at education with respect to the material of the first three sections of this book. Hopefully, we might gain some new insights into the most astonishingly powerful tool of discovery that has ever existed. Education is in the truest sense a tool; it is the tool we use to open-up minds to the possibilities for new discoveries.

UNIVERSAL KNOWLEDGE BASE
Surrounded By a Sea of Potential Knowledge

A MOMENT OF REFLECTION

I believe it is appropriate here we take a moment for reflection. It should be enlightening, if right now we consider what we can distinctly remember from all of those things that we were taught during our approximately twelve years of Primary Education.

Yes, try to make a detailed list. I do not mean, listing just the names of the subjects in which you have been instructed. I mean exactly, exactly, what do you specifically remember from each of them. Take your time and do the best job you can of remembering.

If you are currently, or have recently been a teacher, you should disqualify yourself from this project. The reason is, you have so repeatedly been exposed to the subject material, that it would be impossible to be sure if you remembered it from your original Primary Schooling or from your re-exposure to it during your teaching career.

For those who are not teachers, I'm sure without much doubt, that after considering your list, you must be wondering what happened during all of the time that passed in those twelve years. Or, maybe it is appropriate to wonder just how significant to our later lives were the things that we were supposed to have learned? Or, did we really learn them in the first instance? Or did we, after repeated training, remember them for a long enough time to pass a course test? Or, remember them for a long enough time to pass some overall qualifying test?

TYPICAL
MALE PERSONAL KNOWLEDGE BASE

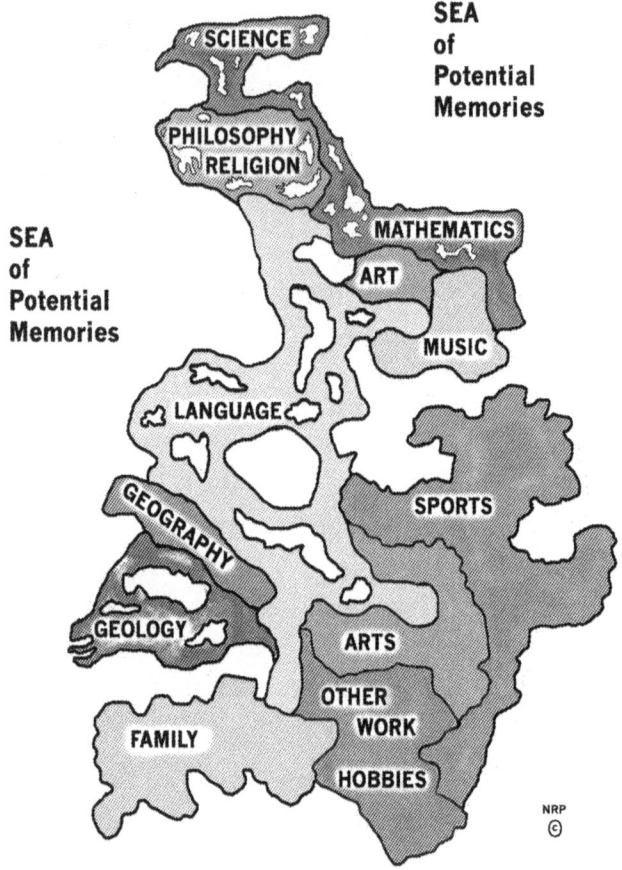

We did of course learn some things that are not easily descriptive, things that surely are the remaining kernels of much of all of the learning that we have forgotten. These are like ghosts. They are the remains. They are the connective paths. They are the logical structures that tied together the specific memories of closely related material. They remain inside our minds after the specifics have faded. They are still there because we use them daily. It is by use of these various sets of generalized logical structures that we have the power to logically evaluate new situations.

$$* \qquad * \qquad * \qquad * \qquad *$$

Education is about constructing mental landscapes, those territories that define the geography of the mind, and the regions in which the individual is free to roam and to strive at discovering unknown lands upon a Sea of Potential Memories.

THE PURPOSE OF EDUCATION

The first and primary element that is a prerequisite for a Nation to proceed with a good, safe and dynamic future is an overall philosophy that is nurturing to the diversity of the human character and establishes social order with justice.

A seconded element, which is indispensable, if the first is to survive, is an Educational System that compliments and succors the first element, with both of these elements reinforcing each other.

Therefore in the most general sense education should stand on five pillars:
1. Guide us at discovering and understanding our universe.
2. Guide us at discovering and understanding ourselves.
3. Guide us at discovering and understanding each other and our societies.
4. Guide us at discovering and understanding the scared value of tolerance.
5. Guide us at discovering and understanding the scared value of diversity.

AIMS OF EDUCATION

What is ultimately necessary within an educational system is that all students are allowed unlimited opportunity to discover and pursue the learning possibilities that are available for them to fulfill their desires and find a meaningful place within the social structure and life.

Although it is necessary that each student acquire a working understanding of the reading, writing and arithmetic, it is not necessary that every student be highly accomplished in mathematics or reading or writing or any of the great curricular idols of today's world. In these basic areas we should assist the students to reach their best attainment.

An aim of education must be to prepare, as best as possible:

1. The individual student for a successful fit into society. We define a successful fit into society as an individual who feels they are an integral part of society, and can find purpose, happiness and continual hope for an ever-interesting life.
2. An individual who can understand society's need for people to work together for the common good, but who is not subservient to the common purpose to the extent of not questioning its philosophy.
3. An individual who questions the status quo and thereby might give society hope for an even better future.
4. An individual who realizes the near sacred nature of diversity and the tolerance of that diversity.

Sadly it is true that within every species, it is those individuals who are noticeably different from what is common that most often suffer the arrows of misfortune. Yet it is necessarily true, that only those Individuals who are different are the ones that can lead to a new and hopeful future.

TYPICAL
FEMALE PERSONAL KNOWLEDGE BASE

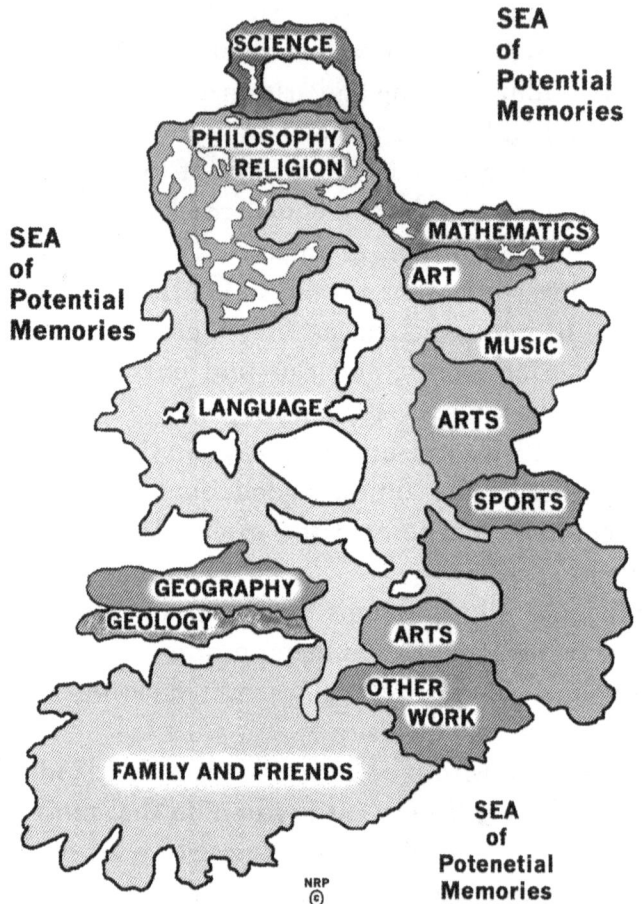

Discovering the Individual Beneath the Student

Education is the primary tool that society has for helping individuals find what they might feel is a meaningful and satisfying position for themselves in life. If society is to be a hopeful place and the future is to be seen as having hopeful possibilities, then it is the primary responsibility of education to give sufficient opportunities to all students to discover their best possibilities and their interests and to offer them the opportunity to develop those interests to the fullest extent.

EDUCATION'S CURRENT SITUATION

Disparity Between Districts

There is a serious problem when the schools within a nation are spread across a wide range of performance from great successes to near total failure. A major part of the problem is the methods of raising money to finance the school systems. Areas that are made up of persons who are the most economically successful have the greatest moneys for their local school system. When this is true, it is also true in general, that those schools have the best facilities, buildings, classrooms, equipment, accessory learning materials and many times the best or most qualified teachers. They also have most importantly, what we might think of as the most qualified students, generally happy and healthy boys and girls who have come from richly endowed home environments.

Other schools within the nation have none of these advantages and necessary requirements for an educational system to be the most successful. Within the worst cases of this extreme are those whose buildings and physical plants are so old and inadequate as to interfere with the teacher's ability to deliver an optimum or even minimal instruction and aid to their students.

It is difficult to believe that such a divergence of quality could exist within the boarders of such a Great Nation as ours. It's a situation that is mindful of a fragmented and unbonded social structure, almost anarchistic. It's a situation that servers no one well, but resides as an ever self perpetuating condition, a condition that results from everyone seeing it as, "That's the way it's always been." and "We want local control of our schools"...Please give that bird another cracker.

Local Control

Let's seeeee,——Local control,——State's control,——Aren't those the very things that led to the perpetration of the long, long history of inhuman atrocities committed against some of our Nation's Noble Citizens? I think it was. **Does that mean that the States or local communities don't necessarily know what's best? That in many instances, they cater to what in fact might be the worst? That they might, more often than not, cater to their own narrow views of what is best? That politicians would bow down to the symbols and costumes of power in total disregard for what is true and right? Yes, I think, yes. The evidence is everywhere throughout our history, that the answer is, Yes.**

It has always been politically popular to support local control of the local educational system. To what good effect this local control brings to the educational system is highly questionable. It would seem quite obvious, that what is actually involved behind this demand for local control, is the perceived need to maintain the propagation of local morals, taboos and religious biases. None of these reasons give an educational system any advantage at accomplishing its primary purpose of giving every student the best possible chances for a good education.

Local control also means, that the curriculum from school district to school district and from state to state is not uniform. Such differences can and do lead to serious problems for the student who moves from one school to another. As an example, we might have a student who is living in an economically poor rural school district. In kindergarten this student may be mainly playing with toys, modeling clay and taking naps. Then the student's family moves to an urban setting and in the new school the student is dumped into a class that is well on its way to reading. The student is at a loss in this new setting and is considerably behind the other student's learning. Then, the family moves again and the student is in a class that is well into learning the methods for performing long division. At this point the student feels buried by their own inadequacy. Then, the family moves again and now the student is dropped into a music class where the other students are reading musical notes aloud from a musical score. The student is beginning to think, that the other students must have been born with this ability. When the student is called upon by the teacher to read the notes for the class, the best the student can do, with great embarrassment, is guess at each note's name.

The reverse situation is also many times true. Where a student transfers to another state and discovers that they are within a class that is far behind their level of attainment. A student may then become dissatisfied and bored, ignoring the presentations in the classroom, which can lead down a trail where without noticing the student has actually fallen behind the other students.

This system of non-uniform curriculums between school districts, and between states was more or less acceptable during the past, when many if not most people were more settled in one place and the family was likely to reside there for a lifetime. But times have changed very much from that more static society. It is past time that the educational system should change to a system of uniform curriculums throughout the Nation. Don't let this suggestion upset your feelings about a need for diversity, because it can be accomplished and accompanied by more diversity than you can dream.

The Things We Teach

I believe that educational systems worldwide bear an undeniable testimony to the general principals of my view of what intelligence is all about. They are, all of them, primarily consumed with delivering known patterns to students and then judging the student's learning performance by asking the students to demonstrate their ability to recall the patterns. There is a need for some of this in education, but we would be better off if we tilted the learning of patterns and their manipulation to what Alfred North Whitehead suggested at the beginning of the 20th century. His suggestion was essentially, that we teach the generalization of pattern manipulation and cease to endlessly belabor the specifics. The Arts exemplify the ultimate of pattern manipulation. It is a fact that most of the endless memorized but unassociated specifics acquired during our years in elementary education are what are soon forgotten in adulthood.

If the educational system is to change for the better, for the society as a whole and for the individual, we must demand that the Arts with their obvious ability to encourage the student to exercise their creative imagination becomes a major part of a student's education. This of course needs to be carried over into all possible curriculums, including arithmetic, mathematics and all of the sciences, wherever possible.

The Things We Don't Teach

Many times cultures have established beliefs that are regarded by most as forbidden to critical examination. Nearly everyone feels required to worship at the shrine of those beliefs, as if they housed nothing but the best values and eternal truths. The Family in most societies is one of those shrines. But in many cases it is within that shrine where is bred and perpetuated some of the worst biases and hatreds that are later perpetrated against particular members of humanity. It is in truth, primarily within some families where unreasonable intolerant attitudes are fostered against various religions. It is primarily within some families where racial and other social bigotries are taught and passed from one generation to the next. It is within some families were all kinds of esoteric dark hatreds are nourished and perpetuated.

It is important that if these most antisocial hatreds are to come to a final end or at least begin to be truncated, then educators must be alert to any signs of them within their students.

Educators must be active at countering these antisocial biases. They must work at countering them from the time of a student's very beginning within the Educational System.

More Things We Don't Teach

We foolishly do not teach our children, beginning from their earliest age, the exacting art of speaking their native language and of precisely communicating whatever exists within their mind.

Because we do not extensively teach diction and pronunciation our ability to communicate with our peers suffers with inadequacy. You only need to observantly listen to any extended conversation between peers to notice the many weakly understood and completely misunderstood ideas that mare the conversation.

Learned mispronunciation leads to great difficulty when children are trying to learn the correct spelling of words, this is beyond the difficulties associated with spelling that the language has inherited from the incorporation of foreign words.

We do not spend enough time in developing a real expertise in descriptive writing and speaking. It is terribly important, that we make a concentrated effort to allow children to exercise this aspect of communicating. It can be an easy and exciting game for children to try to communicate with only words something that they would like their peers to discover and understand.

There are simple handheld and inexpensive electronic devices that can assist children in learning correct pronunciation to a most exacting degree.

More Things We Don't Teach

We mainly teach by directing information to the visual or auditory senses.

This is simply because these senses are the most receptive to the very complex pattern structures that students are attempting to learn. We severely neglect the purposeful teaching of a variety of possible pattern inputs to the other three senses. The senses for Feeling, Smelling and Tasting are all willing to accept the learning of an infinite variety of new patterns. For any individual to grow to their fullest possible mental potential, all of the senses should be busy at discovering the new possible patterns that they can accept. Society has wrongfully placed either directly or indirectly powerful taboos against a person's freedom to learn the infinite variety of patterns that are there for these other senses to discover. Truly, some of this discovery of the world that is available to these senses probably should not be undertaken within the structures of the Primary Educational System, but there should be some place within the Society where a person could go to enhance the learning experiences directed to these other senses. Such learning would serve to enrich and broaden an individual's understanding of themselves and their place within an environment of richly textured patterns that are selectively available to each of the senses.

More Things We Don't Teach

When we teach children to recognize the symbols that represent the Alphabet of the Written Language, at the same time we teach them the spoken language names for the symbols. But, when children on their own, at an early age, begin learning the Visual Alphabet of Patterns, they are left to their own devices. We need to instruct children about the Visual Alphabet in the same way as we do for the symbols of the Alphabet of the Written Language. A good basic understanding of the Visual Alphabet of Patterns would facilitate the teaching and better understanding of the Alphabet of the Language. It would also significantly increase the general understanding of the complex patterns of the visual world.

Some thought should be given to defining the most basic elements of the Visual Alphabet and to devising the simplest spoken names for each of these most basic symbols.

A Note: About Spelling

I believe it is past time for a new convention to be assembled to re-accomplish what Webster originally did for unifying the spelling of English words. The time has come to look at this subject again. It might even be appropriate to introduce a new letter or letters in to the English Alphabet or maybe to remove some letters.

When we are teaching students the correct spelling of words, we are forcing the student to examine and learn the exact letter patterns that make up the overall symbol that is the word. This kind of learning, although necessary, works against one of the most basic axioms of an intelligent system; that axiom is that an image of a Real World Object should only be resolved until it can be distinguished from a similar object. Learning to see the general symbol that represents a word by looking at all of the exact ordering of the letters that make up the word, is counter productive in a situation that requires proficient reading. To become a proficient reader, a student must learn not to look carefully at the exact internal structures of words, but instead must be able to recognize only the most generalized structure (pattern) that can represent the word but still differentiate that word structure from different words. The most proficient readers and readers who can capture the greatest depth of the ideas that underlie the symbols on the written page are those readers who are capable of seeing the words written on that page as the absolute minimal symbols of the words that they represent.

*   *   *   *   *

A CHILD'S PRAYER

Please God, save Me from the Spelling Test Monster

*   *   *   *   *

Student Neglect

It is all too frequent that we see some students, who are bored and or perform poorly by a school's standards. Then later we see, that it is these very same persons, who in the real world of life, make surprising major breakthroughs of discoveries that change the world. These students who are unhappy and unsuccessful in school are many times extremely successful in the real world of industry, finance, entertainment and any and all fields of human endeavor. There is a very serious problem within the educational system revealed here. Clearly the system is neglecting what is required for these disenchanted students to be nourished by the system. After the fact, we can clearly see that they were valuable individuals for society. Yet the educational system was blind to their needs or unwilling to meet them.

Class Characteristics

Consider that within a single class there may be a wide range of different learning disabilities that the teacher and school must deal with. It does seem striking that students with such a wide range of disabilities could be in the same class. It is logical that to efficiently solve any problem, the nature of the problem should be reduced to as few variables as possible. The best way to accomplish this, if the problem is complex to the point of being unreasonable to manage, is to reduce the problem, if possible, to a group of separate problems, each with a minimal number of variables. This solution is both appropriate, reasonable and gives maximum benefit to all of the individuals in a learning situation. In the social environment it is not acceptable, but within the learning environment it is a necessary.

Classes by Age

It can be understood that in an Educational System that is made up of classes of students of the approximate same age, that there will be noticeable differences in the abilities of the students. These differences will necessarily span across the full ranges of social behavior, intellectual ability, physical ability and mental temperament. The only approximate constant in this system of classes is age. **Age has no value as a system of categorizing and regimentation for the purposes of learning, no value whatsoever, none.** We would find such a system in the adult working environment as ridiculous to the extreme. Yet we accept it without question in the Primary Educational System. **The class structure based on** student age is itself one of the major problems within the modern Educational System.

The System brings in a group of a certain age, moves them through the System until the class reaches a certain age and then classifies them as finished. So what exists is a capsule called a class that moves through a larger capsule called the Primary Educational System. Such a system has no appropriate relationship to real life.

This System leads both the students and the teachers to believe that they are part of a group and that the group proceeds as one into the future. It therefore makes for unnecessary personal conflict, when an individual stands out either for positive or negative reasons from the standards of the group. And if an individual by necessity is forced to leave the group either because of advancement or decline, then they also suffer a tragedy of dislocation.

We need to make the moving into or out of certain learning situations be seen by all as the natural consequence of learning.

The Educational System must recognize, that being part of a group is not in itself what is objectionable, but the artificial grouping of classes by age into a group that progresses as a whole through the System of Education is the problem. It is greatly desirable that students and teachers feel they are part of a group. It is the definition of the group itself that needs to be changed. The nature of the group itself must be redefined to be the whole group of the School, the College or the University. In most College or University situations this is the case in fact, although students associate themselves with a certain graduating class year. The truth is, they proceed through that educational system as free individuals seeking out the individual learning experiences that they desire or are dictated by the curriculum of their degree.

Open Door System

All elementary and higher level Educational Systems should each be totally open at any and all levels of accomplishment to students who wish to enter or leave the system at any time in their life. A great Educational System is a continuous system that extends from its most elementary beginnings in a continuous path with connected branches to each and every field of learning and discovery, with doors for entrance or exit at every level, where citizens may enter or leave at any time of their life. It is a System for the continual education of the entire population. The only requirements for entry at any door are Real World prerequisites for entering at that particular level. But since any door is available to anyone who meets the prerequisites, the prerequisite are obtainable at one door or another.

Escape by Voucher

A voucher system that would allow some students, by their own choice or their parent's choice, to escape from a public school system to a private school is a guaranteed method for first destroying the Public Educational System and then leading to the establishment of an economic and religious cast system that would without the slightest doubt fragment our democratic society. It would lead directly without any doubt to the destruction of the separation of church and state. The key word here is "SEPARATION", which by any reasonable argument, is the essence of the meaning of Constitution's Bill of Rights. An education that is about memorizing dogma is not an education, it is an indoctrination. **Education and indoctrination are at divergent purposes.**

We will consider an interesting alternative to the voucher system in the section of Recommendations.

Immortal Institutions of the Herd

Today's educational system is still just a reworked copy of the ancient system. We have made no great amount of progress toward change, as is the general case with trying to change any long established institution. We claim progress, but in general very little is actually there. The reasons are simple. The structures of institutions are as imbedded within the brains of the people within a culture and are as much part of them as is being left or right handed. Everyone is always paying lip service to change, especially change for the better. We make great and expensive rituals about change, where there is much blinding smoke and fire, ritualized movements, and loud choruses singing wonderful sounding words, but in the end, after all has settled, nothing, nothing at all, is different. You can see this is true about all long established institutions of every kind; their theoretical constructs seem to have an immortality that can survive beyond the worst social disasters or any effort to change them.

Look, as an interesting example, The Communist's over throw the Czarist government. And what did they, the people, actually get? They got a government with a different name, but exactly the same hierarchy as before, exactly the same; only the titles of the tyrants were changed. Their function and methods were the same as before the revolution. And finally when the communist government fell, born down by its own rotten inefficient weight, there was great hope for a new system. But what was this new government like? Exactly like before, just new names for the new tyrants.

Just one example you say, but history is loaded with such examples. Here is another, a sad case, where the hopes for a meaningful change by force were just a foolish dream. It was Iran before the recent Iranian revolution. It was clear that the coming revolution was just going to exchange one tyrannical system for another. Iran has been ruled by one tyrant after another since the dawn of recorded history. At least the

Shaw, was a progressive person. He tried to eliminate the ancient religious taboos that had held his country in ignorance for over 1200 years. It is clear that the Shaw was a tyrant, who resorted to terrible tactics to force his will upon the people and the Nation. I do submit, that some of his tactics may have been necessary to break the powerful hold that the established religion had on the properties and minds of his people. But, what happened when the religious supporters gained control of the government? Where was the great change the people were hoping for in this new government? There was no real change. A progressive tyrant was simply replaced by religious tyrants with their philosophy of " We are always right because we rule in the name of god".

OK, so there are real problems in trying to make meaningful changes to any long established institution. But there are ways to get it successfully accomplished. In the educational system meaningful change has been an illusive rascal, but there may be good ways to actually get significant change accomplished, even revolutionary, change that might be acceptable to society. Possibly the times are ripe for such change.

Special Student Requirements

Within any grouping of persons there are many differences that require attending to within the Educational System. Understanding the differences, we should and must make arrangements such that each student can receive the best benefits from their schooling.

All students should not have to suffer the misfortunes of others, or suffer because of the misfortunes of others.

Needs Outside of the School

There are some individual needs that are common to every student. These needs must be satisfied in the best ways possible. All students need to be able to have a restful sleep at night or they are at a very severe disadvantage for learning. All students need to be free from hunger and have proper nourishment. All students need to be healthy and free from physical pain or mental anguish. That children are healthy, well nourished and well rested is as important to their ability to learn, as is the quality of the curriculum and teachers. Any Great Nation has the ability and the responsibility to see that these needs are satisfied for all of its children.

Pushing Learning That is of No Value to Anyone

If we can clearly see that a student has only one leg and that leg is severely deformed, then we would seem foolish beyond all reason if we insisted in trying to teach this student to be a great dancer. If after years of tortuous practice, this student were graduated with a certificate of accomplishment in dance, both the teachers and the student would have to understand, that this certificate was a fraud and would add no prestige to either.

RESULTS OF A POOR EDUCATION

Crippling by Neglect

There are some serious self-sustaining short falls in our current Educational System. There are segments of our population that are significantly, very significantly, short changed in being able to obtain the best possible education. These segments of the population, who for one reason or another are systematically cheated, are those of a low monetary income, and those who are members of some minority group within the general population. Not only are these segments of the population forced to the poorest sidelines of the educational dinner plate, but also after a lifetime of being educationally malnourished, Society points a finger at them as adults and accuses them of being underachievers. And in truth they have become underachievers in all respects compared to the healthy economic and social life of the general community. If we had raised a child that was severely nutritionally malnourished during all of their developmental life, we would find it easy to understand why they are under performers as an adult. But since a lifetime of educational malnourishment is not on a day-to-day examination physically apparent, we do not relate the resulting disastrous effect on their performance to its root cause. It is one of the saddest situations within the education system, and it is a situation that is self-perpetuating, a situation that requires our every effort at changing.

Drop Outs

Many students who might be greatly talented, but for reasons that the current Educational System cannot cope with, are left adrift in an system that is directed at mass education to the exclusion of the needs of the few. Sometimes the potential drop out student has family or social problems with which the system declares it is not equipped to resolve. Sometimes the potential drop out is an individual who is starving for challenges that the system cannot or will not provide. Sometimes the potential drop out is just plain bored with everything the system does provides.

It is sure that some of the students, who drop out from the Educational System, take up revengeful pursuits against the society that neglected them during their time of need. The cost to the individual and to society can be enormous in terms of pain and money in comparison to what it would have taken to assist the individual in solving whatever might have been the nature of their problems. Here again the root cause, with not solving these problems at their beginnings, is a limited foresight associated with a real economic near-sightedness.

Children who either drop out of the educational system or are forced out of the system, must not be left floating in society without any guidance or hope for a better future, also they must not be sent to "alternative schools", where they are forced into an even more second rate educational environment. All children must be required to be in some kind of structured learning environment during those very formative years of their lives and none of them should be abandoned to struggle alone. Some children absolutely require a strictly controlled and very structured environment for them to discover their own capabilities and when this is the case such an environment must be provided.

TESTING AND GRADING

Learning Test Taking Skills

It should be a suspicious situation, when a student's learning performance as measured by some standard test is indicated as satisfactory or as always improving, but when one is given the opportunity to communicate face to face and one on one with these same students, it becomes shockingly apparent that their level of overall knowledge is actually many grade levels below where the standard test showed them to be. It must be considered that instead of students actually improving their overall knowledge, they have in fact improved their test taking skills, or, maybe they have been directed towards the very particular requirements needed to get through the test's hoops.

We further waste a student's valuable time and the Educational System's limited funds by establishing classes that actually teach test taking skills. It is far more appropriate that such time and moneys be put to purposes, that are not directly dictated by those **Test Taking Monsters, who are blowing their Horns so often, and so load, that they have made Test Taking a Central Idea around which they require Education to Dance.**

I remember that at the university I attended, there was a professor of Mathematics, who liked to take the multiple-choice tests for classes for which he had no background knowledge. He always performed above average on these tests, because he understood how these kinds of tests were formulated irrespective of the body of knowledge they were supposed to be testing.

Standardized Testing

Educators and other pushers of standardized testing must realize that the teachers and the students being tested are all members of the cleverest species that nature has yet produced. Because this is true, they will find many ways of meeting whatever goals are set for them. This is especially true if the goal is simply the passing of some written test.

The greater the consequences that are placed on either passing or not passing some test, the greater will be the efforts of those being tested to find some way, any way of passing.

Testing is a way of reducing the need for actually knowing the individual student to the knowing of some quantitative number that is supposed to represent that student. Anyone should be sure this is a very poor and demeaning representation of any individual, a representation that can never be successful. It is a result of an overly populated, overly busy society that pays lip service to the sacredness of the individual and then in everyway tries to reduce the individual to a representative number.

If great consequences are to be placed on knowing an individual's learning accomplishments, then justice can only be fulfilled if great care is taken at discovering those accomplishments. No simple written test will ever be able to fulfill this requirement.

It is clear that within a society that is unwilling to provide the very best resources for educating its people, standardized testing is an attempt at limiting expenditures, with the consequence of handicapping part of the population.

Anxiety about Testing

There are students, students that have learned the course material in great detail, but when the time comes for them to face taking a written test, become so anxious and physically and mentally upset, that they are unable to even read and understand the test questions. Written or verbal testing in general does not show what a student has learned about the course material. At its very best situation it can only give an indication about the knowledge of a specific question.

What is Testing all About?

For the teacher and the student, testing in any form should be about diagnostic discovery, whose sole purpose should be to enhance the teacher student relationship towards continued learning.

Everyone outside of the direct teacher student relationship wants testing to fulfill all of their desires for propping up images of themselves or the student or the system. When those images are not sustained, all Hell can break lose. Parents interested in how well their children are performing want to see specific quantified ratings, because they mistakenly feel that these give a real picture of the status of their child. The parents want the best for their own and each believes that their own is best. But, this is not a place where the Educational System should be caught in the middle of a fight over an imaginary image.

There exists within each individual student an image they have of their state of understanding of a particular subject. They pretty well know their strengths and deficiencies but are not necessarily willing to share this knowledge with others. It is the student-teacher-relationship that allows the student to feel safe in sharing this information. It is this voluntary sharing that holds the best hope for the best results.

Formal written testing, if its results were a real representation of the student's understanding of a subject, should not emotionally affect the student. This is so because the test would reveal something the student already knows. What actually happens is, the test results can never match the reality and so the student is lead in to believe something about themselves that simply is not true. Students that perform exceptionally well on the test might be lead to believe that they know it all, when in fact they know it is not true. Students that perform on the test anywhere below what they feel they know, feel they have been treated unjustly. The students that are in the lowest range of the testing scores feel they have been unfairly marked. It is not that they are not resigned to their score representing somewhat their level of understanding. It is, that in a sense, they feel they have been undressed in front of the other students to reveal to them something they did no want shown to everyone.

Timed Tests

Tests required to be finished within some fixed time period are simply another way of the educational system expressing, that they really don't have the time for giving any special considerations to the individual student and that because of costs they must concentrate on the group not the individual, that consideration of individuality is always of the least importance and is to be disregarded at every opportunity.

What would you think, if in the real world we said, "OK, here we have a serious problem, the major disease of Polio, and you have one week to find a cure? If you haven't found a cure in one week you must drop your research and go on to something else."

The only tests that should be timed are those in which you are seeking to find the fastest at finishing some task, a task whose primary objective is speed, tasks like racing or speed swimming, these are the kinds of things that are appropriate for timed testing.

Tests that are trying to get a handle on intellectual problem solving should concern themselves with the qualities of a student's approach and the proximity of their findings to the problem's solution. Testing should not be about time, but about investigating the processes used for discovery.

Seeing The Truth Without Formal Testing

When small children draw for you their pictures that are representations of the Real World, they are directly allowing you to see through the window of their minds into their Long Term Memories. Their pictures are a true representation of the complexity or simplicity of the visual patterns they have learned and have stored there. We usually see for children within any particular class, that the complexity of patterns displayed within their pictures are remarkably similar. This similarity is primarily because they have learned as a group the same visual images. The simplicity of the patterns is because they have not been systematically taught more complex patterns. The great similarity is because the individuals have not been allowed a free ranging discovery of patterns in a maximally rich pattern environment. The fact is, that even for college graduates we can see in the exhibition of their work that there is a kind of mature professionalism, but an over riding similarity of their styles with very few examples of individual expression.

Whenever students display their talents to you by painting, or writing, or telling stories, by singing, or dancing, or playing a musical instrument, they are opening a window that views directly into their Long Term Memories. By interactions through these various windows anyone can discover in exacting detail what has been stored there. There are no kinds of limited testing that can take the place of these complex interactions between individuals.

Grading

There presently are no practical systems of testing or grading that can show with accuracy either what a student has learned or of what value it might be to an individual's future life. **Nor can any testing or grading discover those things learned that will soon be forgotten and therefore of little or no consequence.**

We are falsely led to believe that some structured system of grading has some direct correlation to the quantity and quality of things inside of a student's head, that by grading a student with an A, B, C, D, or E we somehow have established a meaningful representation of the student. Consider that if we allowed someone to rate works of art with this grading system, could anyone successfully argue that there would be some added significant mean to Michelangelo's Pieta by attaching a letter grade to it? How much more beautiful and complex is the individual's knowledge? Therefore believing that affixing it with a letter grade has somehow explained everything is really beyond good reasoning.

If a parent or any person is seriously interested in how a student is supposedly exactly performing at their studies, they should take the time to have a conversation with the student. By spending an appropriate time in discussion with the student, a person can discover to their hearts delight and to whatever depth they want to pursue the details that lie hidden there. But instead parents and others want some simple mark that they can believe, without expending any of their own effort, represents the overall state of a student's learning. No such magic mark exists. Hopefully, no such magic mark will ever exist.

It is both sufficient and reasonable that the most general terms be used in rating a student's performance within a specific subject. These ratings might be: "Completed" or "Not Completed". They are simple and define well enough the actual existing situation.

Conclusions

It is important that if testing of any kind is going to be representative of anything of value that the testing mechanisms themselves must be flexible, flexible, flexible.

Testing in any form should be about diagnostic discovery, whose sole purpose should be to enhance the teacher student relationship towards continued learning.

Testing should never be about marking students with permanent banners to be displayed to the world. They are always necessarily false banners.

Student Grading should always be related in the most generalized terms and have an absolutely minimal structure.

IQ

As we have already considered in the section of "Testing and Grading", there are no reasonable or appropriate letter, number or any other symbols that can give us any representative meaning to either an individual's overall knowledge or to the value of that knowledge or the individual's worth to society or their probability of becoming accomplished at whatever they undertake. There is no value of any known significance to how fast or slowly an individual is as a learner of new material. No Value at all in how fast or slow an individual is at repeating back learned material or playing at timed puzzle solving games.

IQ ratings are only of value to those persons that need something to grip in their hands to falsely believe, that they have a real hold on what is without doubt ethereal.

For all of those who love to wave their banners of IQ, I say, get them all together for a beach party at Zimmy Beach.

The evidence is clear, most all of Humankind's great discoveries and achievements have been made by so-called average persons, who were tenacious dreamers. The most that can be said of many of those elite IQers is, they can either entertain or bore you to death with an endless array of facts.

The IQ testing should have long ago faded into history along with the so-called Lie Detector Tests, now camouflaged as Polygraph Tests, which are within themselves a lie and are in fact simple **Stage Fright Tests.**

TEACHING AND LEARNING

*   *   *   *   *

**Bring a Hungry Mind to a Place of Discovery
And It Will Feast**

*   *   *   *   *

Teaching

Teaching should involve a sacred bond of trust between the teacher and the student. A trust where the student allows the teacher to take them along a path of learning, a path, a journey, that is unfamiliar and unknown to them, a path from which they can never return to where and what they were before.

A great teacher must win the student's confidence. The teacher must make it believable to the student that the teacher knows the way. Then, help the student carefully and step-by-step along a path that leads to discovery and learning. It is important to emphasize, that the student must be carefully guided. No reasonable teacher would consider taking a student on a path through a great complex forest, where with a wrong turn the student could plummet off a cliff, or by moving on too quickly, could leave the student far behind, lost and helpless to wander through an unknown landscape. But it is true that every day this equivalent crime is committed within every classroom throughout the world.

Nor is it reasonable that one teacher should try to take a class of many students through this same great and complex forest, for surely in nature's world, many would become disorientated, lost and susceptible to tragic disasters. Yet, we ask teachers to do this equivalent everyday. We close our eyes and hope, without hope, for the best results.

Learning

Learning, for any creature that learns, is a painfully slow process. There are no quick alternatives to the long slow and careful observation of the real world to discover the major patterns that exist there, together with all of the subtle nuances associated with those patterns. I am quite certain that no computer program will be written that can sum up all of the real patterns of nature and in a short time jam them into a pseudo intelligent machine. When a machine is built, that is truly intelligent, it will have to use the same logical structures that are used by biologically intelligent creatures. It is the slow long and careful combing through of nature's patterns, which allows them to be discovered as intelligible, then stored into memory in an order of related classifications.

The primal conditions that lead to discovery and learning are Motivation and Inspiration. Any student that must be forced or dragged to the learning experience is usually better off not to be involved in that experience.

Every new thing a student learns, changes them forever and allows them to see the Universe in a different way than they could see it before. **In the surest sense, those of us with a background of limited learning are partially blind to the vast Universe that lies at the tip of our senses.**

The ancient Egyptians had as part of their funerary ceremony, the ritual of the opening of the mouth of the dead. The symbolic opening of the mouth was to open the way for rebirth of the deceased's soul. **In a similar way, teaching and learning are the ways we open up the Senses of the living to a kind of continual rebirth for discovering the Universe.**

Learning Distractions

It should be quite obvious that the immediate environment of learning should be limited to those sensual stimulation's that are directly a part of the patterns to be learned. It's very difficult to discover new patterns within an extremely chaotic background. Any patterns that are present and are not directly related to the learning experience are potential distractions from learning. If there is a high intensity of chaos, it seriously disrupts the learning process. Such distracting patterns are: noise, the sound of voices, confusing environmental motions, unpredictable sudden sounds, lighting that flickers in a random fashion. These are all deadly for the learning process.

Many times the most prevalent distractions to the learning experience are those things that are going on inside of the student's head, things that might be worlds away from the material to be learned.

To minimize the distracting thoughts that might be running through a student's head, it is important that the student must be prepared before their learning experience begins. Students must be stimulated and motivate for the journey they are about to undertake.

Mentors

There is no good equivalent substitute for a one-on-one relationship between a Teacher and a Student. Students need to be understood. Where those needs are so potentially varied, it really requires a mentorship, but not a relationship like a mother breast feeding the student and nurturing them through the entire educational system, but more as a wise friend and advisor, one that can establish a rapport with the student. It should be a person, or better persons, that the student can rely on for advice and assistance throughout the whole time they are in the school system. We might think of it as a group of flesh and blood Personal Educational Guardian Angels.

Nurturing

A friend was telling me how his young son at a very early age would like to sit on his lap and watch him working at constructing electronic circuits with his hands. He said he could clearly see the joy his son was getting from learning while watching. He said, he understood that learning something new gave a person great pleasure and satisfaction. I disagree somewhat with his comment, that the learning of something new gives the learner pleasure and satisfaction while they are learning. The father was observing his son in a very special situation, where the child had strong feelings of complete loving safety. I believe that in other situations the opposite may be true. The learning experience when the individual is isolated and without a feeling of protection is only entered into with a degree of fear and anxiousness and any satisfaction only comes as a great relief after the learner has passed through the leaning experience without major harm.

You can see a quite similar philosophy exhibited by persons who have just survived some major disaster in their lives and you hear them giving thanks and being relieved that the situation wasn't worse. It seems that no matter how bad the disaster, they are expressing their gratitude and great relief that it wasn't worse.

Every individual is born into this world with not a clue as to the real nature of the world existing around them. Every part of their environment is strange, unknown and of potential danger.

The smallest infants are totally clueless about their world. They are also completely fearless of any benign appearing environment. The basis of their fearlessness is a total ignorance of essentially all things. In their infant state they must be guarded by some adult, so they do not befall every possible accident. Once they have had the time and opportunity, while under adult guidance, and have learned enough information, they are allowed to begin exploring on their own.

It is a necessary condition that the world must be approached by any young individual with great suspicion and care. Everything to the young individual is a mystery with potentially fearful implications. Nature has selected to survive those who carefully approach any new situation; this is true even to this day. It is with a careful balance between fear of the unknown and curiosity for discovery that leads to learning. But it must be clearly realized, that some bit of anxiety or fear is an inbred condition to the approach of any new situation; especially when the individual is on their own and unprotected, or even when an individual is within a group and they feel that if they are unsuccessful at learning the group will show them some hostility.

The fact that my friend's child liked to set in his father's lap and watch his father make new things with his hands tells us something extremely important about the best conditions for learning. We can easily note this by watching young primates. We might see a youngster in its mother's arms, curious about some object it hasn't seen before. While still in its mother's arms and clinging to her, the youngster will reach out to the object, almost touching it, and then suddenly withdraw its hand in fear. Then again, realizing nothing detrimental has happened, the youngster will reach out again for the unknown object, this time coming closer to touching it, but again withdrawing its hand, as if to indicated that the closer to the unknown, the more fearful the situation. During this entire time, the mother has not indicated any alarm at what her child was doing; this being an important sign to the youngster that the situation is not too dangerous. Finally the youngster will grasp the object with its hand. It is here and now that the satisfaction, the pleasure comes to the individual. It's is not pleasure from the learning experience. The learning experience is always a somewhat fearful and anxious experience. The pleasure comes from our conquest of the fear and anxiety. You might understand this by realizing that merely the relief from an anxious and fearful situation is by itself, comparatively, a pleasurable condition. Most of us can relate to this situation in remembering our own satisfaction, relief and pleasure at the completion of some difficult newly learned task. Think of the first time you took a roller-coaster ride. You were entering a new experience for leaning and I am certain that you did it with great anxiety, but when the ride was finished, and you made it through safe and sound, you were probably filled with joyous excitement.

If we can really understand that learning can be a somewhat fearful undertaking, then we can understand that if children are to have the greatest success at learning, it can be best accomplished only when the individual is in a situation of safe and loving security. It is of crucial importance that children are in the best, comfortable, loving and secure environment for the learning experience to be the least fearful and the most successful.

My friend's child, now age seven, still loves to sit in his fathers lap and watch as his dad makes new an wonderful things with his hands. This young boy is bright, learns quickly and is well adjusted to life, school and society. You must understand something about the father. He is deeply devoted to his children as is the children's mother. If you could rate these parents on how strongly bonded they are to their children, and how dedicated they are to interacting with their children on a scale of zero to ten, they would both be tens.

Few parents could be rated so high in their dedication and bonding to their children. Many factors take a severe toll on how much time parents have to interact with their children. Work, hobbies, the parents feeling that they also need some private time of their own, and many more things affect the time that can be shared between family members. Clearly if we should rate parents on their interaction with their children, let's call the rating the bonding factor; those scores would range from zero to ten. And, you can pretty well guess that the numbers of parents associated with those scores would pretty well fit the standard bell curve.

With all of this in mind it is not difficult to understand, that within the home environment, more than half of all children are short changed in receiving the loving and attention they need to perform at being the best learners that they can be. It is absolutely necessary that teachers in a modern school system be encouraged to give the students, especially the very young students, the loving security that each child needs to function at their best. It is of great importance that a trusting, loving relationship exists between the student and the teacher. Hugs and praise are most valuable tools for encouraging learning.

Appropriate Subjects

Our educational institutions spend too much time trying to pound square pegs into round holes. It is all caused by a system that is determined to teach classes of students instead of teaching students. Maybe, if these classes could proceed forth as a class to take on employment and the other aspects of life, it might be reasonable to teach classes. But, since the real world wants to deal with individuals, it might seem to someone, that it is appropriate for the Educational System to function at the level of the individual.

We need to come to grips with the reality of this situation. Consider that one ten-year-old student might be receptive to learning about geology. Another student might not be receptive to learning about geology until they were thirty years old. Another student may never in their lifetime be interested in knowing anything about geology.

It is a major mistake of the system to try to divert each and every student down the same path of subject matter. It is a monumental waste of the educational resources. It is a waste of the student's resource of time. It is a one size fits all philosophy that by any analysis is a failure for nearly everyone involved. The success of the educational system is not measurable by how many pass through its gates, but only by what quality is in its results.

Learning Unrelated Patterns

The system also has a problem when it teaches too much the memorization of isolated facts with no time for the opportunity to make creative investigations of their connection to other related materials. Students trapped in the system really don't strongly resist the learning of isolated facts, because it is the easiest kind of learning, simple one-shot memorization. The teaching of isolated facts is swift and easy and can be cleanly noted as being accomplished. This leads the System into believing it is step-by-step accomplishing its goals. The most serious problem is, that with no memory cross address linking that ties these memories firmly to other memories, they are sure to eventually fade and be lost, all a monumental waste of time for the student and the system. Well, maybe it's not a complete waste of time, when you consider how good the System felt when it believed it was really accomplishing its goals.

If we look at the very generalized Individual Knowledge Maps at the beginning of this section "Education", we might be lead to believe that the memories within a person's Long Term Memory are all nicely connected. A true-to-life Long Term Memory Knowledge Map for almost all individuals would look very much like a shotgun scatter pattern, where few areas would actually be connected to one another. Because of the Education System's love of teaching isolated material and its inability to allow time to show how this material is connected to other related material, all of our minds are mostly filled with trivia that is of no value for use in any kind of rational creative thinking. Its only value is for us to entertain each other during exchanges of small conversation, whose only purpose is social verbal massage, where we impress each other with our knowledge of bits and pieces of nothing. Since this heavy spattering of isolated trivia makes up most of the memories within the minds of the general population, it has become a very popular subject of Television Game Shows, where the audience is impressed with a contestant's ability to answer questions, whose answers are of no consequence to anyone except to the contestant who can win large sums of money for demonstrating their ability to recall trivia.

Learning Strongly Related Patterns

It is of extreme importance that learning within any subject area involves the learning of patterns that are highly connected. Highly connected patterns are longest remembered, but more importantly there is within their connections the logic of their association. It is the building of diverse groups of various, different logics of association that can lead to powerful kinds of creative thinking.

It may be one of the reasons that learning Mathematics, the Sciences, or a deep understanding of Music and Foreign Languages are not much liked by many students. They all require the learning of long sequences of highly related patterns. This kind of learning of many strongly connected patterns requires real work and concentration, whereas the learning of unrelated and disconnected patterns is easier and there is little or no consequence if some of them are forgotten or never learned.

Some schools are using portfolios of a student's work as a more exacting indication of what a student has learned and the quality of the work they have performed. It would be highly desirable if from the beginning of a child's formal education that their teachers began constructing a Long Term Memory Map of each student's exposure to learning in all of the various subjects. Such an individual map would clearly show, as the student's education progressed, how much of what they had learned was connected and therefore would indicate their understanding of the relationships between all of the things they had learned. If individuals are ever to begin to really understanding the universe and their place within it, then they must have strongly connected bonds between the elements of their memories. This is so, because all patterns within the universe touch or in someway kiss against some other pattern and in this way all of the natural and imaginary patterns of the universe are connected in a kind of universal bonded harmony. It is a situation we cannot understand or appreciate until our own knowledge is representative of that connectivity.

Toys for Learning Strongly Linked Patterns

Children to easily learn strongly connected logic patterns need to play with specially designed toys that clearly display the strong linking of mechanical movements such as toy sets for constructing and observing functional systems of gears, levers and pulleys.

They should also have access to Optical Toy Sets consisting of Light Sources, Colored Filters, Lenses, Prisms and Polarizing filters, all designed to be functional and interesting shapes for a child's play.

They need to be exposed to more interesting block sets than just the common cubes. They particularly need to see and play with toy sets that exhibit the transformations of one shape into another shape.

In general children need to be exposed to all manner of interesting toys that demonstrate strong linkages between objects within the physical world.

STRONGLY RELATED PATTERNS

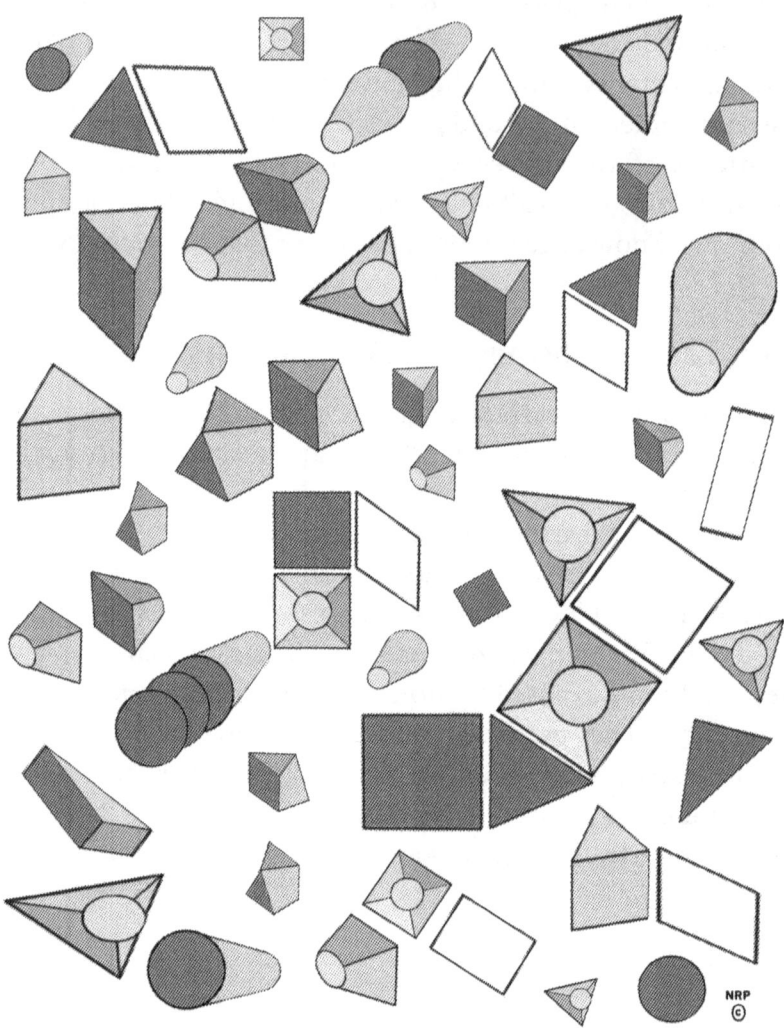

Rotational Transformed Patterns

When small children are learning the visual symbols representing the letters of the language's written Alphabet, they sometimes have difficulty correctly remembering the orientation of the various symbols for the letters.

In the section on Intelligence, we discussed the way the Visual Mapping Function generated a final code that represented an object within the visual field. We also noted that the code was an address location in the Long Term Memory and that the code was in two parts. The left hand part contained the most significant identifiable representation of the visual pattern and the right hand part contained the nuances associated with the pattern. For almost all visual patterns their visual rotation or inversion would produce the same code representation for the most significant part of the code. A rotation or inversion, or reversal of a pattern would normally only affect the least significant part of the code. This is why although we have never seen an Elephant upside-down, when we do see it, we have no difficulty at all in immediately identifying it as an Elephant. Also if an Elephant is pink or green, we can still immediately identify it as an Elephant.

The small child who is just becoming familiar with the visual patterns that represent the Alphabet of Letters may not be observing the minor nuances associated with the spatial orientation of these new patterns. So in whatever orientation they recall the patterns, they always check out OK for the coded address they have stored within their Long Term Memory. They are unable to see any different orientation as being different. It is clear that their Visual Mapping Function is ignoring the nuances associated with these kinds of pattern transformations.

A possible quick solution for pointing out to the child that there exists differences that are associated with pattern orientation, would be to allow the child to view the same pattern in different orientations, while their heads are in a different orientation for each different pattern orientation. This would allow inputs from other senses, other that the visual sense, to alert the child to the differences.

Discovering the Individual's Aptitudes

But, what is to be done in the situation where the teachers with their eyes cannot see the condition of the student's brain? Although we cannot at present see the condition of a student's brain, and cannot clearly even ascertain their true aptitudes, we need some guidance of how to deal with problems of the student, that are clearly observable aspects of their brain's condition as any physical defect is observable to the eye.

Although a student with a single deformed leg will with all reasonable probability never achieve greatness in dance, they might well achieve masterful greatness in some other area, which could have important consequences to both the student and to society. So, it is with this in mind that we can understand that for the best possible results for each student and for the meaningful satisfaction of teachers, it is necessary for either the student or the teacher, and hopefully both, to discover the student's areas of interest and ability. Trying to make such a discovery is much like a group of blind persons seeking out to discover the world on their own.

The prerequisite, for a meaningful discovery that actually can identify a student's interests and abilities, is that their world must be filled with all possibilities. Much of what a student's capabilities and aptitudes are cannot be discovered with any written test. These discoveries take time and much exposure to the multitudes of possibilities that exist.

If there are limits to what the student might be exposed to, then there is always the possibly that the student's greatest interests actually lay outside of those limits. There is no possibility that students will discover an interest in MUSAX, if they have never had the possibility of even knowing it exists. **It is the general case of all Primary Educational Systems in today's world, that they Most Severely Limit the student's environment for discovery.**

The best educational system must allow students to be engaged in a continuous search at discovering their abilities and also discovering their likes and dislikes. Not everyone, that has a certain ability, might like to pursue the development of that ability. It is therefore, equally important that students discover their loves. It will sometimes be the case that a student will have a strong attraction to some subject, where they will have very little demonstrated natural or current abilities. In such a case attraction should rule, because education should be primarily about discovery and learning. It is OK to be about discovering that the student has maybe made a mistake. They might also just discover that their love generates such a strong determination that it drives them to learn and succeed.

Teacher Student Ratios

An important source of improvement in student learning is moving closer to a teacher student one-on-one learning experience. I think that what we need in every school is a mixed situation, a situation that in the first instance has the best student teacher ratio that is economically realistic and secondly where there exists the possibility, whenever the particular situation demands to meet the student's need for a one-on-one teacher to student ratio. I know this means a much greater number of teachers, but that is an absolutely necessary. It also requires that the teachers must have strong specialties where they can truly satisfy the curiosities of the students.

Required Controls of the Learning Environment

Classrooms with large numbers of students who all have different learning abilities and different needs have a high demand for control. Large numbers of individuals do require control and this is a general case within society. The problem is natural and common to any group that is made up of individuals, who truly try to exhibit their individuality. If a population has none or few traits that distinguishes it members, then orderliness is a natural existing condition.

There is a problem that control is many times interpreted as restraint. Instead, it should be thought of as giving constructive direction. Real constructive direction, for a typical class of students grouped by age, would have to be a divergence of directions, directions for individuals to work at learning projects that fit their desires. The problem with this approach is that for the best results it requires some guidance of each group, which means the need for more teachers. What always happens in the real world is a compromise between restraint and constructive direction.

Restraint or constructive direction both give the same general result, that result is order, but in the one case the result is a positive learning experience for the student and in the other it is boredom or stagnation.

Death of the Joy of Learning

We should wonder about the death of the joy of learning and what are its causes and why it never dies in some? It is a mystery. I am sure, there are some students where it had no hope of survival and that cannot be helped. It would seem as if it was apart of their Instinctive Nature. I am also sure this is not the general case, or rather that it need not be the general case.

There is a certain satisfaction that is self-reinforcing, when we feel free at determining the direction of our own lives; it is truly the very basis of the feelings we have of being an individual.

Each child senses that they are truly an individual and strongly desires to seek in directions of their choosing. Our educational system being geared at dealing with classes, by its very design, subverts a child's desired direction into the direction required by the System. Over and over again, they continually subvert the direction to that of the System. It doesn't take much of an imagination to see how this eventually destroys almost all hope of self-determined learning and results in a resignation to accepting without any joy the unwanted direction of the System.

Capitalism cries out against managed economies, because they lack the freedom to compete and therefore seem so unnatural. So why are we willing to accept the same kind of management that is against the individual's free sprit within the Educational System?

For those few who survive and escape the degradation of the individual during their time under the influence of the System, I propose that the joy of learning for them lasts for a lifetime, and that their escaping has much to do with the early coupling of both the elements of art and science within the learning experience. There is a magical power of great strength in science's logic and it leads to much seeking and discovering by individuals on their own which is outside of and separate from the Educational System. There is an equally strong magical power in the primary elements of the Arts, where dreaming and creative imagination together are powerful enough to make pure fantasy, fact. The Arts also lead individuals into much discovering and learning outside of the Educational System. Thus, over a long period of time, individuals who are able to maintain a joy for learning have established a long track record of learning while outside of the normal Educational System and their learning was joyous because it was in a direction of their own choosing.

The magic of the Sciences and the Arts must be experienced by children at the earliest age as a best means of arising in them a curiosity that will flourish even outside of the regular classroom and long survive.

In the coming pages, I have a proposal for a **System of a Universe of Subjects,** which would allow students the free ranging choices they need as a means of maintaining their joy of learning.

COMMUNICATING

Communicating between Nations, between Individuals and between Teacher and Student is not always a totally successful endeavor.

Two people can only maximally exchange and understand the information exchanged, when they both are speaking to the same level of related patterns that they have stored in their Long Term Memories. This is not difficult to comprehend. We might easily understand that a nuclear physicist trying to explain to a pastry baker, the details of a complicated nuclear reaction will find much difficulty in being understood. But we fail to realize, that within our simple daily communications with other people, any attempt at a detailed communication might be a failure, unless they have a repertoire of similar known patterns stored away within their brains. The more closely related is the repertoire of known patterns between two persons, the more completely they can communicate and be understood by each other. Two persons who have lived together for a long period of time can be so closely in tune with each other's known patterns, that they can understand each other's communications almost before they have been completely uttered.

If any two groups have substantially different repertoires of patterns about a subject, it becomes very difficult or even impossible to find common grounds for discussing and coming to a joint common understanding about the subject. Then the only hope for a common understanding is a long period of learning about each other's positions (Known Patterns). In such a situation both sides necessarily sees their point of understanding as the correct one. Sadly, if the patterns are culturally based and acquired over long periods of time, the timeliest solution to this situation is sometimes considered to be the use of physical force.Rather than for all of time to continue to resort to the use of physical force, as a means of by-passing the difficulties of communicating and understanding problems that arise between cultures, it would be wiser and more cost effective if our Ambassadors and other diplomats were well educated in the history and ways of those cultures.

In teaching, teachers must have two important conditions to be most effective at teaching. They must have a number of known pattern memories that greatly exceeds that of their students, they must know the subject they are teaching very well. They must have an intimate knowledge concerning the extent of the known pattern memories of their students. Then, they must communicated at the level their students can understand and use this as a basis for increasing the student's number of known patterns. I hope it is clearly understood that a detailed understanding by the teacher of the student's current knowledge is of a primary importance in guiding the student to new discoveries and new learning. I hope you understand here, that there are no good substitutes for a close personal relationship between the teacher and the student, if they are to be most successful at communicating.

PERFORMANCE REWARDS

Even the performing Whale, Dolphin, Seal or Dog gets a performance award for a good performance. The award they receive must be appropriate to their liking or they will not be happy and will cease to perform. No Whale, Dolphin, Seal or Dog will be happy if you try to reward them with a silken blue ribbon. They all require rewards of immediate personal value.

So why is it, that within the human population we hand out worthless symbols as rewards? Is it because we are so greedy and want to keep the things of real value to ourselves? We like to pat our heroes on the back and present them with a plastic thing, or some ribbon, or a worthless key to the city. We like to make special achievers think they are really appreciated, by presenting them in the presence of a large crowd with some piece of junk, and then with nice words make it all seem so important.

Hey! Wake Up! People also want appropriate rewards, rewards that are within themselves of immediate value. Money can always fit this requirement quite nicely.

But, most seriously, it is of importance that students within the educational system receive appropriate rewards throughout their education as a physical representation of the goals they have achieved. For small children the rewards can be simple, a hug, or appreciative smile, congratulations, or a piece of candy. But whatever the reward is, it must be proportional to the accomplishment and appropriate to the student's real wants.

It should not be necessary to detail a great list of achievements and suggested rewards.

In the last years of their Primary Education the rewards should definitely be money or special distinctions in the social world.

Such a system of rewards is reasonable in that it is the natural system that exists in the world beyond school. Such a system in many cases will go a long way towards enhancing student interest in achieving maximum learning.

A system of rewards for exceptional outstanding performance should apply to the teachers within the Educational System. Here I would suggest that the system, that directs the exceptional achievement award for teaching, must be disassociated from the immediate Educational System. It would be appropriate that whenever a student after leaving school is chosen for some special award, that they name a teacher or teachers that most contributed to their success in learning and then those teachers would then receive an exceptional monetary reward. There would be no popularity contest struggling within this system of rewards, simply because the rewards would be indefinitely delayed into the distant future, much like the infamous "you'll get your rewards in heaven" system used by some institutions.

The best meaningful reward that we can give to the teachers within the educational system is a salary that actually represents their position of highest value within our society. There are no professional teachers within the system that should ever be paid less that the equivalent mean salary that is paid to engineers. They are engineers. They are educational engineers in the truest sense. They are the most important engineers within the body of engineering. They are the ones who trained those other engineers. They are the ones who have helped each of us to become whatever we are. And they deserve our deepest respect and gratitude. **They deserve rewards that are equivalent to their real place of highest value within the social structure.**

CURRICULUM

General

If we can begin to free the Primary Educational System form its entrenched routine of forcing students into classes by age and the belabored teaching of disembodied and disconnected information that is essentially useless to most individuals and soon forgotten, and even if not forgotten is still of no value, then the curriculum of the Primary

Educational System can be significantly expanded, an expansion that should be a joyous reward for all concerned.

Curriculums should be there to fit the needs of the students. The student should never be forced into fitting the curriculum.

Language

Language, written or spoken, is humankind's primary means of communication with other individuals. It is also one of the primary means by which we are able to conduct individual thinking. Further, it is, as we considered in the section about Instincts, a primary identifier in determining if another individual will be accepted as part of the common group.

Language is a fine art and it determines much of how an individual will fare in the many aspects of life. It is a most important binding element of the entire social fabric of any Nation.

It should, without any disabling debate, be one of the prime elements of the educational system's curriculum from the student's first day and continuing throughout their education. Every aspect of the language should be taught and every effort should be made to see that all students in the Nation become a master of the language to their fullest ability.

I hope that with reference to the previous material we have covered, we realize there is a great importance to the leaning of an ever-expanding vocabulary from the earliest years of a child's speaking and writing development and continuing through their entire education.

Language is one of the most primal structures on which thinking, learning and communicating can develop.

Contributors to Logical Algorithms

Every effort should be made throughout the student's education, from the first beginnings to the conclusion, that whenever they are receptive to teach them strongly connected material of every kind that will allow them the ability to develop generalized logical algorithms.

Arithmetic, Mathematics, all of the Sciences and the Arts would naturally be considered to be made-up of strongly connected material. But strongly connected material is certainly not limited to these subjects. Any process that demonstrates a regular systematic solution to a problem is necessarily strongly connected: the assembling of puzzles, the telling of any story that logically unfolds itself, the building of structures. The potential list of strongly connected subjects is actually endless.

Physical Education

Physical Education is important in helping to maintaining the body in a healthy condition. It also has importance in developing social skills related to the understanding of some kinds of teamwork. Most importantly it aids in the development of accurately controlled muscular skills. It may, for some few students, be their ticket to success in life after schooling is completed. For many it is a source of pleasurable experiences within the physical world.

It should be noted, if a student works hard and diligently at developing the strength of their muscles, they might finally succeed in lifting a few hundred pounds over their heads. And, if they worked as hard and as diligently at developing the knowledge within their brain, they might one day be able to lift Spaceships to the Stars.

Homework

Homework is within itself, a tragic indictment of the Educational System. There is no other clearer badge, that the Educational System could hang around its neck, that could better advertise its failure to accomplish it singular job.

Homework advertises, that the assignment wasn't learned, or learned well enough at school, so the schools are shuffling off part of their responsibility to the home environment. It is difficult enough to guide learning within the environment that is dedicated to this work, but to relegate it off to the family at home is just hopeful desperation. It is certainly a way of guaranteeing, that how well a student fares is affected by those economic and social factors that exist beyond the school's control. Yes, for those whose home environment is the best of all possible worlds, things work out pretty well. But, for those who need learning in an environment that allows them to escape an unsatisfactory situation, they are unjustly punished.

The educational system needs to live up to its singular responsibility and do within the system whatever needs to be done to accomplish this responsibility. There are no satisfactory excuses for laying part of that responsibility at an other's doorstep. We simply have all too much of that kind of shuffling of responsibility within society, where everyone is busy blaming others for their own shortcomings or the shortcomings of the System.

The List

The Ideal Primary Educational System should have the most inclusive and general Curriculum that can be economically sustained. I certainly do not mean this in terms of the puny system that is in effect today. It must be a Curriculum that gives the student learning that can contribute to knowing things of immediate value or is preparatory for more advanced leaning. The kinds of subjects it should include, but not be limited to are:

Language studies that cover every aspect of the National Language: Reading, Writing, and Speaking. (Assuming there is a National Language)

The Sciences: Anatomy, Astronomy, Biology, Botany, Chemistry, Electricity, Electronics, Geology, Meteorology, Mineralogy, Metallurgy, Medicine, Optics, Physics, Psychology, and Paleontology.

Arithmetic and Mathematics: Graphing, Geometry, Algebra, Analytic Geometry, Calculus-differential and integral, Matrix Algebra, Mathematical Logic and Digital Logic Systems.

Social Studies: Geography, Histories, Social Morals, and Social Hygiene.

The Arts: Drama, Band, Ceramics, Dancing, Drawing, Etching, Glass Blowing, Music, Movie Making, Orchestra, Painting, Poetry, Playing Musical Instruments, Sculpting, Singing, Live Theater, Weaving, Story and Script Writing.

Computer Skills: Using Computer Programs, Computer Programming, Basics of Computer Design, Automated Control Systems.

Research Skills: Library Skills, Internet Searching Skills, Documentation and Analysis of Evidence, Categorizing Skills.

Practical Machines of the Culture: Refrigeration Systems, Heating Systems, Combustion Engines, Automobiles, Air Craft, Electrical Power Generation, Metal Refining, Machining and Forming of Materials, and Casting Techniques.

Military Science: Philosophy and the Purpose of the Military Structure, Military Organization, Histories of Select Military Campaigns, Weapon Systems and Their Interrelationships, Situations and Strategies, Theoretical Problem Solving, Military Deficiencies and Possible Solutions, Future Weapon Systems and Strategies.

Apprentice Work Studies: Strong relationship with the Business, Artistic or Educational Community, where students would work as apprentices within the actual business environment and would receive specific learning that could apply to their preparation for continued work after their completion of studies within the Educational System.

THE ARTS AND EDUCATION

THE ARTS AND EDUCATION

THE ARTS

Near to the heart of Humankind sits,
Like some ragged unwanted Cinderella step child,
The Arts and Artist of Our Kind.
The Arts whose true awesome power is second not even to science.
The Arts whose very soul is the unheralded other voice of Our Kind.
The Arts whose awesome power has for all of time been bounded and hidden like some invisible Prometheus.
The Arts from whose captured body, mystic philosophies have carefully squeezed like tooth paste the cream of created reality to make fantasy fact and falsehoods believable.
The Arts whose immobilized body has with economic torture yielded to paint history as it never was.
The Arts whose awesome power has with shameful humility bowed to weaker philosophies.
The Arts whose gentle hands have led Our Kind with some dignity through blind and troubled times.
The Arts whose gentle hands can pluck in every way the hidden strings of our emotions.
The Arts whose shrine's doors swing open only by levers of the currency of the time,
Allowing us brief moments of worship when we pay tribute by an individual's coin of true value, smiles, frowns, tears of sadness or joy which are too seldom coaxed from the purse of the most inner being.
And for the Nation that really loves this giant,
Unties its bonds,
Heals its wounds,
Succors it to full life,

And wins its love,
They shall win not just the laurels of the day,
Triumph through time itself shall be theirs.

Arts in Communicating

We have learned everything we know about the Universe from our five senses. Those patterns that we have learned reside within our brains as, at best, skeletal representations of the Real Universe. Our senses detect the patterns, the real part of the Universe, and our mechanisms of Intelligence sort them out, categorize them and file them away into memory. The creative parts of our brains that have the machinery for thinking and day dreaming allows us to make the slightest variations on these known patterns. I do mean the slightest, for in the strictest sense there is nothing new under the sun. There are no insightful leaps to the future, to new ideas. There are only small steps, many, many, many small steps, small variations of what we already know, that eventually taken together lead us to a new idea, to a pattern that we can legitimately call new, a pattern that does not exist in nature or more truthfully, a pattern that we have not experienced in nature. These new patterns that finally arise from our long struggling with the patterns that we already know can be classified into just three categories. Junk or garbage of no apparent redeemable value, like a kind of nightmare, Theories, or Art.

There is something most important to be carefully examined. For all of the patterns gathered up by our senses from the Real Universe, sorted by the mechanisms of intelligence and nicely stored away, then worked on with long struggling by our creative mechanisms to generate some new idea, an idea that is then again hidden away in the skeletal hangings within our brains, there is only one possibility of bringing any of this back out into the Light of the Real World and for presenting them to our fellow humans. That way is by the use of Art. **Art is our only, only, only way of communicating what the five senses have brought into our brains or what our brains have created that is new to the world.**

We have no inverse sense that can directly project on to a screen in the Real World what our eyes have seen. We have no inverse senses that can directly put forth from our bodies the sounds or odors or tastes or sensual things we have learned.

It is the art of language, writing or speaking that we most frequently use to communicate what is inside of us to our fellow humans.

Sometimes the patterns are too complicated to be easily communicated with just words, and then we must resort to communicating by the art of drawing, or painting, or sculpting or theater or motion pictures.

Sometimes the patterns inside of our heads do not relate directly to any material substance and we must resort to music, theater or dance to communicate them to our fellow humans.

In any and every case it is the Arts, and the Arts alone, that allow us to communicate what is inside of our minds to those who are in the world that exists outside of our heads.

Without doubt, the most powerful and sophisticated art medium for communicating the most complex creations of our minds and vicarious representations of the universe is the modern Motion Picture. It, by means of the integrated use of all of the art forms, is the Epitome of Communication.

An educational system that does not incorporate all of the Arts within the curricula is an educational system that is defeating its own aims. Without the Arts we are partially strangled in our ability to communicate whatever it is we have learned or discovered. **If students are not allowed to discover the wonders of all of the Arts, they are cheated in their ability to communicate and lose a most important part of what it is to be human.**

Art and Learning

The Arts offer the special ability for the students to participate in experiencing a unique and most freely creative interaction of their bodies, minds and the mediums of art. It is an interaction of their internal thoughts, their physical bodies and the elements of the external world. There is no other way to duplicate this kind of learning experience. It is also an experience that has truly unlimited possible variations for discovery and learning. It offers learning experiences that uniquely involve the integration of many senses. Its unique kinds of creativity offers immediate and detailed feed back to the brain of exactly what are the effects of its creative actions. It is a kind of active experimentation that brings the experimenter a feeling of real control and joyous amazement at how they can change a piece of the world.

Within the Arts, because of the immediate feedback from the student's creations, students can make some kind of simple pattern, see if it appeals to them, make changes, and continue evaluating what they have created. They soon discover, that what appeals to them changes, simply because they have learned those first patterns and now want something more. They can continually grow their own appreciation for increasingly complex patterns. The Arts allow everyone involved to become ever more appreciative and have more understanding of more and more complex patterns.

I believe a strong argument can be made that the eye detects the visible objects of the real world, but it is the mechanisms of intelligence that is able to see them.

Learning to ever better draw the objects of the real world is the best and most powerful way of actually increasing the ability of the mechanisms of intelligence to see what is really there. Most persons unschooled in Art go through life missing much of the richly textured detail that exists around them.

Art Budget Cutters

It must almost certainly be so, that those persons, who are willing to cut the budgets that support the teaching, learning or demonstration of the Arts, are themselves a representation of how the perceptive intellect can be strangled and deficient in understanding by an education that was lacking in the learning of the Arts. The saddest part of this is, they do not have a clue as to what sins against humanity they are committing, how seriously they are stifling one of the most creative parts of an individual, how they are snuffing out hope for an even more elaborate and interesting life of discovery and rewards.

Those who are Art budget cutters need to be taken out behind the shed and given a new serious and enlightening educational experience.

Conclusion

Art should never be considered a luxury for the educational system. It is in fact a primary element for any meaningful education of an individual.

A WORST CASE EDUCATIONAL SYSTEM

As a means of comparison let's consider what elements might make up the most hellish worst case Education System of which we can conceive. Later, we will consider what might make up the elements of the best system.

Elements of a Worst Case

1. Old or insufficient buildings and physical plants for supporting the system.
2. Old outdated physical equipment necessary for assisting in teaching.
3. Old outdated, damaged or lacking student materials: Books, Microscopes, Telescopes, Computers, Mechanical Tools, Cameras, Furnaces, Video Equipment, Projectors, Film, Paints, Molding Mediums, Electronic Supplies, Physical Testing Equipment, Laboratory Supplies for Biology, Chemistry, Physics, Supplies for live theater and dance, Musical Instruments. You should have the idea; you can add your own preferences to this list.
4. Classes made up of students who are hungry, tired or sick.
5. Classes of students who do not have the prerequisite learning for the new material to be studied.
6. Classes containing students who require specialized learning needs that are outside of the requirements of the general class population.
7. Classes that are so large that students cannot get individual attention, as they require it.
8. Classes of students with so many individual varied abilities and interests that no one subject can ever meet the needs or interests of the individuals.
9. Teachers who are grossly overworked and severely under paid.

10. Teachers who are forced to teach classes instead of students.
11. Teachers who are forced to teach subjects for which they have no love, or interest and are not trained to teach.
12. Teachers who have no aptitude or driving desire to teach.
13. Administrators that enforce the one size fits all philosophy.
14. Severely limited student environment for discovery.
15. Too limited time to teach some subjects
16. No time at all to teach some subjects.
17. A school schedule full of interruptions-intercom- assemblies
18. High student and teacher absenteeism
19. Bussing that gets everyone there late.
20. Inadequate libraries.

A BEST CASE EDUCATIONAL SYSTEM

Here we want to consider what might be the basic elements of a best case for a Primary Educational System, whose elements would be part of a proposed Ideal System.

Elements for a Best Case

1. A building whose design is adequate to meet the most varied needs for discovery and learning. State of the art physical plant facilities for heating, cooling, air circulation and filtering. State of the art internal facilities for communicating within the structure and to and from the outside world. State of the art system for immediate ready access to all physical plant systems, including wiring, plumbing, communication cabling, sewage and other drainage

2. Physical equipment for teachers to use in teaching, that is State of the art, such as Computer Projection Systems, DVD Systems, Electronic Display Microscopes, etc., and within the facility, special projects construction teams with workshops for supplying special demonstration projects that might be required.

3. The newest and best student personal learning materials, Textbooks, Computer Disks, Computer Programs, Microscopes, Telescopes, Computers, Mechanical Tools, Cameras, Furnaces, Video Equipment, Projectors, Film, Paints, Molding Mediums, Electronic Supplies, Physical Test Equipment, Laboratory Supplies for Biology, Chemistry, Physics, Metallurgy, Supplies for Theater, Dance, Musical Instruments of every kind, no shortage of supplies to meet every learning need.

4. Classes made up of students that are not hungry or malnourished, Students who are well rested and are physically and mentally healthy.
5. Students who are enthusiastic and eager for discovery and learning and have the prerequisite learning needed to learn the new material.
6. Classes of students whose special learning requirements are to be found within a class made up of students with common needs.
7. Classes small enough in size that every student can receive individual attention as they might require it.
8. Classes of students who are each interested in learning the specific subject that is being taught.
9. Teachers who have sufficient time to thoroughly accomplish their work and who are appropriately paid for their high position of importance.
10. Teachers who are free to teach to the individual student within their class.
11. Teachers who are both expertly prepared and love the subject or subjects they are teaching.
12. Teachers who love to teach and are able to motivate and inspire their students.
13. Administrators who constantly work to serve the needs of the teachers and students.
14. A boundless environment for discovery within the facility and the Real World.
15. Time to thoroughly learn each subject according to plan and sufficient time for exploring the subject's peripherals.
16. Time, space and materials necessary to teach every subject within the curriculum and time to assist students towards their own desires that may be outside of the curriculum.
17. No interruptions of regular class time would be allowed, except for emergency situations.

18. Minimal student or teacher absenteeism.
19. Transportation systems that are efficient and are always on time.
20. Complete access to the great libraries and museums throughout the world.

The most ideal teacher student relationship is surely a system of mentors, a system where a single student has a supremely knowledgeable mentor, a mentor that has known the student from their earliest formal training, a system where the student and the mentor stay together throughout their time of learning. Such a system is the most efficient for the learning process. This is true, because to most successfully communicate with another person the information communicated must be able to be received by a mind that is receptive to that particular information. Ideally the information must be specifically tailored to be best understood by the student.

RECOMMENDATIONS

Here are the recommendations for a Most Ideal Educational System. These, coupled with those of the previously mentioned Best Case System and those specifically mentioned within the body of the text would form a powerful system for meeting the most ambitious goals of each individual student.

1. It is of the absolute utmost importance that we always strive to be FIRST in Education. It must never be thought, that being second, or third, could be all right. Why not then, maybe fourth, and when being fourth is too difficult, then why not fifth, and so on, and so on. History is littered with those, who once were first, and once were great civilizations.

2. Students must be allowed to engage in a continuous search for discovering and developing their loves and abilities. For many this is a long and slow process, which might continue through their entire Primary Education.

3. The system must always be equipped and ready to give each student the prerequisites necessary to continue the pursuit of their desires.

4. Each student must be allowed the maximum opportunities for exploring the very richest environment for learning that we can provide. To realistically accomplish this goal, will require many learning experiences that are physically outside of the main educational facilities.

5. The Curriculums should be there to fit the needs of the students. Within the Primary Educational System the student should never be forced to fit the needs of the curriculum.

6. What we need is a system that schools "individuals". What we now have is a system that schools "classes". It is important that we do away with the system of classes made by the age grouping of students. Instead for the entire Primary Educational System, there

should be a Universe of Subjects not restricted to any synthetic age grouping, but open to anyone with appropriate ability. The schooling structure would be a collection of subjects and the collection would be uniform throughout the Nation.

7. Certificates of a student's finishing their studies within the Primary Educational System would simply be a list of subjects completed, nothing else.

8. The few subjects that all students would be required to have some knowledge of would be:

8a.Language Studies, which would cover every aspect of the language and would span the entire time the student was within the Educational System. After a student had finished the most rudimentary requirements of the language, they would be free to pursue for the remainder of their time in the system any aspects of the language that they chose.

8b.Arithmetic. Counting, Addition, Multiplication and Division, would be the only required learning about mathematics for every student. Any further mathematical studies would be at the student's discretion.

8c.Arts. Students would be required to take some subject within the Arts from their first days of school until they finished, all at their choosing. Wherever possible the Arts would be integrated with the other non-Art subjects.

8d.Science. Each student would be required to take a basic introduction course to: Chemistry, Physics, Biology, Astronomy and Geology with no requirements for their being tested or rated. Further classes in science would be at their discretion.

8e.Social Studies. Relevant interactions within society, No requirements for testing or rating.

8f.Personal and Social Hygiene. No requirements for testing or rating.

9. All other subjects during the student's time within the Primary Educational System would be taken solely at the student's choice.

10. Since the system is based on a Universe of Subjects, each of which is beginning and completing in a never ending cyclic order, parents would be free at anytime whatsoever to remove their child from the system for vacations or other requirements. This would lend a flexibility to the student's and parent's life that would not have any negative impact on the student's learning.

11. The Primary Educational System would be a system made up of classes by subject matter, classes whose doors would be open to anyone meeting the particular class's prerequisites. Students would be free to depart from the system at any time and to return at any time of the beginning of a particular subject's teaching cycle.

12. The Primary Educational System would be accessible to anyone at any time during their lifetime.

13. There would be no fixed duration of time associated with completing a student's studies within the Primary Educational System. Each student would be free to leave and move on to further studies or pursue the other activities of life.

14. It is clear that this system would require many more numbers of teachers than are within the present System. There would be a requirement for teachers that are very specialized in certain areas not presently taught within the current System, to meet this requirement we need to entice teachers that are specialists within specific fields, but do not necessarily have a teaching certificate. We must begin to build a system of specialists, not certificates. In this new expanded curriculum, we should make every effort to draw new teachers from the ranks of retired persons, where there is a treasure trove of persons with expertise about new areas to be included within the curriculum. Within the community of retired persons are the valuable resources we need to supplement our certified teachers.

15. Students that do not want to participate in anyway with the freely structured Primary Educational System would be required to attend the Special Section for Military Science Training Programs, where the curriculum would be fixed by military personnel and strictly adhered to by all students. This Special Section of The Primary Educational System would also be open to all students by their choice. All students would be free to move between this Special Section and the main Primary Educational System by their own free choice.

16. The System must have extensive Special Sections that are dedicated to assisting students in learning who have particular learning requirements that are not common to the general student population.

17. There should be a special group of counselors who are expert at understanding and resolving problems that are not subject matter related.

18. Education is one of the primary elements that government should be devoted to nourishing. It's the element that is of the uppermost importance to the individual citizen and to society. It therefore should be introduced to the individual student at the earliest possible age. Individuals should hopefully be in school by at least the age of two years. Some parents will not be willing to send their children to school at this early age and that should always remain their prerogative. All Children should be involved in formal schooling by five or six years of age. But, it is important that the new Educational System be prepared to care for the two year old child's physical and educational needs. The advantages for a two year old entering into a safe, caring, rich and stimulating educational environment should outweigh its drawbacks. It would also free many parents from the need to place their small children in expensive day care facilities, where their educational experiences are haphazard at best.

*   *   *   *   *

A major part of the proposed Ideal Primary Educational System would be the physical building or buildings that housed the system. These physical structures would provide all of the facilities for educating the student population which in the current public system is usually spread between three separate facilities, a separate facility for grade school, one for middle school or junior high, and one for high school. These would all be brought together at one site. This would allow for consolidation of all physical plant facilities and all transportation facilities. It would also allow for the consolidation of all those special facilities not directly involved in the student's learning of a particular subject, facilities such as food preparation, libraries, auditorium, physical exercise, athletic fields, parking, medical and many others. The facility's design should be accomplished keeping in mind that areas of usage most common to all students should be central. And the design should take into account that each particular subject would have sections ranging from basic introduction up to the most advanced classes for that particular subject. So the most basic sections of each subject would be within a physically related area. And the next more advanced classes of a subject would be in a physically related area and so on.

The physical facilities should have special areas for boarding some of the student body. Boarding would be allowed either for a short or long-term basis. Boarding at the Educational Facility would be as a means to facilitate the student who might have temporary or long term conflicting outside requirements. Boarding would also serve the student that might have other special requirements of any type that could be assisted by means of the student being available at the facility.

There should be complete facilities for food preparation and consumption. Food consumption areas should not be open military style mess halls, but offer groups some minimal quiet and privacy. Present school cafeteria areas are undignified and noisy beyond control. Many students choose to avoid these chaotic conditions at nearly any cost. Even children like to have a civilized meal with their friends. The school should provide free meals to all students who might require them. We do this for our Nation's military personnel and we can do it for our students.

*   *   *   *   *

There is a need for a National Educational Techniques Research and Development Facility, a single National Facility that would be exceptionally well equipped and staffed with creative persons, devoted to researching methods and developing techniques for enhancing our ability to educate our students. The facility would necessarily have a student population that would contribute to the verification of the facility's research.

The facility would also be tasked with the development of special teaching aids to supplement those developed at the local Federal Schools. Such aids would necessarily include the production of video media for use in the instruction of individual subjects.

The Facility's staffing would include permanent staff and also a staff made up of visiting teachers. Teachers would be invited to attend the facility and to make contributions of their insights and suggestions. In essence, it would be central meeting ground for persons and ideas that should give the facility a dynamic environment in which to test and analyze the greatest variety of ideas.

*   *   *   *   *

New Primary Education Schools should be constructed and financed with Federal Tax moneys with a part of the source originating from a Federal Lottery System, a system where every dollar of lottery profit would go directly to these new Federal Primary Educational Systems. As more schools are built and activated, the State Governments should be slowly relieved of their financial support of education. This would be on the assumption that the States dropped any taxation of the population that was earmarked for the State's Public Educational System. Some further funding of the new Federal Educational System would come from other appropriate sources.

It's a system that can be easily tested for its success. Within each State one of these schools could be built, supplied and staffed.

To begin with students, within the city where the new Federal Schools are constructed, could of their choosing enter a lottery as means of possibly being selected as the first body of students to enter this new system.

I believe that it would very soon become evident, that these schools would be so superior to any public or private schools that everyone would be demanding that their children could attend such a school.

I also believe, if such schools become established, and you then ask any child what is your favorite thing to do? They will enthusiastically answer, "Going to School."

CONCLUSIONS

Currently the Educational System turns out a product that is unprepared to assume a meaningful place within the Economy or within Society. It dumps upon Society a person that is in every sense an adolescent to the real needs of life, a person that is not even prepared to serve at defending the Nation or its Philosophies.

  *   *   *   *   *

Education must ultimately be about meeting the needs of the student everything else about the Educational System must be planetary to this first concern.

  *   *   *   *   *

There are no tests, no examinations of any kind, that can identify that individual or individuals who might rise up in Humankind's hour of most desperate need, and bring us to salvation. We therefore need to honor each individual with the best education we can bring to them, as anyone of them, might one day be the seed of our survival.

  *   *   *   *   *

We must finally begin to clearly see exactly the place that Education occupies as compared to the hierarchy of Nature's evolution.

The absolutely most important lesson to be gained from all of this speculation is the lesson that is critical to our understanding, to our realization, that **Education is the one undeniable supreme master key for our survival against ourselves and against and with nature.**

Look at the situation this way: for nearly two and a half billion years nature has evolved us to finally produce the mechanisms of our wondrous bodies and our Instincts. We have relied on those aspects of evolution to bring us through times of almost unbelievable hardships and suffering. With only those wonderful complex physical and mental attributes, we have looked at nature and learned the ways of survival. Any and all animals existing in nature interact with it to maximize their chances for survival. But, It must be realized that with these magnificently dexterous hands, our eyes and their ability to resolve the finest detail, with all of our wonderful specialized physical aspects and our complex Instincts, even with our intelligence and creativity, Our Kind wondered through the world suffering every outrage that nature brought against us.

It is only the teaching of our cumulated knowledge that has brought us by leaps and bounds away from the pain and suffering of nature's whims.

It is not our magnificent eye that has been our salvation, not any physical or mental capability. We wandered for a million years with our wonderful physical and mental abilities with only the fewest and slowest successes against the torments of nature.

It is Education, our system of teaching all that we have experienced and learned to our children that has lead to our skyrocketing progress in understanding the world.

Education has turned out to be a more powerful force for our survival than all else before.

Even though all our physical and mental talents have led us to great discoveries, if each of us had to discover them again on our own, then Our Kind would be on an endless treadmill leading us finally, nowhere. **But, because we can teach what we have learned to our children, Our Kind can ride the enormous ever-growing tidal wave of knowledge. A knowledge that is the most sacred heritage from all of our ancestors, a knowledge that represents all that has survived from them, through the ages of destructive time.**

*   *   *   *   *

Here I must say once more, it is the very nature of an economy that is in the midst of a technological revolution that society finds itself involuntarily caught up in the midst of another kind of revolution. It is the nature of powerful technological based economic revolutions that new demands are placed upon the existing Educational System; they are necessarily demands for talents that are not supplied by the existing System. They are demands whose basic requirements exceed the quality and quantity of knowledge that students have customarily been required to know.

It is during these times that pressures are put on the Educational System to deliver results that are applicable to the needs of the Real World. It is at these times that parents who have the monetary means are busy removing their children from the Public Educational System and are placing them in private schools as a means of fulfilling their desires for a better education. It is during these times that cries rise up from many in the population for any means to escape from the Public Educational System into any alternative, that they believe can better deliver the educational results they desire.

Such times are dangerous times for a democratic society. They present situations whose unchecked direction can lead to exasperating the spread between those of sufficient economic means and those of minimal means, situations that lead to the further exaggeration of the distance between those with the knowledge to compete within the newly emerging economic world and those with little knowledge to aid in their economic survival.

Our greatest concern should be that this growing situation is self-reinforcing. Unless timely steps are taken to correct its root cause, it will without doubt lead to an ever-increasing gulf between what will become just two identifiable classes within society, one class representing wealth in all its forms and one class representing poverty in all its forms.

There is an immediate need that steps must now be taken, so that we have some leverage of time, towards making our Educational System one that delivers to society, students that are immediately prepared to take a meaningful place within the society and its ever-changing economy.

*   *   *   *   *

Economic Models pay little attention to the place within the economy of the Educational System. Economic theorists are so taken by their theory's mathematical statistics and manipulative razzle-dazzle that they ignore the ultimate basis on which rests the very foundation of every economy. That foundation is the Educational System, no matter how poor or how excellent.

The most basic strength of any and every economy is at the ultimate mercy of the quality of the Educational System, which props up its foundations.

*   *   *   *   *

Give me a Land rich in all of the World's natural resources, and fill it with an uneducated people, and you will soon have a Land where its riches have been squandered and its resources depleted.

Give me Land with nothing but Sea Water and Sand, and fill it with a well-educated people, and you will soon have a Land filled with all they can dream.

*   *   *   *   *

We should try to understand that any view that anyone holds about anything is with certainty Biased. Biased is not the problem. What we need is to slowly shift the bias to a newer one. We are all biased about everything, but some people's biases are fixed.

*   *   *   *   *

There are within our society those who continually parrot, that the so-called "Cold Logic of Science", unguided, as they say, by moral concerns, is the greatest danger to civilization. The verifiable historical facts show a quite different situation, that it is humankind's primitive uncontrolled Instincts and their emotions that are the greatest danger to human survival.

Illogical philosophies to which persons emotionally commit their allegiances are our single greatest danger for a continued understanding of nature, our place within it, and to our and our children's long-term survival.

*   *   *   *   *

For Humankind, the Real World is that World that exists within our minds. It contains all of those Territories both Physical and Ethereal for which we are willing to fight and even sacrifice our lives.

*   *   *   *   *

We should hopefully be willing to admit, that no super projects directed towards any particular discovery or endeavor of any kind, can ever reap the greater rewards of our spending our moneys and time on developing the best Educational System that the world has ever known. There is no Manhattan project, or Moon Landing project, or any Military Weapons Systems development project that can compare to the rewards that can be produced by investing in a Great Educational System.

*   *   *   *   *

No Nation or Peoples has an indigenous trait of superiority for the talents of creative discovery. It is only by their commitments to a philosophy of the nurturing of diversity and tolerance, and their willingness to provide social order with justice, and the quality of their Educational Systems that can guarantee that superiority.

*   *   *   *   *

If we as a Nation, that is the richest and most powerful Nation in existence in the present world, continue to say we cannot afford the changes necessary to make our Educational System the best it can be, then I say we are a most foolish Nation. And, if we continue to deny that we can afford a great effort to improve the Educational System, then the time will surely come, when in fact we cannot afford the improvements. If that time comes, then it is far too late to lament our past mistakes, mistakes that were in fact based upon blind selfish greed. Then, our Nation will already be on the historical path of slow decay, where its citizens are doomed to eventually live amongst the ruins, of what once was their splendor.

*   *   *   *   *

Here hopefully is not the end, but a new beginning.

UNUSUAL APPENDIX

UNUSUAL

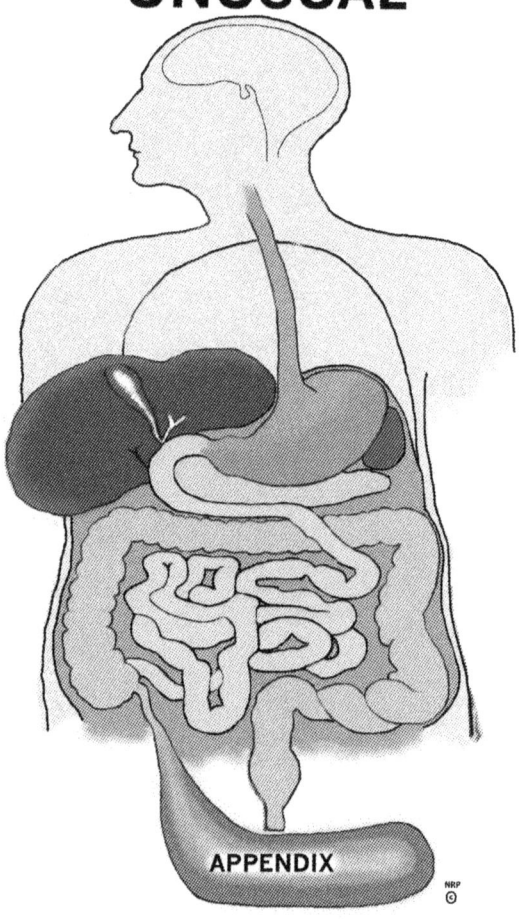

APPENDIX

REFLEX SYSTEMS

Hopefully, we can look from a distance of time and perspective and begin to see the general structures that are essentially common features to all of the Systems we have here considered. Seeing within those systems the commonality that exists, we should begin to understand that they are all evolutionary improvements upon the most primitive Simple Motor Reflex Systems that are a part of every living Creature.

Each of the three main topics we have considered are just nature's repeating in a more complex and sophisticated way the design of its Basic Reflex System. Each of the more complex reflex systems sits or rides upon the back of a more ancient and a more primitive Reflex System.

The hierarchy of the systems must be essentially this:

Upon the most primitive Motor Reflex Systems sits the elements that are the Hereditary Instinctual System, then upon the Hereditary Instinctual System sits the elements that make up the Mechanisms of Intelligence, then upon the Mechanisms of Intelligence sits the elements of the Mechanisms that are the Dream Machine and **we might suspect that the elements that make up the Mechanisms of Consciousness are just another even more complex Reflex System that Rides upon the backs of all of the other Reflex Systems.**

*   *   *   *   *

WHAT WE ARE

What we are is determined by:

1. Our intelligence and specifically by the nature of the individual mechanisms that make up a functional intelligent system.
2. Those Instinctual mechanisms that we have inherited.
3. Those things we have learned and have stored as memories within our Long Term Memory and the Cross Address and Cross Sensory Address Linkings that we have made there.

There are no magical or hidden ingredients that can make us more or less than are defined by these mostly deterministic elements of our basic nature.

We are Creatures like all other Creatures in that our general characteristics are definable and the most variable parts of our individual natures are solely made up from those things we have learned, remembered and linked by associations to other memories.

We must begin to look at our institutions; cultures, societies and nations with a new critical eye whose information sieve contains those three basic propositions.

If we are willing to use this method and can truthful admit to the reality of the discoveries that we find, we are surely going to be greatly shocked at the most tragic wounds that are laid bare to our inspection and also to the truth of the only available rational means to heal those wounds. We must be brave and strong enough to look with this new critical eye for it is manifestly past the time when the old way of seeing has any hope of revealing any truthful understanding of ourselves and all of those that came before us who have struggled along history's long path where pain and the grossest blind injustices were the rocks and barriers that marked its bitter way and mark it to this very day

*   *   *   *   *

Consciousness and Instincts

It would seem that buried somewhere within the structures of both Consciousness and Instincts, are those various structures that are the determining elements that define what we refer to as an individual's general personality. Consciousness attempts to be the primary structure to rule the overall rational mental functioning of a Creature, but the Instinctive Mechanisms seem to have some major sway in the real out come of just how rational are a Creature's actions.

*   *   *   *   *

Pronoun Usage

I often use "they or their" as the pronoun of choice when the noun of reference is an indefinite third person singular antecedent, where the singular noun is without gender. It is illogical to be forced to use a gendered pronoun such as "he" or "she" or even "he or she" or any other gendered form to refer to a non-gendered singular noun.

Use of the word Linkings

By "Linking" I mean the act of making a link and by the use of the word "linkings" I mean the separate but repeated act of linking or referring to many different links.

Cake

If you baked a chocolate cake and then with white frosting you wrote on the top of the cake any simple paragraph and then gave the cake to a person whose life's long work was involved with grammar, spelling and punctuation, they would never, ever, discover the cake.

*   *   *   *   *

Resistive Nature of Higher Reflex Systems

It is a necessary part of the overall nature of the higher reflex systems that we have considered, that they are at every level of their mechanisms resistive to the in-flow or out-flow of data. This resistance is necessary as a means of protecting the integrity of Creatures from becoming over-whelmed with either chaotic or inappropriate data from the natural environment and for the general reserved control of any actions a Creature might undertake.

DECIMAL and BINARY NUMBERS

DECIMAL	**BINARY**
Elements of the Decimal System	Elements of the Binary System
0,1,2,3,4,5,6,7,8,9,	0,1
Element's name "Digit"	Element's Name "Bit"

EQUIVALENT NUMBERS

DECIMAL	BINARY
0	0
1	1
2	10
3	11
4	100
5	101
6	110
7	111
8	1000
9	1001
10	1010
11	1011
12	1100

Capitalization

Sorry, I use Capitalization much like a musician would emphasize the strength of the strike of a piano key.

Unchanging Sensory Inputs

Sensory inputs that are essentially constant or with very little change, we usually think of as simply boring. We should consider that these continuing nearly unchanging inputs could have the detrimental effect of overly stimulating the Mapping Function by repeatedly activating the same neural areas. This could cause the repeated similar patterns to be placed over and over again into the Short Term Memory and thus rapidly filling the Short Term Memory with the same repeating pattern and causing it to become over burdened. The over burdened Short Term Memory would then activate the Instinct To Sleep as a means of relieving its memory burden.

Little Creatures Mechanisms

None of the Little Creature's Mechanisms of Intelligence are intended to physically represent those same kinds of systems within biological Creatures, but their functioning is meant to be representative of the same commonality of functioning within biological Creatures.

Pattern Addresses in Long Term Memory

On page 74, I said, "Similar object patterns relating to visual images lay next to each other in Long Term Memory" I made this statement because I thought to confuse the reader with the real possibility that adjacent addresses might not be adjacent physical locations would complicate too much their ideas about how addresses in the real world are laid out. In truth adjacent codes for sensory address might be somewhat physically separated within the Long Term Memory but still be within each other's neighborhood.

Forming Powerful Complex Strongly Related Patterns

The best and simplest means for creating powerful strongly related patterns, which are the most useful elements when conducting Creative and Analytical Thinking, is to exercise and generate mental linkings of complex visual images to your spoken language.

The Cross Sensory Address Linkings that are logically formed when complex visual images are linked to their descriptive spoken language patterns are those elements that are commonly used by the Mechanisms of Thinking when they are in the process of constructing new ideas or critically analyzing any idea.

A simple example for exercising and creating this kind of linking would be: The verbal telling of a story that creates the story's images within the story- teller's and the listener's mind.

A more rigorous exercise would be to have one person view any complex image that was unseen by another person, then by using spoken language try to convey in detail the contents of the image to the other person, who would attempt to draw what they understood was the nature of the image being described to them.

I'm sure you can understand that there are multitudes of possibilities for establishing these kinds of linkings.

Chewing Gum while Walking

You may have sometime heard the joke indicating that some persons are unable to do two things at the same time, such as chewing gum while they are walking. This little joke has some connection to understanding that the functioning of the five sets of sensory inputs and their respective Mechanisms of Intelligence may not be totally isolated in some persons. This is a condition that should be carefully examined for any person that might show signs of learning impairment. If any of these various Mechanisms of Intelligence are not independently functional, this could severely jeopardized the ability for learning patterns that are normally uniquely supplied by each individual sense.